Communicative dynamism is a central feature of the Prague School theory of functional sentence perspective (FSP), which is concerned with the distribution of information as determined by all meaningful elements. Jan Firbas discusses the distribution of degrees of communicative dynamism over sentence elements and how this determines the orientation or perspective of the sentence. He examines the relation of theme and rheme to, and implementation by, syntactic components, with particular attention to word order. Professor Firbas considers the place of intonation in the FSP factors of spoken communication and establishes the concept of prosodic prominence.

STUDIES IN ENGLISH LANGUAGE

Executive Editor: Sidney Greenbaum
Advisory Editors: John Algeo, Rodney Huddleston, Magnus Ljung

Functional sentence perspective in written and spoken communication

Studies in English Language

The aim of this series is to provide a framework for original studies of present-day English. All are based securely on empirical research, and represent theoretical and descriptive contributions to our knowledge of national varieties of English, both written and spoken. The series will cover a broad range of topics in English grammar, vocabulary, discourse and pragmatics, and is aimed at an international readership.

Already Published

Christian Mair *Infinitival complement clauses in English*
Charles F. Meyer *Apposition in contemporary English*

Forthcoming

John Algeo *A study of British–American grammatical differences*

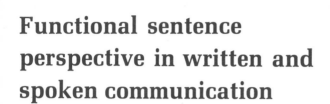

Functional sentence perspective in written and spoken communication

JAN FIRBAS

Professor Emeritus, Department of English and American Studies,
Masaryk University, Brno, Czechoslovakia

CAMBRIDGE
UNIVERSITY PRESS

Published by the Press Syndicate of the University of Cambridge
The Pitt Building, Trumpington Street, Cambridge CB2 1RP
40 West 20th Street, New York NY 10011-4211, USA
10 Stamford Road, Oakleigh, Victoria 3166, Australia

First published 1992

Printed in Great Britain at the University Press, Cambridge

A catalogue record for this book is available from the British Library

Library of Congress cataloguing in publication data

Firbas, Jan.
Functional sentence perspective in written and spoken
communication / Jan Firbas.
        p.   cm. – (Studies in English language)
Includes bibliographical references and index.
ISBN 0-521-37308-5
1. Grammar, Comparative and general – Topic and comment.
2. English language – Topic and comment.   I. Title. II. Series.
P298.F57   1992
415 – DC20   91-3787 CIP

ISBN 0 521 37308 5 hardback

Contents

Preface

A number of colleagues have asked me to prepare a synthesis of my publications on functional sentence perspective (FSP), which have appeared in various periodicals but are not always easily accessible. Among the British scholars it is especially Professors Sir Randolph Quirk, Sidney Greenbaum and Geoffrey Leech who have urged me to present such a synthesis. This is why I have gratefully accepted Professor Greenbaum's invitation to publish my book on FSP in the present series.

Inspired by the work of Vilém Mathesius, Josef Vachek, František Daneš and Maria Schubiger, I published my first paper on FSP in 1957, at a time when it was particularly Czechoslovakia where the problems of FSP were considered to be of special importance for a better understanding of how the sentence functions at the moment of communication. Since then, I have been gradually developing a theory of FSP covering both the written and the spoken language. I have been doing so predominantly on an empirical basis, concentrating on English but frequently comparing it with other languages, especially Czech, German and French. In the meantime a veritable explosion of interest in FSP has taken place (its problems being treated also under such headings as 'theme–rheme structure', 'topic–focus structure', 'information structure').

My endeavour to accompany my arguments by as many examples as possible and also limitations of space have prevented me from making my synthesis as comprehensive as I should have wished it to be and from presenting the reader with an all-inclusive and adequate survey of the state of the art. I have therefore not been able to discuss every reaction, favourable or unfavourable, to my writings on FSP. The book I present is primarily to be looked upon as an account of the main results of my enquiry into FSP, an enquiry that has been carried on for more than three decades.

My thanks are due to many. Let me mention at least Professor Josef Vachek, my teacher, who suggested to me the terms 'functional sentence perspective' and 'communicative dynamism', subsequently used by me – I believe for the first time – in the literature; my colleagues in the Department of English, Masaryk University, Brno, especially Aleš Svoboda, who have worked with me in the field of FSP and published their results mostly in the series Brno Studies in English; Professor E. M. Uhlenbeck, President–Founder of NIAS (the Netherlands Institute for Advanced Studies), where I was able to devote myself to my research into FSP for one academic year; Professors Sir Randolph Quirk and Sidney Greenbaum, Directors of the Survey of English Usage in the Department of English, University College London, who made it possible for me to continue my research for another year in London; Professor Peter Newmark, who like myself is a native of Brno, for his interest in my work and all his encouragement; and Jenny Potts for her meticulous attention to the typescript in preparing the book for press. My very special thanks are due to my wife, without whose assistance and understanding I should have hardly been able to carry on my research.

I subscribe to Professor Vilém Mathesius' view that language is a formidable fortress that must be attacked from all sides and with all means. My enquiry into FSP is just an attempt to participate in this attack. I am well aware that the fortress continues to hold out.

Abbreviations

AofQ	ascription of quality
AT	Arnold and Tooley 1972
AV	Authorized Version
B	bearer of quality
BBE	The Bible in basic English (Cambridge, 1961)
Beck	The New Testament, transl. by W. F. Beck (Saint Louis, Miss., 1966)
CCELD	*Collins Cobuild English language dictionary*
CD	communicative dynamism
CFocA	command focus anticipator
CGEL	*A comprehensive grammar of the English language* (Quirk *et al.* 1985)
Chl	see Chládková 1979
Chr	Agatha Christie, *Evil under the sun* (Berne: Phoenix, Scherz and Hallwag, 1946)
Ch–Rh	The New Testament, a revision of the Challoner–Rheims version, in The Holy Bible (Boston: St Paul Editions, 1960)
Corpus	*A corpus of English conversation* (Svartvik and Quirk 1980)
d	context-dependent (used in text analyses)
D	see Dvořáková 1964
DESH	deshading
DTh	diatheme
DTho	diatheme oriented
FSp	further specification
FSP	functional sentence perspective
G	J. Galsworthy, *The Forsyte saga* (London: Heinemann, 1929)

G1	J. Galsworthy, *Die Forsyte Saga*, vol. I, transl. by L. Wolf (Berlin: Zsolnay, 1929)
G2	J. Galsworthy, *Die Forsyte Saga*, vol. I, transl. by J. Schlösser (Leipzig: Kiepenheuer, 1985)
G3	J. Galsworthy, *Sága rodu Forsytů*, vol. I, transl. by B. Kubertová-Zátková (Prague: Melantrich, 1935)
G4	J. Galsworthy, *Sága rodu Forsytů*, vol. I, transl. by Z. Urbánek (Prague: Odeon, 1967)
GCE	*A grammar of contemporary English* (Quirk *et al.* 1972)
GN	*Good News for Modern Man*, 3rd edn (New York, 1971); Good News Bible, 4th edn (London, 1976)
Go	see Golková 1983
Goodspeed	Complete Bible; OT transl. by J. M. Powis Smith and NT transl. by E. J. Goodspeed (Chicago, 1964)
H	O. Henry, *The complete works* (Kingwood, Surrey: Associated Bookbuyers, 1931)
Ho	see Horová 1976
IC	intonation centre
Jer B	The Jerusalem Bible, London, 1968
Knox	The Holy Bible, transl. by R. Knox (London, 1966)
LDCE	Longman dictionary of contemporary English
M	mood/modality
M	K. Mansfield, *The garden party and other stories* (Harmondsworth: Penguin, 1966)
M1	K. Mansfield, *Ausgewählte Werke*, vol. I, transl. by H. Steiner (Leipzig: Insel 1981)
M2	K. Mansfield, *La Garden party*, transl. by M. Duproix (Paris: Editions Stock, 1948)
M3	K. Mansfield, *Zahradní slavnost*, transl. by A. Skoumal (Prague: Vyšehrad, 1952)
MA	K. Mansfield, *Collected stories of Katherine Mansfield* (London: Constable, 1948)
ME	exponent of mood and/or modality
Moffatt	The New Testament, transl. by J. Moffatt (London, 1950)
NAM	The New American Bible (New York, 1970)
NE	exponent of number
NEB	The New English Bible, Oxford and Cambridge 1970
NegFocA	negation focus anticipator
NegPolE	exponent of negative polarity

NIV	New International Version of the Holy Bible, anglicized edn (London, 1984)
N-R INT	non-reevaluating prosodic intensification
NWT	New World translation of the Holy Scriptures (New York, 1961)
PE	exponent of person
PERF CORR	perfect correspondence
Ph	phenomenon to be presented
Phillips	The New Testament in modern English, transl. by J. B. Phillips (London, 1960)
PNE	exponent of person and number
PosPolE	exponent of positive polarity
PP	prosodic prominence
Pr	presentation of phenomenon
Q	quality
QFocA	question focus anticipator
RAV	Revised Authorized Version
REC DESH	recapitulatory deshading
refl. pron.	reflexive pronoun
Rh	rheme
RhPr	rheme proper
Rieu	The Four Gospels, transl. by E. V. Rieu (Harmondsworth: Penguin, 1961)
R INT	re-evaluating prosodic intensification
RSV	Revised Standard Version
RV	Revised Version
Set	setting
Sp	specification
TE	exponent of tense
Th	theme
ThPr	theme proper
ThPro	theme proper oriented
TME	exponent of tense and mood
Tr	transition
TrPr	transition proper
TrPro	transition proper oriented
VE	exponent of voice
Weymouth	The New Testament in modern speech, transl. by R. F. Weymouth (London, 1929)
Williams	The New Testament, transl. by Ch. K. Williams (London, 1952)

Part I

Functional sentence perspective in written communication

1 Introduction

In medias res

What do we understand by functional sentence perspective (FSP)? An analysis of the following four versions – French, English, German and Czech – of the first paragraph of the closing chapter of Victor Hugo's *Les Misérables* will help to answer this question. The concepts used by the analysis as well as others linked with them, and together with them forming a theory of FSP, will be the object of the present study.

(1) Il y a, au cimetière du Père-Lachaise, aux environs de la fosse commune, loin du quartier élégant de cette ville des sépulchres, loin de tous ces tombeaux de fantaisie qui étalent en présence de l'éternité les hideuses modes de la mort, dans un angle désert, le long d'un vieux mur, sous un grand if auquel grimpent, parmi les chiendents et les mousses, les liserons, une pierre. (2) Cette pierre n'est plus exempte que les autres des lèpres du temps, de la moisissure, du lichen, et des fientes d'oiseaux. (3) L'eau la verdit, (4) l'air la noircit. (5) Elle n'est voisine d'aucun sentier, (6) et l'on n'aime pas aller de ce côté-là, parce que l'herbe est haute et qu'on a toute de suite les pieds mouillés. (7) Quand il y a un peu de soleil, les lézards y viennent. (8) Il y a, tout autour, un frémissement de folles avoines. (9) Au printemps, les fauvettes chantent dans l'arbre (Victor Hugo, *Les Misérables*, Paris: Nelson, 1935).

(1) There is, in the cemetery of Père Lachaise, in the neighbourhood of the poor side, far from the fashionable quarter of this city of tombs, far from those fantastic sepulchres, which blazon in the presence of eternity the hideous fashions of death, in a deserted corner alongside an old wall, under a lofty yew upon which bindweed climbs, and amid couchgrass and moss, a tombstone. (2) This stone is no more exempt than others

3

from the ravages of time. (3) Water turns it green, (4) and the atmosphere blackens it. (5) It is not near any path, (6) and people do not care to visit that part because the grass is long and they get their feet wet. (7) When there is a little sunshine, lizards disport themselves on it. (8) All round there is the rustling of wild oats, (9) and in the spring linnets sing on the trees (Victor Hugo, *Les Misérables*, London and Glasgow: Collins; translator and date of publication not given).

(1) Auf dem Friedhof Père-Lachaise, in der Gegend des Massengrabs, fern dem vornehmen Viertel dieser Gräberstadt, fern der mit Bildhauer-phantasie prangenden Gruften, die vor dem Angesicht der Ewigkeit die häßlichen Moden des Totenkults zur Schau stellen, in einer verlassenen Ecke, an einer alten Mauer, unter einer großen Eibe, an der Winden hochklettern, zwischen Quecken und Moos, steht ein Stein. (2) Er ist so wie die anderen vom Aussatz der Zeit versehrt, von Schimmel, Flechten und Vogelunrat. (3) Das Wasser färbt ihn grün, (4) die Luft schwärzt ihn. (5) Kein Pfad ist nahe, (6) und man geht nicht gern nach dieser Seite, weil das Gras hoch ist und man sofort nasse Füße hat. (7) Wenn etwas Sonne scheint, kommen die Eidechsen. (8) Ringsherum beben die Halme des wilden Hafers. (9) Im Frühling singen die Grasmücken auf einem Baum. (Victor Hugo, *Die Elenden*, translated by Paul Wiegler and Wolfgang Günther, Berlin: Verlag Volk and Welt, 1983).

(1) Na hřbitově Père-Lachaise, poblíž společného hrobu, daleko od elegantního oddělení tohoto města hrobů, daleko ode všech domýšlivých náhrobků, které před tváří věčnosti vystavují na odiv nehezké formy zániku, v opuštěném koutě u zdi, pod velkým tisem, po němž se pne svlačec, leží mezi plevelem a mechem kámen. (2A) Ten kámen stejně jako ostatní náhrobky čas neušetřil (2B) a pokryl jej plísní, lišejníky a ptačím trusem. (3) Voda jej barví na zeleno, (4) vzduch na černo. (5) Nevede k němu pěšinka (6) a lidé v tu stranu neradi chodí, protože je tam vysoká tráva, v níž se hned urousají. (7) Když svítí sluníčko, mihají se tam ještěrky. (8) Kolem dokola se chvěje metlice. (9) Na jaře zpívají na stromě pěnkavky (Victor Hugo, *Bídníci*, translated by Zdeňka Pavlous-ková, Prague: Odeon, 1984).

For the benefit of those who are not familiar with Czech, a literal English translation follows.

(1) In cemetery Père-Lachaise, near common grave, far from elegant section of-this of-city of-graves, far from all pretentious-looking sepulchres, which before face of-eternity make of parade (make a parade of) ugly forms of-decay, in deserted corner near wall, under big yew-tree, upon which climbs bindweed, it-lies amid weed and moss stone. (2) This stone (acc.) in-the-same-way as other tombs (acc.) time (nom.) has-not-spared and has covered it with-mould, with-lichen and with-bird-droppings. (3) Water it colours to green, (4) air to black. (5) Leads-not to it path (6) and people to this part not-eager they-go, because is there long grass, in which *refl. pron.* immediately they-draggle. (7) When shines sun, they-dash-to-and-fro *refl. pron.* there lizards. (8) Round about *refl. pron.* they-sway wild-oats. (9) In spring sing in tree finches.

Two perspectives

In each version, the communicative purpose of the first sentence is to present one particular phenomenon – a tombstone (*une pierre/a tomb-stone/ein Stein/kámen*). It is towards this phenomenon that the development of the communication is oriented (perspectived). In each version, such presentative orientation (perspective) is also displayed by sentences 7, 8 and – with a proviso to be taken up below – 9. Sentence 7 is oriented to *les lézards/lizards/Eidechsen/ještěrky*; 8 to *un frémissement de folles avoines/the rustling of wild oats/die Halme des wilden Hafers/metlice*; and 9 to *les fauvettes/linnets/pěnkavky* (for *die Gras-mücken*, see pp. 11–12). Moreover, in each version, 1 and 7 contain subclauses showing the presentative orientation as well; the elements presented are *les liserons/bindweed/Winden/svlačec* and *un peu de soleil/a little sunshine/etwas Sonne/sluníčko*.

The same applies to the German and the Czech versions of 5; they are oriented to *Kein Pfad* and *pěšinka*, respectively. A phenomenon presented is also expressed by the expanded subject of the *protože* subclause in the Czech version of 6: *protože je tam vysoká tráva, v níž se [lidé] hned urousají.*

As for the remaining sentences and subclauses, they display another orientation: they ascribe a quality to a phenomenon, the development of the communication being oriented towards this quality, or towards its specification if it is present as an amplifying piece of information. Quality is to be understood here in a wide sense, covering an action or a state, permanent or transitory, concrete or abstract.

In this way, the French, English and German versions of 4 are oriented towards a quality (*noircit*, *blackens* and *schwärzt*), but the Czech version of 4 towards a specification (*na černo*). The French version of 3 is oriented towards a quality (*verdit*), but the English, German and Czech versions of 3 towards a specification. A quality orientation is shown also by the subclause of 6 in the Czech version (*urousají*).

The rest of the sentences and the subclauses within them are orientated towards specifications; see *les hideuses modes de la mort*, *the hideous fashions of death*, *die häßlichen Moden des Totenkults* and *nehezké formy zániku* in 1; *des lèpres du temps…et des fientes d'oiseaux*, *from the ravages of time*, *vom Aussatz der Zeit*, *von Schimmel, Flechten und Vogelunrat*, *plísní, lišejníky a ptačím trusem* in 2; *voisine d'aucun sentier*, *not near any path* in 5; *haute*, *long* and *hoch*, and *mouillés*, *wet* and *nasse Füße* in 6.

Communicative dynamism and linear modification – one of the factors of functional sentence perspective

The element towards which a sentence or subclause is oriented conveys the information that completes the development of the communication taking place within the sentence or subclause. It contributes most to this development and is therefore the most dynamic element within the sentence or the subclause.

It is important to note in which sense the words *orient* and *orientation* have been used here. They have been used with regard to the completion of the development of the communication within the sentence. In this respect, the point of orientation is the element that contributes most to the development of the communication and in this way consummates or completes it. Used in this sense, the words *orient* and *orientation* have helped to explicate the meaning in which *perspective* is employed in my writings. If this sense is involved, I shall henceforth replace *orient* with *perspective* in the present study.

It may be asked in what way and to what extent the elements that do not complete the communication contribute towards its development. Among them, it is necessary to distinguish between those conveying information retrievable, and those conveying information irretrievable, from the immediately relevant preceding context. It is undoubtedly the former that contribute *less*, and the latter that contribute *more*, to the further development of the communication. The former are less dynamic than the latter. Retrievable information is conveyed by *cette pierre/this stone* of 2 and the pronominal references to it, *la, elle, y, it,* in 3, 4, 5 and 7; *de ce côté-là/that part* of 6 and the pronominal reference to it, *y,* in 7; and the relative pronoun *qui/which* of 1.

A particular kind of retrievability is shown by the pronominal constitutents of the existential construction *il, y* and *there* (see 1, 7 and 8) and the general subjects *on* and *people* (see 6). It is worth observing that the pronouns mentioned are not pronominalizations of notions previously occurring in the text. This points to their permanent retrievability from the immediately relevant situational context. In this respect, *people* serving as a general subject corresponds to *on.*

Coming back to irretrievable elements, let me emphasize that those of them that do not complete the development of the communication are less dynamic than those that do. This will be illustrated by the role played by the finite verb in the development of the communication.

In the texts under examination, all the finite verbs convey irretrievable information. But a finite verb completes the development of the communication and hence serves as the most dynamic element only if it operates in the absence of an element expressing a phenomenon to be presented or one expressing a specification. In this way, such elements act as successful competitors of the finite verb in the dynamics of communication: they prevent it from becoming the most dynamic element within the clause, independent or dependent. In the texts under examination, the following finite verbs have no competitors: *verdit* of 3; *noircit, blackens, schwärzt* of 4; and *urousají* of 6. (The term *competitor* was suggested to me by Valerie Adams.)

All this shows that the elements of a clause, independent or dependent, differ in the extent to which they contribute towards the further development of the communication. In the act of communication some elements are more and others less dynamic. This induces me to speak of communicative dynamism (CD), a phenomenon constantly displayed by linguistic elements in the act of communication. It is an inherent quality of communication and manifests itself in constant development towards the attainment of a communicative goal; in other words, towards the fulfilment of a communicative purpose. Participating in this development, a linguistic element assumes some position in it and in accordance with this position displays a degree of communicative dynamism.

It follows that by a degree of communicative dynamism I understand the relative extent to which a linguistic element contributes towards the further development of the communication.

Let me add some comment on the notions 'element', 'relative' and 'development'. 'Element' is used in a broad sense. Together with the hierarchy within which it operates, it will be accounted for on pages 16–20. Any linguistic element can become a carrier of CD as long as it conveys some meaning, and hence information, in the development of the communication. ('Information' covers not only purely factual content, but also attitudes, feelings and emotions.)

The qualification 'relative' is important. The degree of CD carried by a linguistic element is not measured or measurable in terms of bits of information. In the course of the development of the communication perspectived towards the fulfilment of a communicative purpose, in other words, towards the goal of the communication, a linguistic element may attain, come close to, or merely approach, this goal. The position it assumes in this process in relation to the other elements engaged in fulfilling the same communicative purpose (attaining the same goal of communication) determines the relative extent to which it contributes towards the further development of the communication. It follows that the degrees of CD are 'relative' in that the degree of CD carried by an element within a sentence is always determined in relation to the contributions that the other elements within the sentence make to the further development of the communication.

It is important to note that 'development' is not understood here as a purely linear notion. Sentence linearity is undoubtedly involved, but it cannot be claimed that the actual linear arrangement of sentence elements is always in perfect agreement with a gradual rise in CD. Let me illustrate this by the following observations.

The involvement of sentence linearity is borne out, for instance, by the fact that the element towards which the communication within a clause, independent or subordinate, is perspectived tends to occupy the final position. This is invariably the case in the Czech text, in which the element that expresses a phenomenon to be presented, or a quality further unspecified, or a specification of a quality, always occupies the final position. In this way, the element carrying the highest degree of CD closes the clause. The French text shows two, the English four, the German eight deviations, *die häßlichen Moden des Totenkults* of 1, *Winden/bindweed* of 1, *blackens/schwärzt* of 4, *Kein Pfad* of 5, *hoch* and *nasse Füße* of 6, *Sonne* of 7, *les lézards/lizards* of 7, and *les fauvettes/linnets/Grasmücken* of 9, not appearing in end position. (Sentence 9 raises a problem to be taken up on pp. 11–12.) In spite of these deviations, the presentative perspective and the quality/specification perspective remain unaffected in the four languages. This is due to the semantic character of the verb as well as the character of the semantic relationship between the verb and its competitor expressing the phenomenon presented, or its competitor expressing the quality or its specification. With a proviso concerning sentence 9, which will be discussed below on pp. 11–12 and 29–30, this relationship asserts itself irrespective of sentence position (linearity).

Unaffected by sentence position are also the degrees of CD carried by elements conveying retrievable information. Irrespective of sentence position, the degrees of CD carried by them are lower than those carried by elements conveying irretrievable information; compare, for example, the positions of *that part* and *v tu stranu* in *people do not care to visit that part* and *lidé v tu stranu neradi chodí* (6); and those of *la* and *it* in *l'air la noircit* and *the atmosphere blackens it* (4).

As the above observations illustrate, the development of the communication, which is reflected by the distribution of degrees of CD over the sentence elements, is not invariably signalled by sentence linearity, in other words by the actual linear arrangement of the sentence elements. Nevertheless, even if not to the same degree, there is evidence of a tendency to arrange the sentence elements in accordance with a gradual rise in CD in each of the four texts under examination.

In these texts, for instance, all the clauses (independent or subordinate) perspectived towards a quality or its specification place the expression of the entity to which the quality is ascribed (the quality bearer = B) before the expression of the quality (Q) as well as that of its specification (Sp) if it is present. In each case the quality and the specification (if present) convey irretrievable information; compare, for example, *people* (B) *do not care* (Q) ... *because the grass is long and they get their feet wet* (Sp); *the grass* (B) ... *long* (Q); *they* (B) *get* (Q) *their feet* (Sp) *wet* (Sp); in 6. The quality bearer carries a lower degree of CD than either an irretrievable quality or its irretrievable specification.

If, in the Czech clauses perspectived towards and closed by a phenomenon presented (Ph), the expression of such a phenomenon concurs with an adverbial element expressing a local or temporal setting (Set) against the background of which the presentation takes place, the Set always precedes the Ph (see sentences 1, as well as its second subclause, 5, 6, 7, 8 and 9). The same feature is displayed in the French text by four clauses (see 1, its second subclause, 7 and 8), in the English text by two clauses (see 1 and 8) and in the German texts by two clauses (see 1 and 8). The order described places an element carrying a lower degree of CD (a Set) before the element carrying the highest degree of CD (the Ph).

An interesting example is provided by the string of settings occurring in sentence 1. The settings identify the place of the tombstone, gradually narrowing down the location originally stated to the very spot in which the stone is situated. By gradually narrowing down the location the narrator actually leads the reader step by step to the spot occupied by the phenomenon that he wishes to present: the cemetery – one of its sections – a corner within this section – the yew in this corner – the place beneath it – the tombstone occupying it. In all the four texts, the development of the communication tallies with the linear arrangement of the settings and the phenomenon presented. Their linear arrangement displays a gradual rise in CD.

This raises the question of the relationship between degrees of CD and sentence linearity. Bolinger's important paper 'Linear modification' (1952) has demonstrated that linearity is endowed with modificatory power. He holds that 'gradation of position creates gradation of meaning when there are no interfering factors' (1952: 1125). His observation can be squared with the observations on the texts examined. In terms of degrees of CD, linear modification as a factor gradually raising degrees of CD can assert itself provided no other factors work counter to it.

If no other factors work counter to it, linear modification can fully assert itself, and the resultant distribution of CD has come to be referred to as basic. As viewed in my approach, the basic distribution of degrees of CD, reflecting a gradual rise in CD, is not language specific. It is implemented in every Indo-European language, but the extent to which it is implemented can differ from language to language. 'Basic' does not therefore necessarily mean 'the most natural', 'most frequent' or 'unmarked'.

The analyses of the written texts adduced point to two factors capable of operating counter to linear modification. One is semantic and the other contextual. It follows that in assessing degrees of CD, the analyses of the written texts have taken into consideration (i) linear modification, (ii) the character of the semantic content of the linguistic element as well as the character of the semantic relations involved, and (iii) the retrievability of the information from the immediately relevant preceding context. An interplay of these three factors determines the distribution of degrees of CD over the written sentence. It determines the perspective in which a semantic and grammatical sentence structure is to function in the act of communication; that is, it determines its functional sentence perspective.

But language is not a rigidly closed system. It cannot therefore be expected that the outcome of the interplay of factors will always be invariably unequivocal.

Potentiality (= ambiguity?)

If equivocal, the interplay of factors potentially leads to more than one interpretation. To some extent, the English version of sentence 9 can serve to illustrate. But let us first have a look at the Czech, French and German versions of this sentence.

In the French and the Czech versions, the adverbials *dans l'arbre* and *na stromě* refer to the yew tree mentioned in 1 (*un grand if/velký tis*). They convey retrievable information and hence irrespective of sentence position and semantic content carry low degrees of CD. They serve as settings. Settings are also expressed by the adverbials *Au printemps* and *Na jaře*. In the presence of these settings, the verbs *chantent* and *zpívají* perspective the communication towards the notions – phenomena to be presented – conveyed by the subjects *les fauvettes* and *pěnkavky*. Though not expressing existence or appearance on the scene explicitly, the verbs do so at least implicitly. In this way the subjects complete the development of the communication and act as competitors of the verbs. In Czech, linear modification asserts itself through placing the subject in end position. The dynamic function of the subject as well as the unequivocal outcome of the interplay is thereby underlined.

In the English and the German versions, the adverbials *on the trees* and *auf einem Baum* are not co-referential with the yew tree of 1 (*a lofty yew/einer großen Eibe*). This makes them convey irretrievable information. In spite of it, the German adverbial is best treated as a setting. Treating it as a specification and thereby perspectiving the sentence towards it would produce an undue emphasis. The reader's attention would be drawn to the fact that the linnets (*die Grasmücken*), of whose existence the reader is informed for the first time, congregate on one particular tree. It is worth noticing that the definite article (*auf dem Baum*) would render the adverbial co-referential with *einer großen Eibe* and mark it unequivocally as retrievable and as a setting.

Containing a plural noun, the English adverbial *on the trees* would not produce undue emphasis if interpreted as a specification. It appears, however, more adequate to interpret it as a setting. This is because the preceding sentences 7 and 8 are presentational. These are the phenomena presented by them: a little sunshine, lizards, and the rustling of wild oats. It is quite natural to assume that 9 will continue this string by presenting the linnets. Nevertheless, the possibility of interpreting the adverbial *on the trees* as a specification cannot be excluded.

Potentiality can be removed in the sphere of the spoken language. By placing the intonation centre (IC) of the sentence, i.e. the most prominent prosodic feature within the sentence, on *les fauvettes/ linnets/die Grasmücken/pěnkavky*, the speaker unequivocally signals the presentational interpretation. This interpretation is now co-signalled and corroborated by intonation, which joins the interplay of FSP factors as an additional factor at the level of the spoken language.

Actual linear arrangement and interpretative arrangement

The present chapter has demonstrated that linguistic elements differ in the extent to which they contribute to the development of the communication. It has outlined what is meant by functional sentence perspective and by degrees of communicative dynamism.

The distribution of degrees of CD necessitates making a distinction between actual linear arrangement and interpretative arrangement. By the latter I understand the arrangement of the sentence elements in accordance with a gradual rise in CD. The two arrangements may, but need not, coincide. Under the contextual conditions stipulated above, the sentences placed in the left-hand column have the interpretative arrangements given in the right-hand column. (For a necessary refinement of the interpretative arrangements, see p. 73.)

(4)	l'air la noircit	la l'air noircit
(4)	the atmosphere blackens it	it the atmosphere blackens
(4)	die Luft schwärzt ihn	ihn die Luft schwärzt
(7)	Quand..., les lézards y vien- nent	y Quand..., viennent les lézards
(7)	When..., lizards disport themselves on it	on it When..., disport themselves lizards

(7) Wenn..., kommen die Ei-   Wenn..., kommen die Eidechsen
dechsen

Organization of the present study

The following chapters offer a discussion of the concepts involved, and do so on an empirical basis. They will enquire into the interplay of the FSP factors, delimiting the ranges of their operation within the interplay. They will establish a degree of CD carried by a linguistic element as a communicative feature (communicative value) acquired by the element in the course of the development of the communication, i.e. in the dynamics of the communication, and delimit and hierarchize the linguistic elements acting as carriers of degrees of CD.

The interrelation of the FSP factors within their interplay reveals that FSP constitutes a system. The first part of the present book will deal with the operation of this system within the written language and the second with its operation within the spoken language. The first part will contain a special chapter on the relationship between FSP and word order.

Especially when dealing with the written language, the empirical approach adopted in the book makes use of the contrastive method, frequently comparing English with other languages, especially German, French and Czech. (A similarly extensive comparison at the level of the spoken language must be left to further research.) The contrastive method proves to be a useful heuristic tool capable of throwing valuable light on the characteristic features of the languages contrasted; compare the method of linguistic characterology advocated by Mathesius (e.g. 1928 and 1975) and Vachek (e.g. 1975) and subscribed to by me.

The views of other scholars will naturally also be discussed, although, for reasons stated in the Preface, not to an extent required by a study surveying the state of the art. My study does not claim to present such a survey.

2 The sentence and the carriers of communicative dynamism

The sentence as a field of relations

Before starting a discussion of the problems of FSP, the question must be answered of how to interpret the relation between the semantic contents and the semantic ties interlinking them within the sentence on the one hand, and the grammatical (syntactic) structure of the sentence on the other; and of how to interpret the relation of this semantic and grammatical complex to FSP. In my approach I have adopted the following assessment of these interrelations.

The communicative needs of the speaker are satisfied through a twofold process: elements of thought – reflecting the extralinguistic reality, concrete or abstract – are denominated by naming units, which are combined to produce sentences. The former process consists in selecting – or if need be, in coining – naming units (and is covered by Mathesius' functional onomatology; see Mathesius 1975); the latter consists in syntactic structuration (and is covered by Mathesius' functional syntax; see ibid.).

Either process involves meaning and form. This may be obvious in regard to the onomatological process, but perhaps less so in regard to the process of syntactic structuration. But the latter does not merely combine forms: as has been emphasized by Reichling (1961: 1) and subscribed to by Daneš (1968: 55), syntactic structuration effects a semantic connection, i.e. a connection of meanings. In this way syntactic structure (and grammatical structure in general) is ultimately rooted in meaning (Poldauf 1954). Trost speaks of grammatical structuration effected on a semantic basis (Trost 1962: 268; in Sgall's translation, semantically grounded grammatical articulation; Trost 1987: 147).

As I see it, the communicative (functional) perspective of a sentence is implemented in the course of the twofold process outlined above. It

is _not_ imposed on a sentence already existing as a finished product. It is
in this sense that I speak of a semantic and grammatical sentence
structure resulting from the twofold process and functioning in a definite
kind of perspective. This conception is in harmony with Vachek's
modified version of Mathesius' definition of the sentence. Vachek
regards the sentence as an elementary reaction to any extralinguistic
reality, existing both objectively and subjectively (Vachek 1975: 85).

Further comment is necessary on the concept of sentence. Trost holds
that the sentence can be delimited as a field of syntactic relations which
are either determinative or non-determinative, i.e. copulative. They do
not extend beyond the sentence. A word syntactically unrelated either to
words that precede or to words that follow constitutes a sentence (Trost
1962: 267; 1987: 148). Such delimitation recognizes the existence of
verbless sentences (1962: 268; 1987: 149). Nevertheless, Trost
emphasizes that sentencehood is a relative value: for instance, in contrast
with the sentence _Přijde_ ('He/She/It-will-come'), the sentence _Bratr
přijde_ ('Brother he-will-come') has a structure more solidly built up
owing to the presence of a subject implemented by a separate word
(1962: 269; 1987: 149). More comment on the relative value of
sentencehood is offered below.

As I see it, the sentence, delimited by Trost as a field of syntactic
relations, also serves as a field within which the degrees of CD are
distributed, the distribution inducing the sentence to function in a
particular perspective, i.e. perspectiving it towards the element carrying
the highest degree of CD.

Lastly, Trost's conception of the sentence as a field of relations is also
applicable to the sentence as bearer of prosodic (intonational) features in
the spoken language. In this sphere, but not in that of the written
language, the sentence serves as a distributional field of prosodic
prominence (weight). The question of the relationship between the
distribution of degrees of CD as determined by the non-prosodic FSP
factors and the distribution of degrees of prosodic prominence will be
taken up in the second part of the present study.

Like sentencehood, distributional fieldhood is a relative value.
Distributional subfields are provided by subclauses, semiclauses and
even by nominal phrases (Svoboda 1968, 1987; see this volume pp.
83–5). The central position, however, is occupied by distributional
fields provided by independent verbal sentences. It is in relation to them
that other distributional fields are evaluated. (Let me add that by a

semiclause I understand a non-finite verb form together with the elements expanding it.)

The relative value of sentencehood/fieldhood manifests itself also in regard to the distinctness with which one sentence/field is delimited from another. For instance, in *After the row, he went to bed and slept. Fast and soundly* the full stop and capitalization distance the adverbs from the verb to such a degree as to create a new sentence/field. Though their relationship is not totally effaced, the adverbs and the verb are practically severed from one another. In the spoken language, intonation takes over and asserts itself in clarifying the internal organization of the sentence/field and in delimiting it from its neighbours.

In the present study, I consistently link the designation 'sentence' with fieldhood serving a communicative purpose under certain contextual conditions. In the absence of such conditions, linguistic elements organized into an integrated field of syntactic relations do not represent a structure actually serving as a sentence in the functional sense of the word. They represent a structure capable of performing such a task, but not actually carrying it out. Seen in this light, they merely represent a (semantic and grammatical) sentence structure that is communicatively inoperative: they do not represent a sentence in a truly functional sense of the word.

Comparing the semantic and grammatical sentence structures in actual use, we find that one and the same structure can appear in different functional perspectives. This means that a semantic and grammatical sentence structure can operate under varying contextual conditions. It shows a range of contextual applicability. I shall discuss this phenomenon on pages 110–14 and 214–16.

The wording 'definite perspective' covers two aspects. It refers to the actual perspective in which a sentence functions in the act of communication and/or to the type of perspective implemented in such an act. One aspect applies to the sentence serving as an utterance event, the other to the sentence implementing an utterance type. (I owe this distinction to the writings of Daneš.)

The hierarchy of carriers of communicative dynamism

The distribution of degrees of CD within a distributional field involves carriers of degrees of CD, i.e. linguistic elements that convey some meaning and hence participate in the development of the communication and according to the extent to which they contribute to this development are assigned degrees of CD within the distributional field.

The expression 'linguistic element' is used here in a wide sense. Any linguistic element – a clause, a phrase, a word, a morpheme or even a submorphemic feature (e.g., the vowel alternation *sing, sang, sung*) – can become a carrier of CD on account of the meaning it conveys. In fact, even a semantic feature without a formal implementation of its own is a meaningful 'linguistic element' and is therefore to be regarded as a carrier of CD; consider the contrasts conveyed by *Peter stayed in London, and Paul decided to go to Edinburgh*. In the written language, the contrast between *Peter* and *Paul* and that between *London* and *Edinburgh* are additional pieces of information and raise the degrees of CD carried by the proper names, but do not affect their written form. For convenience, 'element' will be frequently used in my discussions, but only when context makes it sufficiently clear what type of linguistic element is spoken of.

In the process of syntactic structuration a CD carrier constitutes or – together with another CD carrier or other CD carriers – co-constitutes a communicative unit. This requires an explanation. I agree with Svoboda (1968) that a sentence, a clause, a semiclause and even a nominal phrase serve as distributional fields of CD in the act of communication, and that their syntactic constituents (e.g., subject, predicative verb, object, ... head element, attributive element ...) serve as communicative units. This means that the sentence structure *Peter decided to learn foreign languages/that he would learn foreign languages* provides a distributional field. With an important modification to be adduced below, the syntactic constituents within this field – the subject *Peter*, the predicative verb *decided* and the object *to learn foreign languages/that he would learn foreign languages* – serve as communicative units.

In their turn, the clause *that he would learn foreign languages* and the semiclause *to learn foreign languages* provide distributional subfields, their communicative units being respectively the conjunction *that*, the subject *he*, the predicative verb *would learn*, the object *foreign languages*; and the non-finite verb *to learn* and the object *foreign languages*.

The nominal phrase *foreign languages* provides a subfield as well, its communicative units being the headword *languages* and the attribute *foreign*. Being itself a communicative unit within a subfield, it represents a distributional field of third rank. (The sentence structure under discussion provides a basic, or first-rank, distributional field and the clause/semiclause occurring within it a second-rank distributional field.)

The important modification concerns the predicative verb, which is regarded by syntacticians as one communicative unit. But for reasons to be accounted for in detail later (p. 91), it is considered to represent two communicative units in FSP, one constituted by its notional component and the other by its categorial exponents, i.e. its formal signals conveying such indications as those of tense, mood, modality, person, number, gender, voice, aspect, polarity. (I accept Halliday's distinction between mood and modality, mood being the selection by the speaker of a particular communicative role in the speech situation reflected as a statement, question, command or exclamation, and modality a form of the speaker's comment on or assessment of what he is saying. But in my discussions of the FSP functions of the categorial exponents of the finite verb, I use only 'mood' and 'modal', both terms covering both concepts.)

The categorial exponents are implemented as separate auxiliary words (cf. *would* and *have* in *would have decided*), affixes (cf. *-ed* in *you have decided* and *ge-* and *-en* in *du hast gesehen*), endings (cf. *-s* in *reads*), submorphemic features (cf. *spring, sprang, sprung*), or zero features (cf. the bare stem form *sing* used as imperative).

Singling out the implementation(s) of an indication (indications), I speak of an exponent of person (PE), an exponent of number (NE), or exponents of person and number (the PNEs), an exponent of tense (TE), an exponent of mood (ME), or exponents of tense and mood (the TMEs), etc.

With the exception of the exponent of negative polarity (NegPolE), the exponents frequently coincide in form: for instance, *-s* of *goes* in *He usually goes for a walk in the afternoon* simultaneously serves as PE, NE, TE, ME, VE (exponent of voice) and a PosPolE (exponent of positive polarity).

As the TMEs convey the basic predicative categories, they are regarded as representatives of a subgroup which they form together with the exponents of V, A and PosPol. As will be demonstrated, this subgroup plays a particularly important role in FSP. For convenience, I will speak only of the TMEs, and I beg the reader to bear in mind this simplification.

The assessment of the positions of the communicative units in the development of the communication, i.e. their degrees of CD, will be discussed in the following chapters. Anticipating these discussions, let me just say every distributional field is perspectived towards the communicative unit that carries the highest degree of CD: every distributional field has its functional perspective. The sentence structure *Paul decided to learn foreign languages/that he would learn foreign languages* would be interpreted as follows. Provided only *Paul* conveys retrievable information, the basic distributional field is perspectived to *to learn foreign languages/that he would learn foreign languages*; the first-rank subfield is oriented to *foreign languages*; and the second-rank subfield to *foreign*.

It follows that (i) a communicative unit can carry more degrees of CD than one and in this respect be heterogeneous in regard to CD, and (ii) while a communicative unit is always a carrier of CD, a carrier of CD need not constitute a communicative unit. This means that a communicative unit always has its form, which does not invariably apply to a carrier of CD. Not every discernible semantic element (which on account of its meaningfulness participates in the development of the communication) has its special form.

The communicative units, and the CD carriers in general, are organized through syntax, which induces them to operate in hier-archically ranked distributional fields. At the same time, however, it permits them to be hierarchized in accordance with the requirements of FSP (cf. the subordinate clause in *Peter decided that he would learn foreign languages*, serving as a subfield towards which the basic distributional field is perspectived).

Generally speaking, the number of degrees of CD carried by a sentence (or the number of carriers of CD occurring in a sentence, for that matter) is not fixed. Nor is the number of communicative units. There are as many communicative units and as many carriers of CD in general as provided by the semantic and syntactic sentence structure.

As for the syntactic constituents (sentence/clause components and phrase components), I am aware that problems of interpretation may arise. There may, for instance, be disagreement as to the line of demarcation between objects and adverbials; prepositional objects may not be recognized at all. (I retain the concept of prepositional object, because I find it convenient to do so in my contrastive approach.) In regard to FSP, however, the semantic character of a communicative unit is, as a rule, of greater relevance than its syntactic status.

In non-Indo-European languages other types of syntactic components may occur than in Indo-European languages, but I venture to assume that in non-Indo-European languages the syntactic structuration plays the same role in delimiting the communicative units as in Indo-European languages.

3   The contextual factor

The introductory chapter has given a rough sketch of the interplay of the three factors that determine the distribution of degrees of CD over a written sentence and in this way its FSP (see p. 11). The present chapter will concentrate on the operation of what for convenience is termed the 'contextual factor'; what is actually in play is the retrievability/irretrievability from the immediately relevant context (see ibid.). Since context is a complex phenomenon, the chapter will have to deal with a number of questions (see Daneš 1974b: 109–10). As Daneš has pointed out (ibid.), one of them is the relative and very broad (if not vague) character of the notions of given (known, old) and new (unknown) information. This question will be taken up first.

Known information and the structure of context

An examination of the function of the articles in FSP (Firbas 1957, 1966) shows that information marked by the definite article as known cannot always be regarded as such from the point of view of FSP. The following sentence will illustrate.

> Beryl stepped over the window, crossed the veranda, ran down the grass to the gate. He was there behind her. (M 62)

(For abbreviations following example sentences or passages and indicating the sources, see the list of abbreviations, pp. xiii–xv. The number after the abbreviation indicates the page of the source.)

In view of the development of the narration, the elements *the window*, *the veranda*, *the grass* and *the gate* convey new information, although they have already occurred in the story and in this sense convey information that is known. But they introduce new information by telling the reader the place Beryl ran to (the gate) and how she got there (over the window, across the veranda and down the grass).

Proper names behave in the same way as appelatives.

[...and a very gay figure walked down the path to the gate.]
It was Alice, the servant girl, dressed for her afternoon out.
(M 40)

Alice, the servant girl, is a character already familiar to the reader, but it is announced now that it was just she who was coming down the path.

Roughly speaking, there are two types of known information that can be conveyed by the sentence in the act of communication: (i) information that, though conveying knowledge shared by the interlocutors, must be considered unknown in regard to the immediately relevant communicative step to be taken and in this sense irretrievable from the context; and (ii) information that not only conveys common knowledge shared by the interlocutors, but is fully retrievable from the context even in regard to the immediately relevant communicative step.

In regard to FSP, the concept of known information must be considerably narrowed. This necessitates the introduction of the concept of the immediately relevant verbal and situational context, immediate relevance being assessed in relation to the point in the flow of communication at which a new sentence is produced and/or taken in and which separates the mass of information accumulated so far from the mass of information to be further accumulated (see Daneš 1974b: 112). Henri Weil was well aware of the relevance of this point when he said: 'Car dans la parole, ce qu'il y a de plus essentiel, c'est le moment de la conception et de l'énonciation: c'est dans ce moment que se trouve toute la vie de la parole, avant ce moment elle n'existait pas; après, elle est morte' (1844: 27).

In Czech, Vilém Mathesius felicitously used the qualification *aktuální* in reference to the organization of the sentence as implemented and/or perceived at the moment just described. Like French *actuel* and German *aktuell*, Czech *aktuální* conveys the meaning of 'being of immediate interest and concern'. Unfortunately, this meaning does not associate so readily with English *actual*, which primarily suggests the meaning of 'existing in fact', 'real'. This was decisive for the introduction of the term *functional sentence perspective*, which I now regard as an equivalent of *aktuální členění větné* (*division actuelle de la phrase, aktuelle Satzgliederung*), coined by Mathesius.

The immediately relevant context, verbal and situational, is only a fraction of the complex phenomenon of context. It is embedded in a sphere formed by the entire preceding verbal context and the entire situational and experiential context accompanying it. In its turn, this sphere is embedded within a still larger one constituted by all the knowledge and experience shared by the interlocutors, which then forms part of the general context of human knowledge and experience.

The complexity of context is increased by possible borderline areas between the spheres. Of particular importance is the borderline area between the immediately relevant context and the rest of the complex of context.

So far the context following the sentence has not been mentioned. Strictly speaking, it is only at the level of the written language that such context is available at the moment a sentence is to be taken in. Contrary to the listener, the reader may move backwards or forwards in the written text and spend some time on the interpretation of the sentence. The listener has not normally the following context at his disposal (Vachek 1976: 411–12). This is only the case when the spoken text has been recorded and can be replayed. In any case, if available, the immediately relevant following context, written or spoken, can help to throw valuable light on the communicative purpose fulfilled by the sentence produced and/or taken in. (This point will also be discussed in greater detail later; see p. 51.)

The immediately relevant context

As the immediately relevant context and retrievability/irretrievability from it play significant roles in FSP, they deserve to be discussed in greater detail. Let me open the discussion with two questions. (i) For how long a stretch or span in the flow of communication can a piece of information remain retrievable (and in this sense known in regard to the immediately relevant communicative step to be taken) without being mentioned again? And likewise in respect to the situational context: (ii) how narrow is the sphere yielding referents suggesting pieces of information that can be considered retrievable and in this sense known in regard to the immediately relevant communicative step to be taken?

(i) As to the length of the retrievability span within the preceding verbal context, Svoboda's observation is of special interest. Analysing an Old English homily, he came to the conclusion that after its last occurrence in the text an element remains retrievable for the span of seven clauses (Svoboda 1981: 88–9). Hajičová and Vrbová's enquiries into spoken texts carried out from the viewpoint of the hierarchy of activation (1981, 1982) point in the same direction, i.e. to very short stretches of text.

It is perhaps not feasible to give a generally valid exact number of distributional fields that can intervene between two occurrences of a piece of information and do not obliterate the retrievability of the earlier occurrence. Further, borderline cases permit different interpretations and in consequence evoke the phenomenon of potentiality (to be discussed later, see pp. 108–10). However, as will be demonstrated, uncertainty about the retrievability of an element need not affect the interpretation of its degree of CD, for this may ultimately be determined through the interplay of the FSP factors. Moreover, as will be shown presently, more light can be thrown on the length of the retrievability span if the problem is approached from a different angle.

(ii) As to the immediately relevant situational context, it has to be described, because of its non-verbal nature, in terms of non-linguistic referents. I find that it is constituted by two groups of referents, strikingly different in character, but both retrievable.

The chief representative of the first group is the speaker/writer. As producer, he or she is permanently present in the ever-changing situational context. Another important representative is the listener/ reader, to whom the sentence is addressed. When the sentence is perceived, he or she is even present in the flesh. Of all the other notions, it is that of people in general and that of nature in general which, in regard to permanent obviousness, come close to the notions of speaker/writer and listener/reader. These four notions are frequently referred to by such pronouns as *I*, *you*, the impersonal *it*, *one*, German *man*, French *on*, etc. (see Svoboda 1983: 55; Firbas 1986a: 56). It is worth noting that these pronouns can be introduced into the discourse directly, not pronominalizing any antecedents (predecessors). (An observation suggested to me by a formulation of Daneš; see 1985: 202 note.) This bears out the permanent places that the notions involved occupy in the ever-changing immediately relevant situational contexts. With due alterations, the same applies to the pronoun, or rather proadverb, *there* of the existential construction. Though semantically very weak, it is not totally stripped of all meaning. As an integral part of the existential construction, it acts as an indicator of a scene expressed by a genuine adverbial of place (*There were books on the table*; *There were books there*). Further research may add one or two other notions belonging to this group, but on the whole their total number will remain small. Their common denominator is a high degree of permanent obviousness.

The second group of referents is constituted by such items of the extralinguistic reality as are of immediate, *ad hoc* concern both to the speaker and to the listener. For instance, the attention of two friends walking along the street has been drawn to a boy falling off his bicycle; their interest has been aroused by the noise caused by the fall: 'I hope he hasn't hurt himself', one friend may say to the other, *he* conveying information retrievable from the extralinguistic situation at the moment of utterance. Or they may see a ferocious dog, which naturally becomes the object of their immediate concern: 'I do hope he won't bite us', one says to the other, once again making the pronoun *he* express a referent that is retrievable from the situational context. This type of operation of the immediately relevant context is restricted practically to the sphere of the spoken language.

Let me further clarify the concepts of immediately relevant context and retrievability/irretrievability by analysing two short texts – the English version of the Victor Hugo text (see pp. 3–4) and a short extract from a story by Katherine Mansfield ('At the bay', ch. 6; see below).

Developing a text, the language user keeps on introducing information previously unexpressed into the flow of the communication. Once introduced, a piece of information can pass out of this flow without being re-expressed, or it can stay in it and be re-expressed once or more times after a shorter or longer intervening stretch of text.

The analyses of the two texts will establish the frequency of notions (pieces of information) newly introduced, and the frequency of those re-expressed; and also which of the notions re-expressed have the status of retrievable information, and which stretches of text can be accorded the status of retrievability spans. (For the purpose of the present analyses the expression *newly introduced* is to be understood to mean 'appearing for the first time in the text specimen under analysis'.)

An analysis of the Hugo text reveals that the notions newly introduced heavily outnumber those re-expressed. Of the 66 words making up the long complex opening sentence, only six re-express notions already introduced; see *this city of tombs* referring back to *the cemetery of Père Lachaise, which* to *those fantastic sepulchres*, and *which* to *a lofty yew*.

Of the 79 words making up the rest of the text, only seven re-express notions already introduced; see *This stone* of 2 (i.e. the second sentence of the text) and the *its* of 3, 4, 5 and 7, all referring back to *a tombstone* of 1; *they* of 6 to *people* of 6; and *that part* of 6 to the scene depicted in 1–5.

Of particular interest are the distances between two co-referential elements, a predecessor and its re-expression. In terms of basic distributional fields (see p. 18), a re-expression occurs within one and the same field as its predecessor, or within a field adjacent to that of its predecessor, or within a field separated by one or more fields from that of its predecessor. In the English version of the Hugo text, the distance between two co-referential elements does not exceed one basic distributional field – a distance that certainly does not obliterate retrievability. It follows that the re-expressions occurring in the text convey retrievable information. They all undoubtedly occur within the retrievability spans opened by their predecessors.

A tabular analysis of four paragraphs of a text taken from Katherine Mansfield's short story 'At the bay' and adduced below yields a similar result. The analysis follows the text.

(1) In a steamer chair, under a manuka tree that grew in the middle of the front grass patch, Linda Burnell dreamed the morning away. (2) She did nothing. (3) She looked up at the dark, close, dry leaves of the manuka, at the chinks of blue between, (4) and now and again a tiny yellowish flower dropped on her. (5) Pretty – (6) yes, if you held one of those flowers on the palm of your hand and looked at it closely, it was an exquisite small thing. (7) Each pale yellow petal shone as if each was the careful work of a loving hand. (8) The tiny tongue in the centre gave it the shape of a bell. (9) And when you turned it over the outside was a deep bronze colour. (10) But as soon as they flowered, they fell and were scattered. (11) You brushed them off your frock as you talked; (12) the horrid little things got caught in one's hair. (13) Why, then, flower at all? (14) Who takes the trouble – or the joy – to make all these things that are wasted, wasted... (15) It was uncanny.

(16) On the grass beside her, lying between two pillows, was the boy. (17) Sound asleep he lay, his head turned away from his mother. (18) His fine dark hair looked more like a shadow than like real hair, (19) but his ear was a bright, deep coral. (20) Linda clasped her hands above her head (21) and crossed her feet. (22) It was very pleasant to know that all these

bungalows were empty, that everybody was down on the beach, out of sight, out of hearing. (23) She had the garden to herself; (24) she was alone.

(25) Dazzling white the picotees shone; (26) the golden-eyed marigold glittered; (27) the nasturtiums wreathed the veranda poles in green and gold flame. (28) If only one had time to look at these flowers long enough, time to get over the sense of novelty and strangeness, time to know them! (29) But as soon as one paused to part the petals, to discover the underside of the leaf, along came Life (30) and one was swept away. (31) And, lying in her cane chair, Linda felt so light; (32) she felt like a leaf. (33) Along came Life like a wind (34) and she was seized and shaken; (35) she had to go. (36) Oh dear, would it always be so? (37) Was there no escape?

(38) Now she sat on the veranda of their Tasmanian home, leaning against her father's knee. (39) And he promised, (40) 'As soon as you and I are old enough, Linny, we'll cut off somewhere, we'll escape. (41) Two boys together. (42) I have a fancy I'd like to sail up a river in China.' (43) Linda saw that river, very wide, covered with little rafts and boats. (44) She saw the yellow hats of the boatmen (45) and she heard their high, thin voices as they called... (Mansfield 1966: 31–2).

The left column in the chart below records elements newly introduced in the flow, elements expressing notions re-introduced into it after a longer absence from it (indicated by ˅˅), and elements newly introduced into the flow, but referring to the group (i) phenomena of the immediately relevant situational context (indicated by ˅; see p. 24). The right column records re-expressions of notions conveyed by elements listed in the left column. The numbers in parentheses indicate the sentences (basic distributional fields) in which the elements occur. Square brackets enclose words serving as attributes within noun phrases the heads of which convey irretrievable information.

The chart presents co-referential links formed by two, and co-referential strings formed by more than two, items. It is worth noticing that the distance between two co-referential elements does not amount to more than three basic distributional fields – a distance that once again does not obliterate retrievability. The re-expressions occur within the retrievability spans of their predecessors.

First paragraph

Linda Burnell (1)   She (2), She (3), her (4)

a manuka (1)   that (1), the manuka (3)

a tiny yellowish flower (4)   [those flowers] (6), they (10), they (10),
                                    them (11), the horrid little things (12),
                                    all these things that are wasted, wasted
                                    (14)

one (6)   it (6), it (6), it (8), it (9)

you (6) ˅   [your] (6), you (9), you (11), [your]
                                    (11), you (11), [one's] (12)

Each (7)   each (7)

Second paragraph

Linda Burnell (1) ˅˅   [her] (16), his mother (17), Linda (20)
                                    [her] (20), [her] (20), [her] (21), She
                                    (23) (as for *herself* of 23, see p. 35),
                                    she (24)

lying (16)   lay (17)

the boy (16)   he (17), [his] (17), [his] (17), [his] (18),
                                    [his] (19)

fine dark hair (18)   [hair] (18)

Third paragraph

the picotees (25), the golden-   these flowers (28)
eyed marigold (26), the nas-
turtiums (27)

time (28)   time (28), time (28)

one (28) ˅   one (29), one (30)

Life (29)   Life (33)

Linda Burnell (1) ˅˅   [her] (31), Linda (31), she (32), she
                                    (34), she (35)

Fourth paragraph

Linda Burnell (1) ˅˅   she (38), [her] (38), you (40), we (40),
                                    we (40), Linda (43), She (44), she (45)

father (38)   he (39), I (40), we (40), we (40), I (42),
                                    I (42)

a river (42)   that river (43)

the boatmen (44)   [their] (45), they (45)

An item of special interest is the notion of 'Linda Burnell'. It occurs in the following fields: 1, 2, 3 and 4; 16, 17, 20, 20, 20, 23 and 24; 31, 32, 34 and 35; 38, 38, 40, 41, 43, 44 and 45. Note the gaps between fields 4 and 16, and 24 and 31, the first amounting to ten fields and the second to six fields.

The fields 5–15, which form the first gap, convey Linda Burnell's meditative soliloquy on the tiny flower that had dropped on her from the manuka tree (see 4). Throughout this passage, the reader is aware of Linda Burnell's presence in the flow of communication, for the generalizing *you* of the *you*-string (6, 6, 9, 11, 11, 11 and 12) includes the soliloquist. In this manner, the *you*-string efficiently fills the gap and keeps Linda Burnell in the flow of communication, and thus, the gap has in fact been removed.

The fields 25–30, which form the second gap, continue to convey Linda Burnell's meditation. Within this portion of the text, it is the generalizing *one*-string (28, 29 and 30) that produces the same effect as the *you*-string. In this way, even the second gap has in fact been removed.

In consequence, the *you*-string, the *one*-string and the three *Linda Burnell* strings actually form one long string, which keeps 'Linda Burnell' in the flow of communication throughout the passage. An analysis of the text shows that 'Linda Burnell' remains retrievable in the narrow sense of the word throughout the flow of the communication till the end of chapter 6 (of which the passage examined represents about two fifths).

It follows that even within the 'long' *Linda Burnell* string the retrievability span does not exceed three basic distributional fields. This conclusion does not establish the maximum length of the retrievability span in general, but corroborates that it is normal for the retrievability span to be very short. Returning to the Hugo text, we find that this is also borne out by the following observation.

In the French original there is a comparatively long distance between *un grand if* (1), an expression introducing a new notion, and its re-expression, *l'arbre* (9): it amounts to seven basic distributional fields. A careful reader will notice the co-referential link between the two, regard the second as conveying retrievable information, and perspective sentence 9 towards the irretrievable *les fauvettes*. This reader will be right in doing so, for *l'arbre* conveys part of the background against which the notions expressed by *les fauvettes* (9), *les lézards* (7) and *un frémissement de folles avoines* (8) are set off. A less careful reader, however, may overlook the co-referential link.

The English and the German translators have actually done so and translated *l'arbre* by *the trees* and *einem Baum*, respectively. The Czech translation and a recent English one render it correctly by *stromě* and *the tree*, respectively.

> In sunny weather lizards visit it, there is a stir of grasses all around it and birds sing in the tree. (Victor Hugo, *Les Misérables*, translated by Norman Denny, Harmondsworth: Penguin Classics, 1984, p. 1200)

The example demonstrates how, on account of its length, retrievability span can become less distinct and almost obliterated and in consequence reduce the effectiveness of the communication.

The shortness of the retrievability span is undoubtedly also due to the continuous influx of new, irretrievable information into the communication. New information continuously opens up new retrievability spans, obliterating those that are not efficiently maintained. Like the Hugo text, the Mansfield text shows an overwhelming preponderance of irretrievable over retrievable information.

Counting all the words occurring in chapter 6, we find that their total number is 1,167. Irretrievable information is conveyed by 969 words, i.e. 83 per cent, and retrievable information by 198, i.e. 17 per cent. If co-referential words repeating retrievable information are not counted, the ratio of irretrievable and retrievable information is 969 (95 per cent) : 56 (5 per cent). The numbers would be somewhat different if they were not based on words, but on communicative units. (This is because a communicative unit can consist of more words than one and because its rank must be taken into account as well.) But the relationship between retrievable and irretrievable information would remain essentially the same.

Under the circumstances, this relationship is also unaffected by a phenomenon that will be discussed in greater detail later (pp. 32–9). For instance, on account of its co-referentiality with *flowers* (6), *the horrid little things* (in the string introduced by *a tiny yellowish flower*; see p. 28) conveys retrievable information. At the same time, however, it is not devoid of irretrievable information – the speaker's emotional characterization. This raises the problem of heterogeneity in regard to retrievability/irretrievability and that of predominance of one or the other type of information (see pp. 32–9).

It is through information retrievable from the immediately relevant verbal and situational context that a sentence is embedded in the flow of communication and rendered dependent on this immediately relevant contextual sphere. Irretrievable information, on the other hand, is independent of it.

True enough, a piece of information may be retrievable or irretrievable from the part of context outside the immediately relevant contextual sphere, and hence dependent on or independent of this part of context. However, in regard to the immediately relevant communicative step, in other words in regard to the immediately relevant communicative orientation of the sentence (its FSP), it is not the wider, but the immediately relevant, context that plays the decisive and determinative role. In the present study, the expressions 'context-dependent' and 'context-independent' are to be understood – unless specified otherwise – as retrievable and irretrievable from the immediately relevant context, respectively.

Signalling of context dependence

How is retrievability, which renders an element context-dependent, signalled? First, those cases should be mentioned in which retrievable information is conveyed (i) by a repetition of a non-pronominal expression, (ii) by a pronoun, (iii) by a morphological exponent, or (iv) by ellipsis. As has been pointed out by other scholars (e.g., Daneš 1985:192ff.; Halliday 1985: 287ff.), all these devices signal co-reference.

Naturally, only such co-reference is relevant as occurs within the retrievability span. Uncertainty as to the extent of the retrievability span and/or referential identity (i.e. whether two or more elements have the same referent) and/or the predominance of co-referential or non-coreferential information within one element (see the discussion of heterogeneity on pp. 32–7) opens the door to potentiality and hence to equivocal interpretation.

The devices listed under (i) to (iv) above can all be found in the four Mansfield paragraphs.

For (i), see, for instance, the repetitions *Linda* (20, 31 and 43), echoing 'Linda Burnell', *manuka* (3), *flowers* (6), *Life* (33), and *river* (43).

For (ii), see, for instance, the personal pronouns (e.g., *she* in 2, 3, 23, 24, 32, 34, 35, 38, 44 and 45, and *you* in 9, 11, 11), the possessive pronouns (e.g., *her* in 16, 20, 31, 38) and the relative pronoun *that* in 1.

For (iii), see, for instance, the exponent of person and number in *was* (24), co-referential with *She* of 23.

For (iv), see the ellipted *she* in *Linda clasped her hands above her head and* [o] *crossed her feet* (21).

Close to non-pronominal expressions identical in form with their predecessors (see (i)) stand expressions that show some formal similarity and some co-referentiality with their predecessors; compare *reader* and *reading* in *Peter is a voracious reader, but I just don't see any sense in his reading*; and *lay* (17) and its predecessor *lying* (16).

Another large group is constituted by synonyms and a wide range of co-referential expressions of other types. Members of this group convey some additional meaning, which is irretrievable. In this way, they are not fully context-dependent; they are heterogeneous in regard to retrievability/irretrievability, and in consequence in regard to context-dependence/independence.

The following comments can be made on an English version of a Czech example adduced by Daneš (1985: 202).

> In the introduction the author characterizes the personality of Ernest Hemingway. This admirer, adorer and worshipper of Africa, hunter, fighter and writer is here presented as...

The element *This admirer, ... and writer* is co-referential with *Ernest Hemingway*. Nevertheless, it conveys a considerable amount of irretrievable information, though not the information towards which the sentence is perspectived.

Retaining the introductory sentence of the example, let us alter the sequel sentence in the following way.

> In the introduction, the author characterizes the personality of Ernest Hemingway. He presents him as an admirer, adorer and worshipper of Africa, hunter, fighter and writer.

The additional information 'admirer, ... and writer' remains the same, but it has become the information towards which the sequel sentence is perspectived. The element expressing it is no longer co-referential; nor is it heterogeneous in regard to context dependence and context independence: it is entirely context-independent. Note the replacement of the demonstrative *this* by the indefinite article *an*.

In either version, the perspective of the sequel sentence is unequivocal. This cannot be said about the third version, which follows.

> In the introduction the author characterizes the personality of Ernest Hemingway. And who would not like to read something about this admirer, adorer and worshipper of Africa, hunter, fighter and writer.

This is because the co-referential character of the element *this admirer, ... and writer* may not fully assert itself. If it does, it induces the element to recede into the background and permits the sentence to be perspectived to the notion of 'reading'. If it does not, it permits the considerable amount of irretrievable information conveyed by the element to serve as a characterization towards which the sentence is perspectived. This perspective can actually be regarded as heralded by the verb *characterize*, occurring in the preceding sentence.

The two interpretations point to potentiality. Under the contextual conditions intonation would decide which way the sentence is perspectived. In an overwhelming majority of cases, however, it is without the disambiguating aid of intonation that either the retrievable or the irretrievable feature predominates for one reason or another. It is one of the tasks of the enquiry into FSP to establish these reasons. The following observations are a contribution to such an enquiry.

Apart from the co-referential expressions, there are others that, strictly speaking, are not co-referential, but merely convey associative meaning; compare *restaurant* and *lunch*; *summer* and *vacation, science* and *investigators*; *school*, and *pupils* and *teachers*.

If within the retrievability span *lunch, vacation, investigators, pupils and teachers* follow *restaurant, summer, science* and *school*, respectively, they convey information that is related to that conveyed by their predecessors and in this respect share a kind of semantic associative feature with them: 'catering', 'the warmest holiday season of the year', 'research' and 'education'. When expressed by the second member of the pair so associated, this feature becomes retrievable, but is evidently not strong enough to predominate and to make its bearer behave like a context-dependent element. In contrast to a fully context-dependent element, which on account of its context dependence is prevented from expressing the information towards which the sentence is perspectived, the bearer of the associative semantic feature does not lose its capacity for conveying such information.

> I have been to all three restaurants in that strange place. At the most expensive of them I had breakfast, at the least

expensive dinner, and at a third, with prices just acceptable, lunch.

In these sentences, *breakfast*, *dinner* and *lunch*, each of which is associated with *restaurant*, convey the information towards which the communication is perspectived. We can, however, ring the changes and use them in a different way:

I have been to all three restaurants in that strange place. Breakfast, I had at the most expensive of them; dinner, at the least expensive; and lunch, at the third, with prices just acceptable.

After this rearrangement, *breakfast*, *dinner* and *lunch* express the starting point of the communication, not its goal.

On account of their associative relations the elements *restaurant* and *breakfast*, *restaurant* and *dinner*, *restaurant* and *lunch*, etc., display cohesiveness. They do so irrespective of functional perspective. In my approach, the concept of cohesive relationship is therefore not identical with that of context dependence: it is a wider concept. Fully and predominantly context-dependent elements do not convey information towards where the communication is perspectived.

Even if contextual boundness is also a wider concept than context dependence, it cannot be equated with cohesiveness either. In terms of the contextual boundness approach, which speaks of topic and focus (see, e.g., Sgall, Hajičová and Panevová 1986: 352), elements express cohesiveness irrespective of whether they occur in the topic or the focus. Contextual boundness is only linked with topicality.

Let me return to the problem of heterogeneity and the predominant feature.

I have been to all the hotels in that place. There are three of them. I have been to the Continental, the Grand and the International. But they are not to my taste at all.

In regard to the closing sentence, the items of information 'the Continental', 'the Grand' and 'the International' are retrievable. They are referred to by the pronoun *they*, which is fully context-dependent.

A different situation is reflected by the sentence below.

There are three hotels in that place, the Continental, the Grand and the International, but the one I like most is the Grand.

In the *but*-sentence, the information 'the Grand' is undoubtedly context-dependent. Nevertheless, the element *the Grand* cannot be regarded as fully context-dependent. This is because it has become a vehicle of additional irretrievable information, that of selection, which predominates. It is, in fact, this piece of information to which the sentence is perspectived.

With due alterations, the same applies to the elements *the Continental*, *the Grand* and *the International* in the second sentence of the following example.

> There are three hotels in that place: the Continental, the Grand and the International. I liked the Continental and the Grand, but I did not like the International.

In the second sentence the elements *the Continental*, *the Grand* and *the International* have becomes vehicles of additional irretrievable information, i.e. that of selection and/or that of contrast. (To my knowledge Sgall was the first to point out the important role played by contrast in FSP.)

We can go on ringing the changes.

> There are three hotels in that place: the Continental, the Grand and the International. I liked the Continental and the Grand, but the International I did not like at all.

The wording no longer perspectives the last sentence towards *the International*. It perspectives it to the information 'absolute dislike'. The adversative *but* affects the meaning of the entire sentence, but the contrast is no longer the most important piece of information. Owing to the way *the International* is presented, the information conveyed by it actually exhausts the list of three hotels. It is a case of exhaustive listing (Kuno 1972) and in this respect context-dependent.

Another example of a carrier of predominating irretrievable information is the emphatic pronoun *herself* in field 23 of the Mansfield text (see p. 23). Apart from conveying the retrievable notion of 'Linda Burnell', it comes to express the irretrievable notion of 'exclusive property', towards which the communication is perspectived.

By way of closing this section let me add a note on a special type of co-referentiality and a summarizing note on heterogeneity. It may be argued that in the sentence *His father was the famous musician*, both *His father* and *the famous musician* have the same referent and are therefore to be regarded as context-dependent. It has, however, to be borne in mind that, even if at the moment when the sentence is to be produced and/or perceived both the notion 'his father' and the notion 'the famous musician' were retrievable, the identity between them has not yet been established and is therefore irretrievable. It is the communicative purpose of the sentence to establish the identity of the two. It is on this account that the sentence is perspectived to the element which conveys the additional irretrievable result of the selection or identification and in consequence behaves in the same way as an entirely context-independent element would do. It depends on the immediately relevant context which of the two notions is the one to be indentified and which the one to convey the result of the identification. Let me add that if perspectived to *the famous musician*, the sentence would create an unmarked effect. If it were perspectived to *His father*, the effect created by it would be marked.

Turning to heterogeneity, I find that the kind of heterogeneity under discussion can affect communicative units of all ranks. The following examples will illustrate. For instance, in their most natural use the communicative units provided by the clauses and semiclauses adduced below are heterogeneous, the pronouns conveying retrievable, and the other elements irretrievable, information.

> In order to meet him, I went to Prague.
> I went to Prague in order to meet him.
> As he was ill, we could not see him.
> We could not see him, because he was ill.

Irretrievable information unmistakably predominates in the subclauses and semiclauses, which therefore act in the same way as entirely context-independent communicative units. Under favourable conditions (see p. 54), the subclause or semiclause conveys the information towards which the basic distributional field is perspectived. (This applies to the second and the fourth sentences.) A communicative unit that is entirely context-dependent or predominantly context-dependent cannot convey such information.

In *He did not praise your paper, but my paper*, the possessives *your* and *my* serve as communicative units within the subfields provided by the noun phrases *your paper* and *my paper*, respectively. *Your* and *my* are heterogeneous, because in addition to conveying retrievable information, they also convey irretrievable information – that of contrast. In either case, irretrievable information predominates, and irrespective of the status of *paper*, the possessive, *your/my*, conveys the information towards which the distributional subfield *my paper*, and in fact the entire basic distributional field, is perspectived.

Heterogeneity as to retrievability and irretrievability does not do away with the dichotomy of context dependence and context independence. This is borne out by the fact that communicative units dominated by retrievability behave in the same way as those which are entirely context-dependent, whereas communicative units dominated by irretrievability behave in the same way as those which are entirely context-independent.

More thoughts on context dependence

Criterion of context dependence

It has been demonstrated that, in regard to the immediate communicative step, information is given (old, known) if it is present in, and hence retrievable from, the immediately relevant preceding context and/or if the referent suggesting it is present in, and hence retrievable from, the immediately relevant situational context. The emphasis on the actual presence induces me to prefer the qualification 'retrievable' (or 'recoverable') to the qualification 'derivable', for the former suggests actual presence more forcefully than the latter. It follows that my criterion of given or new information cannot be equated with that applied by Chafe (1976: 30; cf. Firbas 1987d: 54). In his approach givenness is conditioned by the assumption of the speaker that the information is present in the addressee's consciousness. This means that his criterion is based on the speaker's assumption of the state of the addressee's consciousness. My criterion, on the other hand, is based on the actual presence of an element in, or its absence from, the immediately relevant context.

Context dependence and contextual boundness

In this connection it could be asked whether my 'context dependence' can be equated with 'contextual boundness' as conceived of by Sgall, Hajičová and Panevová (see, e.g., 1986: 349). To a certain extent, 'context dependence' as used by myself and 'contextual boundness' as used by them cover the same ground, but strictly speaking they are not co-terminous. The concept of context dependence is narrower than that of contextual boundness.

From the point of view of context dependence, for instance, the pair *me* and *you* and the pair *last week* and *this morning* do not perform the same FSP function if used in a sentence opening a discourse. While *you* and *me* are regarded as context-dependent on account of their referents being present in the immediately relevant situational context, *last week* and *this morning* are looked upon as context-independent. From the point of view of contextual boundness, however, they are all treated alike. This is due to their indexical character, on account of which they are regarded as highly activated and therefore contextually bound (see Sgall, Hajičová and Panevová 1986: 187).

Similarly, *last Christmas, three years ago, twenty miles to the north, in my native town* and *on your favourite beach* can be used as contextually bound elements in a sentence opening a text. The notions conveyed by these expressions are interpreted as highly activated because of their connection with one of the main referential indices (*now, here, I, you*).

The criterion of contextual boundness legitimately permits this interpretation. In accordance with the narrower criterion of context dependence, however, only *me* and *you* of the expressions adduced for discussion can serve as context-dependent elements either at the beginning of discourse or in the course of its further development. As for the other expressions, they are normally context-independent at the beginning of discourse. In the course of its further development, they convey either irretrievable or retrievable information, and in consequence are either context-independent or -dependent according to the contextual conditions. As context-independent elements they could even express the piece of information towards which the sentence is perspectived. They could do so even in opening sentences as in the following examples.

> I wish I were sitting on my favourite beach.
> I wish I were back in my native town.
> The events I am going to tell you about happened last Christmas/ten years ago/twenty miles to the north/in my native town/on my favourite beach.

The determination of context dependence or independence is based on an enquiry into the facts of the immediately relevant context, verbal and situational. The determination of contextual boundness is based on an enquiry into the notions that at the moment a sentence is produced and/or perceived are activated from the stock of knowledge shared by the interlocutors.

Contextual boundness is a wider concept than context dependence. A contextually bound element may be irretrievable from the immediately relevant context; if irretrievable, it is context-independent. As I see it, the results of the enquiries into contextual boundness could be exploited for a better understanding of the borderline area between the immediately relevant verbal and situational context and the rest of context as well as for a better understanding of the language user's choice of the element(s) starting the communication within a distributional field ('starting' being used here in reference to the interpretative, not to the actual linear, arrangement).

Context – a graded phenomenon

The fact that context is a graded phenomenon is borne out in many respects by my discussion. In the first place, let me recall the existence of the contextual spheres, of which the immediately relevant context plays the decisive role in FSP. The borderline area adjacent to this sphere must also be taken into consideration. Moreover, the immediately relevant context itself is a graded phenomenon. A notion not re-expressed in the flow of the communication gradually loses its retrievability status. But even notions that are clearly established in the immediately relevant context and therefore undoubtedly retrievable are gradable.

This applies, for instance, to the notions conveyed by the pronouns in the sentence structure *I have read it there* in its most natural use. In such a case, it is the notion of the speaker that is most firmly established in the immediately relevant context; *it* refers to some text mentioned in this portion of context; and *there*, though conveying a retrievable notion too, further expands the information concerning the text. It is worth noticing that the three grades – speaker, text, location – are reflected by the actual linear arrangement. This applies also to the German, French and Czech versions of the sentence.

> Ich habe es dort gelesen.
> Ich las es dort.
> Je l'y a lu.
> Četl jsem to tam. (Read (past participle active) I-am it there.)

To what extent and under what conditions the actual linear

arrangements of context-dependent elements and their interpretative arrangements coincide must be left to further research. What is, however, of particular interest to us at the moment is that even context-dependent elements differ in the extent to which they contribute to the further development of the communication. They, too, carry different degrees of CD. The more firmly an element is established in the immediately relevant context, the lower is the degree of CD carried by it. This means that it is the degree of embeddedness in the immediately relevant context, in other words, the immediately relevant context itself, that decides the degrees of CD. It does so irrespective of the actual linear arrangement (cf. *L'y as tu lu?*). It is, of course, in harmony with linear modification if the actual linear arrangement shows a gradual rise in CD.

Presenting elements as context-dependent

Against the objective background of retrievability and irretrievability as offered by the immediately relevant context, verbal and situational, an irretrievable piece of information may be induced to suggest context dependence. It is not context-dependent, but only presented as such. It is in this sense that the words 'presenting as context-dependent' are to be understood in this study.

Under the heading of such presentation comes the *in medias res* effect, instanced by the following sentences. Each of them opens a short story written by O. Henry.

> At midnight the cafe was crowded. (H 10)
> The policeman on the beat moved up the avenue impressively (H 69)
> He really was an impossible person. (H 172)
> And then, after six years, she saw him again. (H 181)

In each case, the subject (and in the last sentence also the object) conveys information that, though irretrievable, is presented as retrievable. The reader is 'plunged into the midst of things'. He or she is well aware of this effect and knows that the information is not present in the immediately relevant context. (For Halliday's concept of presentation, which is not identical with mine, see pp. 99 and 178.)

4   The semantic factor

The verb and its successful competitors

The preceding chapter has shown that in determining degrees of CD, linear modification cannot assert itself if the contextual factor operates counter to it. Another factor capable of operating counter to linear modification is the semantic factor. Its operation will be discussed in the present chapter and in the chapter to follow. In the spoken language, the interplay of factors is joined by intonation. But intonation does not operate in the written language. It will be dealt with in the second part of the present study – in the part devoted to FSP in spoken communication.

The designation 'semantic factor' has been chosen for the sake of brevity. What it actually covers is the impact that the semantic character of a linguistic element, as well as the character of its semantic relations, has on the distribution of degrees of CD. The present chapter will concentrate on the role played by the semantic content of the verb and its semantic relations.

We already know that it is only in the absence of certain elements that the verb completes the development (see p. 7) of the communication within a distributional field. In other words, there are elements that, if present, take the development of the communication further than the verb and so come closer to, or even effect, the completion of the communication. In consequence, they prove to be dynamically stronger; they carry a higher degree of CD than the verb. In regard to the dynamics of the communication, they can be looked upon as successful competitors of the verb.

In order to be such a competitor, an element must be context-independent. What further matters is the way its semantic character, together with the character of its semantic relations, reacts to linear modification. On the one hand, these semantic characteristics can be such as to induce the context-independent element to exceed the verb in CD irrespective of linear modification; on the other hand, they can be such as to make successful competitorship dependent on linear modification. Occasionally, a significative co-determinative role is played by what will be termed a suggestive clue, a semantic feature offered by the immediately relevant – preceding or following – context.

The context-independent object

As a rule, context-independent objects, direct or indirect, non-prepositional or prepositional, exceed the verb in CD irrespective of sentence position. True enough, no matter whether context-dependent or -independent, the information conveyed by the object amplifies the information conveyed by the verb. It does so by stating the goal or result, or in any case the recipient, of the action named by the verb. But while this amplificatory information necessarily recedes into the background when context-dependent, it asserts its weight and comes to the foreground when context-independent. Compared with the verb, the context-independent object then develops the communication further and – in the absence of stronger competitors – even completes it. In this respect, the information conveyed by the object becomes communicatively more important than that conveyed by the verb and in consequence dynamically stronger: it carries a higher degree of CD. With provisos to be stated below, all this holds good irrespective of sentence position.

In the sentences adduced below, the verbs (finite or non-finite) of the verb–object combinations are context-independent. Their objects are either context-dependent or -independent. If the former, the object recedes to the background; if the latter, it takes the communication further than the verb. This holds good irrespective of sentence position. In the examples displayed below, the element carrying the higher degree of CD within the object–verb combination has been italicized. (In a complex verb form, only the notional component has been so marked.) The sentences are quoted from John Galsworthy's *The Forsyte Saga* (G) and from two German translations of it (G1, G2). (See the list of sources on pages xiii–xv. The numbers added to the quotations are references to pages.)

> Here, under a parchment-coloured Japanese sunshade covering *the whole end*, inhabitants or visitors could be

screened from the eyes of the curious while they drank *tea* and examined at their leasure *the latest of Soames' little silver boxes.* (G 71)

Hier konnten sich unter einem pergamentfarbenen japanischen Sonnenschirm, der *einen Teil des Raums* bedeckte, Bewohner und Gäste vor neugierigen Blicken schützen, wenn sie *ihren Tee* tranken und in Muße *die neuesten von Soames' kleinen silbernen Dosen* betrachteten. (G1 86)

Hier, unter einem pergamentfarbenen japanischen Sonnenschutz, der sich über die ganze Seite erstreckte, wurden Bewohner oder Besucher vor neugierigen Blicken geschützt, während sie *Tee* tranken oder angelegentlich *die neuesten von Soames' kleinen Silberdosen* inspizierten. (G2 81)

June, in the fulness of her heart, had told *Mrs. Small*, giving her *leave* to tell *only Aunt Ann* – she thought it would *cheer* her, the poor old sweet! for Aunt Ann had kept *her room* now for many days. (G 81)

June hatte es in der Überfulle ihres Herzens *Mrs Small* erzählt und ihr erlaubt, es *nur Tante Ann* zu sagen – sie dachte, es wurde die gute alte Seele *erfreuen*, denn Tante Ann mußte seit vielen Tagen *das Zimmer* hüten. (G1 295)

June, deren Herz voll war, hatte es *Mrs Small* erzählt und gesagt, sie dürfe es *nur Tante Ann* erzählen – sie glaubte, es würde sie *freuen*, die gute, alte, liebe Seele; denn Tante Ann hütete nun seit vielen Tagen *ihr Zimmer*. (G2 89)

He found himself now in the embarrassing position of one who must pay *a compliment* or run *the risk* of losing *a good thing*. Bosinney was just the fellow who might *tear up* the plans and refuse *to act for him*; a kind of grown-up child! (G 108)

Nun befand er sich in der peinlichen Lage, *ein Kompliment* auszusprechen zu müssen, wenn er nicht *Gefahr* laufen wollte, *etwas vorteilhaftes* zu verlieren. Bosinney war ganz der Mann dazu, die Pläne *zu zerreißen*, und sich zu weigern, *weiter für ihn zu arbeiten*; er war ein großes Kind. (G1 127)

Nun befand er sich in der peinlichen Lage eines Menschen, der *ein Kompliment* machen mußte oder *Gefahr* lief, *eine gute Sache* zu verlieren. Bosinney war genau der Mann, der die

Pläne *zerreißen* und sich weigern konnte, *für ihn zu arbeiten,* eine Art erwachsenes Kind. (G2 115)

Soames saw that his suggestion had touched *some unintelligible point of personal vanity.* (G 111)
Soames sah, daß seine Frage *einen ungreifbaren Punkt seiner persönlichen Eitelkeit* getroffen hatte. (G1 130)
Soames sah, daß sein Vorschlag *irgendeinen unverständlichen Punkt persönlicher Eitelkeit* getroffen hatte. (G2 117)

The sentences adduced demonstrate that different orders within the English and the German verb–object combinations do not affect the CD distribution within these combinations. This becomes especially evident if the corresponding constructions are placed alongside each other; see, for instance, the combinations *drank tea* and *ihren Tee tranken/Tee tranken,* and the combinations *must pay a compliment* and *ein Kompliment auszusprechen zu müssen/ein Kompliment machen mußte,* in which the context-independent object carries a higher degree of CD; and the combinations *might tear up the plans* and *die Pläne zu zerreißen/die Pläne zerreißen... konnte,* in which the context-independent verb, or rather its notional component, exceeds in CD the context-dependent object.

With one exception, I have not marked objects implemented by clauses or semiclauses and therefore providing distributional fields of their own; see, for instance, the *that/daß*-clause in the last triad of sentences. In the sentences adduced, all such objects are context-independent and exceed in CD their verbs (e.g., *saw/sah* in the last triad).

Comments on the following simple structures sum up the arguments presented. They apply if the element *She,* occurring in the structures, remains context-dependent.

> *She broke.
> She broke a vase./*She broke it.
> She broke the vase./*She broke it.
> She broke the vase./She broke it.
> She broke it.
> She did it.

The first structure is incomplete both syntactically and communicatively. The addition of an amplification is absolutely essential. If context-independent, the amplification cannot be pronominalized. (The first use of *the vase* is context-independent, the second context-dependent.) When context-dependent, it can, but need not, be pronominalized; in any case it does not complete the development of the communication, but recedes to the background, the development being completed by the verb. The purpose of the last structure is merely to convey assertion. In this way, *She broke a vase/She broke the vase, She broke the vase/She broke it,* and *She did it* are perspectived towards the goal of the action, the action, and the assertion, respectively. It is worth noticing that assertion becomes the information towards which the sentence is perspectived on condition that both the notional component of the verb and all the non-verbal sentence elements have been rendered context-dependent.

It can be expected that further research will discover peripheral types calling for restrictions on the formulation that a context-independent object exceeds a verb in CD. I have so far found four such types.

1 The formulation does not apply to a context-independent object implemented by the unqualified indefinite pronoun *something*, nor, in essence, to a context-independent object expressed by an interrogative pronoun. Neither type of pronoun actually amplifies the meaning conveyed by the verb in the sense that it develops the communication further. It usually acts as a semantic slot filler, leaving it to another element in the flow of the communication to particularize the meaning unexpressed; compare *He wanted to ask her something* and *What did he mean by saying he would have to look into the matter?* (In *She must have seen something dreadful*, the object exceeds the verb in CD because of the qualification *dreadful*.)

2 A context-independent object does not exceed its verb in CD if, in co-operation with it, it introduces onto the scene a phenomenon expressed by a context-independent subject; e.g. *A cold blue light filled the window panes, For a moment or two big tears brimmed her eyes, A dusky orange dyed his cheeks, A dumb and grumbling anger swelled his bosom.* In each case, the communication within the sentence is perspectived towards the information conveyed by the context-independent subject (see p. 61).

3 A context-independent initial object does not exceed its verb in CD if it expresses a notion put in contrast with another notion equally expressed by an initial element, and if the verb is context-independent.

('Initial' includes here also elements occurring immediately after a conjunction.)

> The towns they attacked with tanks, and the villages with aeroplanes. (*CGEL* 975)
> The towns they damaged and the villages they burnt.
> Verdi is splendid in his way, but Mozart's operas I regard as pure perfection. (*CGEL* 1376)
> His face not many admired, while his character still fewer could praise. (*CGEL* 1378)

4 A case of particular interest is a context-independent object that occurs before a context-independent subject; e.g. *Einen Löwen hat ein Jäger erschossen*. Under these conditions, linear modification may assert itself in the interplay of factors through preventing the sentence from being perspectived to the object (*Einen Löwen*) in front position. Such a perspective, however, cannot be ruled out. The type is an example of potentiality (see pp. 108–10).

Whereas the basic formulation and the observations adduced under 1 and 2 reflect the operation of semantics, 3 is a special case of co-operation of semantics (through contrast) and linear modification (through initial position), and 4 a case of equivocal co-operation of the two.

The context-independent subject complement and the context-independent object complement

Other elements that – providing they are context-independent – prove to be as a rule dynamically stronger than the verb are the subject complement and the object complement. Like the object, a complement conveys important amplificatory information. It supplies a description or characterization of the subject or the object to which it is related by the verb. Provided it is context-independent, it has something new to say about either of them, and as a rule proves to be dynamically stronger than they and the verb (which is usually context-independent). It acts as a successful competitor of all of them. In the absence of an element additionally conveying specifying information (see p. 49), it even completes the development of the communication. This applies especially if the subject is context-dependent; compare *He has proved to be an excellent musician, Er hat sich sehr großmütig gezeigt, They have elected Peter/him president, Sie haben Peter/ihn zum Präsidenten gewählt, Wilson his name is* (CGEL 1377), *An utter fool he made me feel* (ibid.), *I felt a proper charlie when I dropped all the plates* (LDCE 1987: 162), *A proper Charlie I felt, too* (van Ek and Robat 1984: 415), *Sehr großmütig hat er sich gezeigt, Zum Präsidenten haben sie Peter/ihn gewählt, Criminal I call it* (ibid.). In each case, the context-independent complement proves to be the most dynamic element in the sentence. It remains so regardless of sentence position.

If context-dependent, a complement exceeds in CD neither a context-independent subject nor a context-independent object. The following examples, quoted from *CGEL* (1381), contain such dynamically weak complements. *CGEL* speaks of the complement making 'comparative reference to something that has preceded' (1381; see also Greenbaum and Whitcut 1988: 386). Let us note that the examples arrange the elements in what may be termed presentation order, in which the initial element is followed by an intransitive verb and a context-independent subject. This presentation order reflects linear modification and strengthens the perspective of the communication towards the context-independent subject, occurring in end position.

> His answer was a disgrace; equally regrettable was his departure immediately afterwards.
> Her face was stony and even stonier was the tone of her voice.

The adverbs *equally* and *even* pertain to the complements, but simultaneously point to the subjects.

Problems arise when both the subject and the complement are context-independent. It could be assumed that by supplying a description or characterization of the subject a context-independent complement always take the communication further than the subject and acts as its successful competitor. But this is not invariably the case when the subject is context-independent. This can be illustrated by another pair of sentences quoted from *CGEL* (1380).

> Especially remarkable was her oval face.
> Faint grew the sound of the bell.

Contexts could be thought of in which the complements of these sentences are context-independent. Nevertheless, the sentences are perspectived towards the subjects, and the sentence constituents are once again arranged in presentation order. Let us note that it is in terms of visual and acoustic perception that the notions conveyed by the subjects are presented to the reader's attention, and in this way induced to appear on the scene (see p. 59). The type under discussion represents a special case of interplay of semantics and linear modification, in which the latter fully asserts itself.

This interpretation does not apply to the structures:

> Especially remarkable her oval face was.
> Faint the sound of the bell grew.

CGEL (1379) questions their acceptability if the nuclear focus is placed on the verb. Under the circumstances, the non-use of the presentation order indeed prevents linear modification from asserting itself, and the context-independent complement can come to the fore. If this interpretation is correct, each sentence is perspectived towards the complement, which then bears the nuclear focus. The awkwardness of the structure noted by *CGEL*, however, remains. The complement does not open the presentation order (as its initial position and its connotations of visual or acoustic perception may suggest), but itself conveys the information towards which the communication is perspectived. (Let us note that the placement of the nuclear focus is determined here by the interplay of the non-prosodic FSP factors.)

Without any awkwardness, such a perspective towards an initial context-independent complement is achieved in sentence 25 of the Mansfield text. The complement indeed conveys a characterization that takes the communication further than the information expressed by the context-independent subject. This interpretation is substantiated by a clue suggested by the perspectives of the two following sentences.

> Dazzling white the picotees shone; the golden-eyed marigold glittered; the nasturtiums wreathed the veranda poles in green and gold flame.

The three sentences display the same communicative purpose: to give a picture of what the flowers looked like. This purpose is fulfilled by the information conveyed by the context-independent complements, not by that conveyed by the context-independent subjects.

Another note on this type of complement behaviour involving

context-independent subjects and complements will be offered below (see pp. 56–8).

The context-independent adverbial

Another successful competitor of the verb can be an adverbial element. This happens if the adverbial is context-independent; but context independence is not the only condition of successful competitorship. The relation of the semantic characteristic of the adverbial to linear modification must be taken into account as well.

Generally speaking, an adverbial is induced to perform one of three communicative (dynamic) functions in the act of communication. Two of them will be discussed presently; the third will be dealt with later (see pp. 77–8). The first two are that of conveying a specification and that of conveying a setting. It is the one conveying a specification that renders the adverbial a successful competitor of the verb. The two functions are exemplified by the following sentences.

(a) He lived in London.
Er lebte in London. Er hat in London gelebt.

He flew to Prague.
Er flog nach Prag. Er ist nach Prag geflogen.

This happened yesterday.
Das geschah gestern. Das ist gestern geschehen.

(b) I met an old friend yesterday. Yesterday I met an old friend.
Ich bin gestern einem alten Freund begegnet.
Gestern bin ich einem alten Freund begegnet.

(What do Londoners do in the evening?) In the evening many people go to concerts in London.
In London many people go to concerts in the evening.
(Wie verbringen die Londoner ihre Abende?) In London pflegen abends viele Menschen Konzerte zu besuchen. Abends pflegen viele Menschen in London Konzerte zu besuchen.

If in group (a) all the non-subject elements are context-independent, the perspectives of the sentences are: *in London, to Prague, nach Prag, yesterday* and *gestern*. If in group (b) all the elements are context-independent with the exception of *I/Ich/ich*, *in the evening/abends* and *in London*, the perspectives are: *an old friend, einem alten Freund, to concerts* and *Konzerte*.

Unlike *in London* and *yesterday/gestern* of group (b), *in London* and *yesterday/gestern* of group (a) express obligatory amplifications of their verbs. In doing so, they complete the development of the communication and prove to be successful competitors of their verbs. On the other hand, the adverbials *in London* and *yesterday/gestern*, as well as the adverbial *in the evening/abends*, in the sentences of group (b), convey only background, concomitant information. Whereas the adverbials conveying obligatory amplifications belong to the core of the message (see p. 71), those that convey mere background information participate in laying the foundation (see p. 71) upon which the core of the message is presented. Whereas the former perform the dynamic semantic function of expressing a specification, the latter perform the dynamic semantic function of expressing a setting.

As we shall see, specifications can also be implemented by context-independent adverbials that do not express an obligatory amplification.

In group (b) the function of specification is also performed by the objects *an old friend, einem alten Freund* and *Konzerte*. I shall come back to objects serving as specifications on page 82, where the concept of dynamic semantic function will be discussed in greater detail.

Before further exemplifying the function of specification and that of setting as they are performed by adverbials, let me outline the way the three factors – the contextual factor, the semantic factor and linear modification – participate in making the adverbial serve as a setting or a specification.

If context-dependent, the adverbial serves as a setting. It does so irrespective of semantic character and sentence position. (For examples, see paragraph 1 below.)

If context-independent, the adverbial serves as a setting, or as a specification, or performs a dynamic function that will be discussed separately (see pp. 77–9).

A context-independent adverbial that conveys an obligatory amplification of the semantic content of the verb functions as a specification and does so irrespective of sentence position. The same behaviour is shown by a context-independent adverbial that does not convey an obligatory amplification of the verb, but an amplification essential enough to be regarded as specifying. It is not always easy to draw a distinct line between the two types. (For examples, see paragraph 2 below.)

A loosening of the relationship of the adverbial to the verb opens the door to the operation of linear modification and may induce a context-independent adverbial to serve as a setting when it occurs initially, or as a specification when it occurs close to end position or finally. (For examples, see paragraph 3 below.)

Another type is the context-independent adverbial whose relationship to the verb is loose and which conveys mere background information. It serves as a setting irrespective of sentence position. (For examples, see paragraph 4 below.)

The difficulty of drawing a distinct line between context-independent adverbials that convey an obligatory amplification and those that, though not conveying an obligatory amplication, nevertheless express a sufficiently essential one is not of such significance as the difficulty of drawing a distinct line between context-independent adverbials conveying an essential amplification and those that do not do so with sufficient distinctness.

A context-independent adverbial, however, becomes a setting or a specification also on account of a suggestive semantic clue offered by the perspectives of the sentences occurring in the immediately relevant preceding or following context. (For an example, see paragraph 5 below.)

Cases in which the interplay of the three factors – the contextual factor, the semantic factor and linear modification – does not unequivocally determine whether an adverbial serves as a setting or a specification are cases of potentiality. This can be removed in the spoken language, when intonation joins the interplay of factors as its fourth participant (see p. 180).

The outline just offered can be exemplified as follows.

1 Adverbials serving as settings on account of their context dependence and doing so irrespective of sentence positions are instanced by *in the evening*, *abends* and *in London* in the group (b) above, and by *on her* and *na ni* in the English and Czech versions of sentence 4 of the Mansfield text.

> and now and again a tiny yellowish flower dropped on her
> a každou chvíli na ni drobný žlutavý kvítek
> (and every moment on her it-fell tiny yellowish little-flower)

The adverbial *now and then/každou chvíli* is another setting in the sentence. It is, however, context-independent and will be commented on below (see paragraph 4).

2 The context-independent adverbials *in London, to Prague, nach Prag,*

to concerts, *yesterday* and *gestern*, interpreted on page 5 as specifications, belong to the core of the message by particularizing points in space or time as the case may be. Let us note that they are linked with verbs of appearance/existence (*live, leben, happen, geschehen*) or verbs of motion (*fly, fliegen, go*). Sentences 1, 6, 12, and 30 of the Mansfield text contain local specifications; sentence 28 of the same text contains a temporal specification.

> a…tree that grew in the middle of the front grass patch (1)
> if you held one…on the palm of your hand (6)
> the…things got caught in one's hair. (12)
> one was swept away. (30)
> time to look at these flowers long enough (28)

Two sentences in the text – 7 and 33 – contain context-independent adverbials (implemented by a clause and a prepositional phrase, respectively) completing comparisons.

> Each…petal shone as if each was the careful work of a loving hand. (7)
> Along came Life like a wind (33)

Sentence 6 contains an adverb in -*ly* that particularizes the manner in which an action is carried out.

> If you…looked at it closely (6)

The examples adduced demonstrate that the dynamic function of specification is not expressed solely by adverbials conveying an obligatory amplification of the verb.

The manner adverb in -*ly* is of particular interest.

> This bus may suddenly stop.
> This bus may stop suddenly.
> It was as though we had been unconsciously driving towards danger. (Chl (Chládková 1979) 80)
> It would be unjust for him to bear personally the great expenses involved. (*CCELD* 1070)
> I have undertaken all the enquiries personally. (*CCELD* 1070)
> Somebody impatiently knocked again.
> Somebody knocked again impatiently. (Chl 89)

Nobody can touch him if he properly does his work.
Nobody can touch him if he does his work properly. (Chl 89)
Karlchen ... put his stick away in a corner as unobtrusively as
he could. (Chl 89)
She shook her head twice, quite seriously. (Chl 89)

Chládková (1979) has compared the English manner adverb in -*ly* with its German and Czech counterparts and demonstrated that these elements are practically always context-independent. In this capacity the manner adverb significantly amplifies the information conveyed by the verb and takes the communication a step further than the verb. In principle, its functions as a specification and keeps up this relationship irrespective of sentence position. It carries a higher degree of CD than the verb.

Simultaneously, however, it is not unaffected by linear modification. It carries a higher degree of CD when occurring after the verb than when occurring before it (cf. Bolinger's observations on adverbs in -*ly* in Bolinger 1952). With the exception of an initial subject that expresses a phenomenon towards which the communication is perspectived (e.g. *A large heavy truck slowly emerged from behind the corner*), the manner adverb exceeds in CD a successful competitor of the verb when placed after such a competitor (see the examples adduced above).

For a detailed discussion of how the adverbial of manner operates within the English, German and Czech word-order systems, see Chládková's study (1979). For a further discussion of the relationship between the verb and the adverbial of manner, see page 58. Let me just add here a note on the adverb of manner in initial sentence position before the subject. For instance, in *Casually, Leslie greeted the stranger*, the relationship of *casually* to the verb is loosened and its relationship to the subject strengthened (see *CGEL* 573). This weakens *casually* as a specification and shifts it towards a setting (cf. *Trying to be casual, Leslie greeted the stranger*). The insertion of a comma after *Casually* is in harmony with this interpretation. But as its relation to the verb has not been entirely severed, *Casually* continues to serve as a specification, though not in a pure and typical way.

The effect of the initial position of *Casually* is facilitated by the system of English word order, which rarely puts an adverb in -*ly* before the S–V–O string. Such an effect is not produced by the German system of word order; cf. *Ungezwungen grüßte leslie den Fremden*. Note the obligatory word-order contiguity of the initial adverb and the verb in second position. *Ungezwungen* serves as a specification.

3 This section instances context-independent adverbials that serve as specifications or settings according to sentence position. In front position they serve as settings, whereas in end position or in a position close to it they serve as specifications. This, however, is not solely due to linear modification, for linear modification asserts itself in this way, as it is not prevented from doing so by the semantic character of the adverbial and the character of its semantic relations. This can be illustrated by the following two pairs of sentence structures, the first containing adverbial clauses of cause and the second adverbial semiclauses of purpose.

> He did not attend the lecture because he was ill.
> As he was ill he did not attend the lecture.

> He went to London in order to visit a friend.
> In order to visit a friend he went to London.

Provided only the pronominal subjects convey context-dependent information, the initial adverbials serve as settings and the final adverbials as specifications. In consequence, the first sentence is perspectived towards the cause of the man's absence from the lecture, but the second towards the fact of his absence. And likewise, whereas the third sentence is perspectived towards the purpose of the man's journey, the fourth is perspectived towards his journey's destination.

In essence, an adverbial expressing an agentive reacts to linear modification in the same way; but it occurs almost exclusively in end position or close to the end and functions as a specification. It represents an interesting type of relationship between linear modification and the semantic character of the adverbial. It has been discussed by Golková (1983, 1985).

> He will not be influenced by family considerations. (Go 38)
> ... it may well be that Mary Warren has been conquered by Satan ... (Go 42)
> ... and /I/ had been summoned by the man next door but one for having a ferocious dog at large ... (Go 46)

Examining the Mansfield text, we find that all the adverbials occurring initially (thirteen in number) serve as settings (all of them operating in basic distributional fields). In an overwhelming majority of cases (seventeen out of twenty in basic distributional fields; four out of four in distributional subfields), the final adverbials serve as specifications. The rest of the final adverbials (see sentences 3, 4 and 11) serve as settings. It follows that in the vast majority of cases this distribution of settings and specifications is in harmony with linear modification. But a full evaluation of the operation of linear modification would have to take into account whether the semantic character of the context-independent adverbial is or is not capable of working counter to linear modification. In the affirmative, the adverbial comes under 4; in the negative, it comes under 3.

4 The difference between type 3 and type 4 can be illustrated as follows. A shift from front position to end position of the *as soon as* clauses in sentences 10 and 29 of the Mansfield text brings about a change in perspective.

> But as soon as they flowered, they fell and were scattered. (10)
> But as soon as one paused to part the petals, to discover the underside of the leaf, along came life. (29)

> But they fell and were scattered as soon as they flowered.
> But along came Life as soon as one paused to part the petals, to discover the underside of the leaf.

In the original versions the *as soon as* clauses convey background information, the communication being perspectived to the deterioration (of the leaves) and the appearance of Life. On the other hand, the re-arranged versions are oriented to the locations of these phenomena (deterioration and Life) in time, an orientation less fitting the flow of the narration. In the former versions the *as soon as* clauses serve as settings, in the latter as specifications. The *as soon as* clauses represent type 3.

A change in the positions of the adverbials *now and again* and *as you talked* in sentences 4 and 11 of the Mansfield text do not bring about a change in perspective.

> and now and again a tiny yellowish flower dropped on her (4)
> You brushed them off as you talked (11)

> and a tiny yellowish flower dropped on her now and again
> As you talked you brushed them off

Irrespective of sentence position the adverbials convey background information, the communication remaining perspectived to the appearance of a tiny flower (*a tiny yellowish flower*) and the action affecting the flowers (*brushed ... off*). Irrespective of sentence position the adverbials serve as settings and represent type 4.

Although this type is not very frequent in the Mansfield text, it is not uncommon in English (see, for instance, Dvořáková 1964 and Horová 1976).

> The dinner in honour of June's engagement had seemed a bore at first. (D 144)
> You would drift into the cafe one evening. (Ho 102)
> so I have put them in here for the time being. (Ho 102)
> that the girls are at school all day. (Ho 102)
> A fly settled on his hair. (D 146)
> Each of these ladies held fans in their hands. (D 148)

The adverbials *at first, one evening, for the time being, all day, on his hair* and *in their hands* can be shifted from end position to front position without changing the perspective to a *a bore, into the cafe, in here, at school, a fly* and *fans*, respectively. (In the last but one sentence the shift necessitates an overall rearrangement: *On his hair settled a fly.*) They serve as settings.

Let us note that they would serve as specifications if the elements that under the present contextual conditions are context-independent and act as their successful competitors became context-dependent. Contrast can strengthen the specifying effect; compare *This time, a fly did not settle on his hair, but on his chin* (see also pp. 45–6).

5 A suggestive semantic clue that is offered by the perspectives of sentences in the immediately preceding context and co-determines the dynamic function of an adverbial can be illustrated by the following passage from the Mansfield text (sentences 25–7) and its German, French and Czech translations. The elements towards which the sentences are perspectived are in italics.

> *Dazzling white* the picotees shone; the golden-eyed marigold *glittered*; the nasturtiums wreathed the veranda poles *in green and gold flame.*

Table 4.1 *Uhlířová's assessment of FSP functions of adverbial nominal phrases*

Type of adverbial	Total of adverbials serving as settings	Total of adverbials serving as specifications	Total
Condition	82	18	100
Concession	74	26	100
Viewpoint	66	34	100
Time	62	38	100
Purpose	57	43	100
Cause	52	48	100
Restriction	47	53	100
Place	35	65	100
Source	31	69	100
Means	30	70	100
Manner	24	76	100
Agent	12	88	100
Measure	7	93	100
Result	3	97	100

Note: The classification is based on Šmilauer (1966). The corpus is constituted by educational and journalistic texts.

Blended weiß leuchteten die Nelken. Die goldenen Ringel-blumen *glänzten*. *In grünen und goldenen Flammen* wand sich die Kapuzinerkresse um die Verandasäulen. (M1 156)
Des fleurettes blanches brillaient *éblouissantes*; les renoncules aux yeux d'or *scintillaient*; les capucines enguirlandaient *de flammes vertes et dorées* les pilliers de la veranda. (M2 24)
Hvozdíky svítily *oslnivou bělí*; zlatooké měsíčky *přímo sálaly*; řeřišnice ovíjela sloupky na verandě *zeleným a zlatým plamenem*. (M3 343)
(Picotees they-shone *with-dazzling with-white*; golden-eyed marigolds *literally glittered*; nasturtium wreathed pillars in veranda *with-green and with-gold with-flame*.)

Cases in point are the English adverbial phrase of manner *in green and gold flame* and its French, German and Czech counterparts. Each of these adverbials acts as a successful competitor of the verb and serves as a specification towards which the sentence is perspectived. The English adverbial and its Czech counterpart occur in end position and are in harmony with linear modification. As for the German and the French counterparts, they occur in front and in penultimate positions, respectively. In spite of the non-final position, however, neither is exceeded in CD by the context-independent element, which occurs in end position. This can be accounted for as follows.

An examination of the English original shows that each sentence is perspectived towards the visual impact produced by the flower: *dazzling white, glittered, in green and gold flame.* (In the second sentence, it is a verb that, in the absence of a competitor, expresses the impact.) It is only the Czech version that places all the three corresponding expressions in end position and is in full harmony with linear modification. But trios of 'impact' expressions are also present in the German and in the French versions. In each of them the semantic homogeneity of the trio aids the adverbial phrase of manner of the third sentence in expressing the information towards which the communication is oriented. A less careful reader may miss this clue operating counter to linear modification and orient the third sentence to the final element, which is not one of the 'trio' expressions. In doing so, the reader would misinterpret the communicative intention of the author. Note that unlike the adverb *casually* in the example discussed on page 53, the initial German adverbial of manner shows no semantic relationship to the subject.

I have been able to give only a rough outline of the interplay of context, linear modification and semantics in determining the conditions under which the adverbials serve as settings or specifications. I trust that an elaboration of this outline will further particularize the interplay and bear out the usefulness and correctness of the distinction between settings and specifications.

A remarkable contribution to the enquiry into the settings and specifications implemented by adverbials has been offered by Uhlířová (1974). She has examined 1,400 Czech adverbial nominal phrases and summarized her enquiries in a table, which is reproduced as table 4.1.

In table 4.1 Uhlířová refers to the settings and specifications as thematic and rhematic elements, respectively. I have employed the former pair of terms, for the thematic and the rhematic functions will be discussed here later (see p. 71). As will become clear, settings are indeed thematic and specifications rhematic (see here pp. 75–7 and Uhlířová 1974: 105–6).

Uhlířová's enquiry testifies to the impact the semantic character has on the dynamic function performed by the adverbial in FSP. An examination of an English, German or French corpus, or of an English corpus containing also clausal and semiclausal adverbials for that matter, may not yield exactly the same results, but will not disprove the role played by semantics in FSP.

It should be added that a sentence may contain more than one element performing the dynamic semantic function of specification. The mutual relation of such elements will be taken up on pages 81–3.

The context-independent subject

In the absence of any of the successful competitors so far discussed, the verb shows a strong tendency to recede into the background and to be exceeded in CD in the presence of a context-independent subject.

> A boy came into the room.
> There was a boy in the room.
> In the centre of the room, under the chandelier, as became a host, stood the head of the family, old Jolyon himself. (G 6)
> A very sweet look had come into the old lady's face. (G 16)
> There was little sentimentality about the Forsytes. (G 24)

In each sentence, the notional component of the finite verb expresses appearance or existence on the scene. It does so explicitly or with unmistakable implicitness. The subject is context-independent and conveys the information towards which the communication is perspectived. (In the case of the *there*-clause, this applies to its 'notional' subject.) The notional component of the verb introduces this information into the communication and in this respect recedes into the background. The adverbial elements serve as settings. (For a detailed discussion of the existential *there*-clause, see Breivik 1983.)

It is of interest to note that under the circumstances the subject carries the highest degree of CD irrespective of sentence position, i.e. no matter whether it occurs initially (*A boy, A very sweet look*), medially (*a boy, little sentimentality*) or finally (*the head of the family, old Jolyon himself*).

Equally consummating the communication, the latest Czech translation of the above-adduced sentences places the subjects in end position.

> Pod lustrem uprostřed pokoje, jak se sluší na hostitele, stála hlava rodiny, sám starý Jolyon. (G4 17)

(Under chandelier in-middle of-room, as *refl. pron.* it-becomes *prep.* host, it-stood head of-family old Jolyon.)

Na tváři staré dámy se objevil velmi sladký úsměv... (G4 25)
(On face of-old of-lady *refl. pron.* it-appeared very sweet smile.)

Ve Forsytech bylo pramálo sentimentálnosti. (G4 31)
(In Forsytes it-was very-little sentimentality.)

A number of verbs of verbal phrases that explicitly convey the meaning of appearance or existence on the scene could be added to those occurring in the above-adduced examples: *exist, be in existence, be in sight, be within view, obtain, appear, arrive, become plain, begin, come forth, come forward, come into sight, come into view, come up, commence, crop up, develop, emerge, ensue, evolve, grow out of, happen, issue, loom, materialize, occur, recur, rise, set in, show up, spring up, stand out, start, surface, take place, turn up, unfold.* The list is not exhaustive.

It is certainly more difficult, if not impossible, to draw up an exhaustive list of verbs and verbal phrases that unmistakably imply, or under certain conditions are capable of unmistakably implying, appearance or existence on the scene. The following examples contain such verbs (*hover, settle, steal over*).

A haze hovered over the prospect. (G 19)
A fly settled on his hair. (G 25)
[But in thinking of his remaining guest,] an expression like that of a cat who is just going to purr stole over his old face. (G 44)
A wave of the azalea scent drifted into June's face, ... (G 133)
A goldfinch flew over the shepherd's head... (M 12)
And now big spots of light gleamed in the mist. (M 11)

In each sentence, the notional component of the verb performs the same presentation function as in the sentences adduced above and the adverbial serves as a setting. Completing the development of the communication, the subject expresses the phenomenon presented.

The verbs of the last three sentences represent an interesting type of implicitness. They display a semantic affinity with their subjects. Thus both *drift* and *wave* express the idea of motion and both *gleam* and *spots of light* the notion of illumination. *Fly* expresses the manner a bird (*goldfinch*) appears on the scene. Through this affinity the verb prepares the way for the phenomenon to be presented.

The examples so far adduced contain only intransitive verbs. But even transitive verbs can be involved in expressing appearance/existence on the scene. (I owe the examples quoted from MA to Jindřiška Svobodová.)

A cold blue light filled the window panes. (MA 250)
[And the night passed. Presently the cold fingers of dawn closed over her uncovered hand;] grey light flooded the dull room. (MA 13)
For a moment or two big tears brimmed her eyes. (MA 179)
[Swithin stared at her;] a dusky orange dyed his cheeks. (G 49)
A dumb and grumbling anger swelled his bosom. (G 46)
[Aunt Ann looked up from her velvet chair.] Grey curls banded her forehead, [curls that, unchanged for decades, had extinguished in the family all sense of time.] (G 11)

In the sentences under examination, the object expresses a phenomenon that is filled, permeated or covered by another phenomenon. The latter appears within the space provided by the former. The latter is the phenomenon to be presented; the former serves as the setting (scene) for the presentation.

A frequent type of sentence has a context-independent subject presenting a phenomenon appearing on a human body, the element(s) expressing the body or some part of it performing the role of the setting; see, e.g., *on his hair* (G 25), *into June's face* (G 133), *her eyes* (MA 179), *his cheeks* (G 49), *his bosom* (G 46), *her forehead* (G 11).

Let me add that in G 49 *dyed* displays a semantic affinity with *a dusky orange*, and that the transitive *closed* in *Presently the cold fingers of dawn closed over her uncovered hand* (the sentence co-constituting the immediately relevant preceding context of MA 13) links a setting (*her uncovered hand*) with a phenomenon covering it and eventually to be presented (*the cold fingers of dawn*).

In the following sentence, appearance on the scene is metaphorically expressed by a verb–object combination.

Through Aunt Ann's compressed lips a tender smile forced its way. (G 12)

A German and two Czech translations in fact use an intransitive verb (*drängte sich, se prodral, pronikl*). They strengthen the subject in its consummative communicative function by placing it in end position.

> Über Tante Anns zusammengepreßte Lippen drängte sich ein feines Lächeln. (G1 22)
> Sevřenými rty tety Anny se prodral slabý úsměv. (G3 18)
> (Through-compressed through-lips of-aunt of-Ann *refl. pron.* it-pressed-through faint smile.)
> Sevřenými rty tety Anny pronikl něžný úsměv. (G4 22)
> (Through-compressed through-lips of-aunt of-Ann it-penetrated tender smile.)

Performing the presentative function, the verb can also appear in the passive. This applies to the verbs used in the sentence structures adduced below provided the subjects are context-independent – a condition characterizing the most natural application of these sentence structures.

> Quite a number of new houses have been built in our town. Powerful machines have been constructed. An uncanny impression is thereby created. A new method has been developed. Ingenious new schemes were devised in various institutes. Monuments will be erected in the centre of the city. Printing was then invented in Germany. A new daily is to be launched next week. An unnecessary mistake was made. Important discoveries were made towards the end of the nineteenth century. Shoes are manufactured there. More food must be produced this year.

Under the contextual condition stipulated, the adverbial elements serve as settings, local or temporal, and the subjects express the phenomenon to be presented. The verbs convey the meaning of production, which unmistakably implies that of appearance on the scene.

These observations by no means belittle the role played by the passive in perspectiving the communication away from the information conveyed by a subject in pre-verbal position. But they are a reminder that it depends on the interplay of FSP factors whether the passive participates in perspectiving the sentence away from the subject or towards it. At the same time they do not disprove the well-known fact that in a majority of cases the passive participates in perspectiving the sentence away from the subject.

The sentences with verbs in the passive demonstrate that the meaning of appearance/existence on the scene is also conveyed by transitive verbs. Bringing a phenomenon into existence (causing it to appear on the scene) is unmistakably implied by sentences expressing production and a goal affected by it. An effected goal is an outcome (result, consequence) of a production process: it has been brought by it into existence. If context-independent, an element expressing an effected goal takes the development of the communication further than the element expressing the production process.

It is Hatcher's merit to have pointed out that the verbs of production imply the meaning of appearance/existence on the scene. But verbs of production are not the only transitive verbs implying this meaning. Hatcher submits to a detailed enquiry five verbs – *give, say, have, make* and *hold* – which represent a group of transitive verbs implying it. (She lists altogether 252 verbs which belong to this group; see Hatcher 1956: 44–5. Her corpus is Spanish, but with due alterations her findings are applicable to English as well.)

According to Hatcher, for instance, the possessive *have* indicates the existence of a phenomenon in somebody's possession. Utilizing this observation and comparing *I have got a book* with *There is a book in my possession*, I find that both *is* and *have got* have *a book* as their competitor, provided it is context-independent. Under this condition, they both introduce *a book* into the communication, and in the absence of other competitors orient the communication towards it. In either case the meaning of existence participates in taking the communication a step further. It follows that it can develop the communication no matter whether the latter is perspective to or away from the information conveyed by the subject.

According to Hatcher, the meaning of appearance on the scene is also implied, for instance, in the semantic content of *bring*. Let us have a look at two versions of Matthew 12.22, which both contain this verb.

> Then they brought to him a blind and dumb demoniac. (JerB)
> Then a blind and dumb demoniac was brought to him. (Moffatt)

Each version perspectives the communication towards the element *a blind and dumb demoniac*. This element is context-independent and acts as the only competitor of *brought*. Its successful competitorship is strengthened through the implication of the meaning of appearance expressed by the notional component of the verb. The elements *they* and *to him* are context-dependent. The adverbial *then* is context-independent, but expresses mere background information. The same perspective of the two sentences holds good in spite of their different actual linear arrangements.

It may be asked whether a goal that is not effected but merely affected by an action can also be related to the meaning of appearance/existence. Indeed it can. A goal (person or thing, concrete or abstract) becomes affected through an effect produced on it. In this way, an affected goal is linked with 'production' and 'effect', and hence with 'bringing into existence'. What is brought into existence is the effect. For instance, the sentence structures *He has offended an old friend* and *He has overtaken every car* express neither the appearance of a friend nor the appearance of a car. What, however, they respectively convey is that an effect has been produced on a friend through the act of offending him and that an effect has been produced on a car through the act of overtaking it. If an element expressing an affected goal is context-independent, the notion of the effect produced on the goal strengthens the element in its competitorship with the verb. As an expression of an effect produced by the action conveyed by the verb, the context-independent element takes the communication a step further than the verb and exceeds it in CD, in the absence of other competitors even becoming the carrier of the highest degree of CD. In this respect, a context-independent goal affected is introduced into the communication in the same way as a context-independent goal effected. Needless to say, this does not apply to an expression of an affected goal or to one of an effected goal if such an expression has become context-dependent and in this way dynamically weakened.

As I see it, this explanation throws some light on the use of the sentence structure *Präsident Kennedy ist ermordet worden/President Kennedy has been assassinated*, discussed at the conference on FSP in Mariánské Lázně (Marienbad) in 1970. The structure could hardly be perspectived to *assassinated* unless *President Kennedy* were rendered context-dependent for some reason or other by the immediately relevant context of situation. (The structure would then be used in reply to the question 'What has happened to President Kennedy?', as it were.) The message would be treated rather as entirely context-independent (in reply to the question 'What has happened?', as it were). In that case it is the effect of the action, indicated by the name of the person upon whom the effect has been produced (i.e. the affected goal) that under the circumstances carries the highest degree of CD and is the piece of information towards which the communication is perspectived. (I shall continue the discussion of the contextual application of the sentence structure under examination on p. 179.)

The present chapter has demonstrated that within a distributional field the verb cannot complete the development of the communication in the presence of a successful competitor. The role of such a competitor can be taken over by a context-independent subject (i) if – with provisos stipulated above – neither a context-independent object nor a context-independent subject complement nor a context-independent object complement nor a context-independent adverbial serving as a specification is present, and (ii) if the verb performs the presentative function. The verb does so (i) if, in the absence of competitors other than a context-independent subject, it explicitly expresses or unmistakably implies appearance or existence on the scene; or (ii) if, in accordance with its tendency to recede into the background, it performs the presentative function even if not expressing or implying existence/ appearance. The occasional difficulty to establish whether in the presence of a context-independent subject and in the absence of any other possible competitor a verb coming under (ii) performs the presentative function or not points to potentiality (see the note on potentiality below).

It is an interplay of factors that makes the subject act as the carrier of the highest degree of CD within the sentence or clause. Sgall, Hajičová and Buráňová are, of course, right in maintaining that the verbs of appearance/existence do not form a clear-cut category (1980: 40). But the meaning of appearance/existence, explicitly expressed or implied, plays an essential role in the development of the communication and it is legitimate to enquire into the conditions under which it does so. The occasional indistinctiveness of clues to context dependence and independence, the presentative and the non-presentative roles, or settings and specifications opens the door to potentiality, which in regard to the FSP function of the subject will be taken up on pages 108 and 183. But potentiality can be removed by intonation, which joins the interplay of FSP factors in the spoken language (see p. 180).

5 The theme and the non-theme

The scales of dynamic semantic functions

The analyses of the texts in the introductory chapter and the discussion of the successful competitors of the verb show that, in relation to the information conveyed by the subject, the information conveyed by the verb, or rather by its notional component (see p. 70), participates in the development of the communication in one of two ways. It perspectives the communication either (i) towards the phenomenon presented by the subject, or (ii) towards the quality ascribed to the phenomenon expressed by the subject or beyond this quality towards its specification. In other words, it performs either (i) the dynamic semantic function of presentation (Pr), or (ii) that of expressing a quality (Q). In consequence, the subject either (i) performs the dynamic semantic function of expressing the phenomenon to be presented (Ph), or (ii) the dynamic semantic function of expressing the quality bearer (B). The discussion of the competitors of the verb has dealt with two other dynamic semantic functions: that of expressing a setting (Set) and that of expressing a specification (Sp).

The qualification 'dynamic' is necessitated by the fact that the semantic content concerned is not viewed as unrelated to the flow of communication, but as linked with definite contextual conditions and as actively participating in developing the perspective of the communication.

As has already been indicated in the introductory chapter, the two types of perspective involve two sets of dynamic functions:

Set(ting), Pr(esentation of Phenomenon), Ph(enomenon presented);
Set(ting), B(earer of Quality), Q(uality), Sp(ecification) and F(urther) Sp(ecification).

The items of the two sets represent dynamic semantic functions performed by context-independent elements. They have been arranged in accordance with a gradual rise in CD and constitute two scales. The first can be referred to as the Presentation Scale and the second as the Quality Scale. They reflect the interpretative, not the actual linear, arrangement. The two arrangements may, but need not, coincide.

> Linnets (Ph) sang (Pr) in the trees (Set). Ages ago (Set) a young king (B) ruled (Q) his country (Sp) capriciously and despotically (FSp).

As in the interpretative arrangement both scales open with a setting and as in the flow of the communication reflected by this arrangement a Ph-element precedes a B-element (see below), the two scales may be combined into one. The Combined Scale reflects the following interpretative arrangement:

$$\text{Set} - \text{Pr} - \text{Ph} - \text{B} - \text{Q} - \text{Sp} - \text{FSp}$$

The placement of the Ph-function before the B-function is justified by the following comments.

It may be argued that, in the sentence *Ages ago a young king ruled his country capriciously and despotically*, *a young king* performs the Ph-function, because the sentence could be interpreted as corresponding to *Ages ago there was a young king, who ruled his country capriciously and despotically*. This is indeed true, but in terms of distributional fields the two sentences are to be accounted for as follows. They both provide basic distributional fields, but the amended one contains a distributional subfield provided by a relative clause. Within the amended basic distributional field its entire expanded subject performs the Ph-function. In this respect, the field implements the Presentation Scale. Within the distributional subfield, however, the subject performs the B-function and the subfield implements the Quality Scale. The original basic distributional field telescopes the Ph-function and the B-function into the subject *a young king* and in this way implements the Combined Scale.

It would be odd to open a story with *He ruled his country capriciously and despotically. Ages ago there was a young king*. If the narrator does so, he or she would have to explain: 'Oh, I mean a young king. There was a young king, you know.'

On the other hand, the narrator may open the story (though not a fairy tale) with the sentence *He ruled...*, adding no apologetic explanation and treating the character as known from the very beginning. He leads the listener/reader into the middle of the story (*in medias res*), using this type of opening as a stylistic device. As follows from the discussion in the previous chapter, *He* is actually context-independent at the beginning of the narration.

The telescoped opening, the odd opening and the stylistically coloured opening indicate that the Ph-function can be implemented simultaneously with the B-function or remain unimplemented (becoming conspicuous by its absence), but cannot be implemented *after* the B-function. 'After' applies to the interpretative arrangement, but the likelihood of coincidence between the interpretative arrangement and the actual linear arrangement is extraordinarily high here.

At this point special mention should be made of verbs that serve as copulas. In their most natural use they do not perform the entire dynamic act of ascribing a quality. They merely perform the ascription in the narrow sense of the word, the quality itself being expressed by a non-verbal element. In such a case they are interpreted as performing the dynamic semantic function of ascribing a quality (AofQ).

A writer (B) felt (AofQ) despondent and disillusioned (Q).

The positions of the AofQ-function in the Quality Scale and the Combined Scale are the following:

$$\text{Set} - \text{B} - \text{AofQ} - \text{Q} - \text{Sp} - \text{FSp}$$
$$\text{Set} - \text{Pr} - \text{Ph} - \text{B} - \text{AofQ} - \text{Q} - \text{Sp} - \text{FSp}$$

A scale need not be implemented in its entirety. Moreover, sentences occurring in the flow of communication are not always entirely context-independent. (Let me recall that, as they have been established here, the scales are constituted by context-independent items.) Sentences are usually embedded in the flow through context-dependent elements. As has been shown, such elements recede into the background and, irrespective of semantics and sentence position, carry low degrees of CD. Under these circumstances context dependence tends to neutralize the dynamic semantic function of an element; it tends to bring it down to the level of a setting. It is only in the presence of clues provided by context-dependent elements that a context-dependent element may still suggest another dynamic function than that of a setting. Its context-dependent character, however, prevents it from exceeding in CD context-independent elements.

For instance, in the presence of context-independent elements, the context-dependent element *He/The young king* still suggests the B-function in *He/The young king ruled his country capriciously and despotically*, and participates in implementing the Quality Scale. The same applies to the context-dependent element *He/The writer* in *He/The writer felt despondent and disillusioned*. A context-dependent B-element, however, does not exceed in CD a context-independent setting; cf. *At the beginning of his reign* (Set) *he/the young king* (B) *ruled* (Q) *his country* (Sp) *capriciously and despotically* (FSp), and *Unable to finish his manuscript* (Set), *he/the writer* (B) *felt* (AofQ) *despondent and disillusioned* (Q).

The problems of the neutralization, distinctiveness and syntactic implementations of the dynamic functions must be further investigated. But as the analyses of texts carried out here and elsewhere (Firbas 1975: 325–6; 1981: 55–66; 1986a: 58–67; 1986b: 859–73; Svoboda 1981) show, the Presentation Scale and the Quality Scale can be regarded as established and looked upon as belonging to the centre of the system of language. A central feature of primary importance indeed are the two communicative perspectives: the Ph-perspective and the Q/Sp-perspective (the frequency of the latter markedly exceeding that of the former). It can be assumed that modifications resulting from further research will remain subject to evaluation against the background provided by the central position of the Presentation Scale and the Quality Scale, or the Combined Scale for that matter.

The foundation-laying and the core-constituting elements: the theme and the non-theme

In regard to the Scales viewed as central phenomena, the following general conclusion is suggested. If not itself completing the development of the communication, the verb is either perspectived towards a phenomenon that is presented, or to some piece of information that acts as a specification or further specification. This involves the dynamic functions of Pr and Ph on the one hand, and those of AofQ, Q, Sp and FSp on the other. In the presence of elements performing these functions, the remaining elements – if any – are backgrounded. With the exception of those that distinctly perform the B-function, the remaining elements are interpreted as performing the Set-function.

The mediatory role of the verb is also borne out by the Mansfield text.

It contains 45 verbs (39 finite, 6 non-finite), but only 8 (7 finite, 1 non-finite) are without successful competitors and complete the development of the communication within their distributional fields: *flowered* of 10i, *scattered* of 10, *talked* of 11i, *glittered* of 26, *to get over* of 28ii, *seized* of 34, *shaken* of 34, *to go* of 35. (The Roman numerals i, ii, indicate distributional subfields.) Out of the 39 finite verbs, only two open the development of the communication within their distributional fields: *flower* of 17 and *felt* of 32.

Performing the Pr, the AofQ or the Q-function, the verb tends to mediate between elements participating in the development of the communication. As a mediator it develops the communication beyond the information conveyed by any context-dependent elements (including context-dependent B-elements and Set-elements and context-dependent elements that have acquired the Set-status through context dependence), by context-independent Set-elements and by context-independent B-elements. It acts as a successful competitor of all these elements and therefore carries a higher degree of CD than they do.

But assessing the communicative function of the verb, we must bear in mind that the verb (finite or non-finite) consists of the notional component and the categorial exponents. It is necessary to distinguish between the information conveyed by the notional component of the verb and the information conveyed by its categorial exponents. For even the information conveyed by the latter participates in the development of the communication. And this information is quite complex, too, for it conveys a number of indications, such as those of person, number, tense, mood, voice, positive/negative polarity (see p. 89). Through one of these indications, it can even complete the development of the communication. This can normally happen if the notional component becomes context-dependent and if there is no other element present that acts as a successful competitor; cf. *Has he ever read such a book? – You will be surprised. He really has*, where in the second sentence of the reply the affirmation conveyed by the categorial exponent *has* is the most important piece of information. (See also the discussion of *did* on p. 44.)

Whereas the notional component of the verb shows a strong tendency to serve as mediator or transition between two types of elements, the categorial exponents of the verb do so invariably. They do so especially through the indications of tense and mood – conveyed by the temporal and modal exponents (the TMEs, for short). In this respect the TMEs are transitional *par excellence* and are regarded as performing the function of transition proper. This function is of paramount importance and will be discussed in greater detail on pages 88–93.

As for the relationship between the notional component of the verb and its categorial exponents, the following holds good. As long as it is context-independent (which is usually the case), the information conveyed by the notional component acts as a successful competitor of that conveyed by the categorial exponents. This relationship applies irrespective of sentence position. German sentences illustrate this point particularly well. Non-finite forms behave in the same way as finite forms. (Even non-finite forms have their categorial exponents.)

> Sie konnte es einfach nicht glauben.
> Da sie es einfach nicht glauben konnte, ...
> Sie behauptete, sie hätte ihn nicht gesehen.
> Sie tat, als ob sie ihn nicht gesehen hätte.
> Ach, Papa, stell dir bloß vor, mit Stanley Burnell verheiratet zu sein. (M1 157)
> Oh, papa, fancy being married to Stanley Burnell! (M 33)

Performing the transitional role in the development of the communication, the TMEs invariably, and the notional component of the verb more often than not, start building up the core of the message on a foundation provided by one or more elements of the following types:

1 context-dependent elements (including context-dependent B-elements and Set-elements and context-dependent elements that have acquired the Set-status through context dependence);
2 context-independent Set-elements;
3 context-independent B-elements.

In this way the TMEs initiate the core-constituting process and at the same time serve as a link and as a boundary between elements that can be regarded as foundation-laying and those that can be regarded as core-constituting. In other words, they simultaneously serve as a link and as a boundary between the foundation of the message and its core.

The foundation has been termed 'theme', and the core 'non-theme'. The core-constituting elements forming the non-theme are (i) the transitional elements and (ii) the elements that develop the communication beyond the transitional elements and eventually complete it. The elements of group (ii) constitute the rheme, the element that completes the development of the communication acting as rheme proper. The transition is provided by the following:

1 the TMEs, which act as transition proper;
2 elements that are regarded as transition proper oriented and will be accounted for presently (pp. 77–9);
3 elements performing the AofQ-function or Pr-function;
4 a Q-element operating in the presence of successful competitors.

In the absence of competitors a Q-element completes the communication and serves as rheme proper. This role is also played by a Ph-element that is linked with a Pr-element. It is also played by a Sp-element or FSp-element in the absence of a successful competitor. In its presence, a Sp-element or a FSp-element belongs to the rest of the rheme.

It follows that the non-theme can be divided into transition proper, transition proper oriented part, rest of transition, rheme to the exclusion of rheme proper, and rheme proper. The parts the theme can be divided into will be discussed later (see pp. 79–81).

Within a distributional field, not all the thematic and not all the non-thematic parts need be implemented. Two parts, however, must always be implemented: rheme proper and transition proper (see p. 93). This answers Sgall's question (justly raised at the Sofia conference on FSP in 1976) whether every sentence has a theme.

Like 'development', none of the concepts 'theme', 'non-theme', 'link', 'boundary', 'transition proper', 'transition proper oriented', 'transition', 'rheme' and 'rheme proper' are position-bound. They refer to the interpretative arrangement. Their implementation may, but need not, coincide with the actual linear arrangement. In other words, thematicity, transitionalness and rhematicity are not invariably linked with the beginning, middle and end of a distributional field, respectively.

As for the relation of thematicity and non-thematicity to context dependence/independence, an element that is context-dependent is thematic; a context-dependent element cannot be non-thematic. A non-thematic element must be context-independent, but a context-independent element may be thematic.

Seen in the light of CD, the thematic elements carry lower degrees of CD than the non-thematic elements. Within the non-theme, the transitional elements carry lower degrees than the rhematic elements. Within the transition, the lowest degree of CD is carried by transition proper, which in its turn is exceeded in CD by transition proper oriented elements (see pp. 77–9) and the rest of transition. Within the rheme, the highest degree of CD is carried by rheme proper, the element conveying the piece of information towards which the communication is perspectived. As the preceding discussions have shown, differences in degrees of CD reflect the competitive relationship between the elements concerned.

In regard to the interpretative arrangement, a thematic element – if present – will constitute the starting point of this arrangement. It will be the element carrying the lowest degree of CD within the theme. In the absence of the theme, the starting point is constituted by the element carrying the lowest degree of CD within the non-theme. This means that the theme, if present, always supplies the starting point of the interpretative arrangement. The opposite, however, does not apply. The starting point of the interpretative arrangement need not be invariably thematic. In the absence of a theme, the starting point of the interpretative arrangement is constituted by transition proper (see pp. 92–3). The fact that the interpretative arrangement may, but need not, coincide with the actual linear arrangement, involves that their starting points may, but need not, coincide (Firbas 1987b).

In principle, the thematic and the non-thematic elements have not been invariably linked with any syntactic functions or any syntactic forms. Nevertheless, relations between FSP functions and syntactic functions and forms can be and have been established. These relations hold under conditions which determine the interplay of the FSP factors (linear modification, the contextual factor and the semantic factor, which in the spoken language are joined by intonation) and they correspond to signals resulting from this interplay. These signals are simple, or more or less complex (see p. 114). A simple signal of paramount importance is provided, for instance, by the TMEs. Invariably performing the function of transition proper, they constitute a simple boundary/linking signal placed in the interpretative arrangement between the theme and the non-theme.

It may have been observed that in delimiting the theme I have not had recourse to the notion of 'aboutness'. This does not mean that I do not subscribe to the view that the theme expresses what the message conveyed is to be about. But the 'aboutness' feature is not the starting point of my delimitation of the theme; it is its outcome that singles out the elements that convey the theme and bear the 'aboutness' feature.

With due alterations the same applies to the notion of communicative purpose. As I see it, the perspective of a sentence towards a particular element acting as rheme proper reveals a communicative purpose. The establishment of rheme proper and the communicative purpose is the outcome of my enquiry into its FSP, not its starting point. Both the aboutness feature and the communicative purpose are encoded by the sentence and wait to be decoded by the enquirer. (For a more detailed account of the development of my views on the theme, see Firbas 1987a).

An analysis of two paragraphs of the Mansfield text, presented below, demonstrates the FSP functions so far discussed, as well as those performed by the transition proper oriented elements, and the question focus anticipator and the negation focus anticipator, to be discussed on pages 77–9 and 101–4, respectively.

An analysis of a text

In the analysis of the Mansfield text, the following abbreviations have been used: Th (theme), TrPr (transition proper), TrPro (transition proper oriented), Tr (transition to the exclusion of transition proper and transition proper oriented elements), Rh (rheme to the exclusion of rheme proper), RhPr (rheme proper), QFocA (question focus anticipator) and NegFocA (negation focus anticipator). In order to underline the linking and boundary function of transition proper, the plus sign is additionally used. (Later, in the second part of the study, only the plus sign will be employed.) The abbreviation 'd' stands for context dependence. The italics are used for rhematic elements. The asterisks indicate subfields provided by clauses and semiclauses. (Subfields provided by nominal phrases are not covered by the analysis.) The subfields are given separate treatment.

For instance, the first sentence of the Mansfield text

> In a steamer chair, under a manuka tree that grew in the middle of the front grass patch, Linda Burnell dreamed the morning away.

has been interpreted as follows. It opens a new chapter in the story and is entirely context-independent. It provides a basic distributional field of CD. On the one hand, its (phrasal) verb *dreamed ... away* is exceeded in CD by a successful competitor: the object *the morning*, which acts as a communicative unit, serves as a specification and becomes rheme proper.

On the other hand, the verb exceeds in CD the communicative units *In a...chair, under a...tree that...*, and *Linda Burnell*. The notional component of the verb, acting as a communicative unit (see p. 91), performs the Q-function and serves as transition; its TMEs, acting as another communicative unit (see p. 91), serve as transition proper. Of the communicative units exceeded in CD by the verb, two (the adverbials) serve as settings and one (the subject) as a quality bearer. All three are thematic.

> In a steamer chair (Set, Th), under a manuka tree that grew in the middle of the front grass patch (Set, Th)*, Linda Burnell (B, Th) dreamed (+, TrPr; Q, Tr) *the morning* (Sp, RhPr) away (Q, Tr).

Within the subfield provided by the *that*-clause, the verb *grew* has one successful competitor; the adverbial *in the middle of...patch*, serving as a specification and rheme proper. On the other hand, it exceeds in CD the subject *that*, serving as a quality bearer and theme. The notional component of the verb performs the Q-function and is transitional; the TMEs of the verb serve as transition proper. (Although, in regard to the preceding context, the entire basic field is context-independent, *that* of the subfield becomes context-dependent in regard to the antecedent to which it relates within the basic field.)

> *[a manuka tree] that (d, B, Th) grew (+, TrPr; Q, Tr) *in the middle of the front grass patch* (Sp, RhPr)

The analysis of part of the Mansfield text can now follow.

(1) In a steamer chair (Set, Th), under a manuka tree that grew in the middle of the front grass patch (Set, Th)*, Linda Burnell (B, Th) dreamed (+, TrPr; Q, Tr) *the morning* (Sp, RhPr) *away* (Q, Tr). (2) She (B, d, Th) did (+, TrPr; Q, Tr) *nothing* (Sp, RhPr). (3) She (B, d, Th) looked up (+, TrPr; Q, Tr) *at the dark, close, dry leaves of the manuka* (Sp, Rh), *at the chinks of blue* (FSp, RhPr) between (Set, Th), (4) and (TrPro) now and again (Set, Th) *a tiny yellowish flower* (Ph, RhPr) dropped (+TrPr; Q, Tr) on her (Set, d, Th). (5) *Pretty* – (6) yes, if you held one of those flowers on the palm of your hand and looked at it closely (Set, Th)*, **, it (B, d, Th) was (+, TrPr; AofQ, Tr) *an exquisite small thing* (Q, RhPr). (7) Each pale yellow petal (B, Th) shone (+, TrPr; Q, Tr) *as if each was the careful work of a loving hand* (Sp, RhPr)*.

(8) The tiny tongue in the centre (B, Th) gave (+, TrPr; Q, Tr) it (Set, d, Th) *the shape of a bell* (Sp, RhPr). (9) And (TrPro) when you turned it over (Set, Th)* the outside (B, Th) was (+, TrPr; AofQ, Tr) *a deep bronze colour* (Q, RhPr). (10) But (TrPro) as soon as they flowered (Set, Th)*, they (B, d, Th) *fell* (+, TrPr; Q, RhPr) and (TrPro) were (+, TrPr) *scattered* (+, TrPr; Q, RhPr). (11) You (B, d, Th) brushed (+, TrPr; Q, Tr) them (Set, d) *off your frock* (Sp, RhPr) as you talked (Set, Th)*; (12) the horrid little things (B, Th) got (+, TrPr) caught (+, TrPr; Q, Tr) *in one's hair* (Sp, RhPr). (13) Why (QFocA), then (TrPro), flower (Set, d, Th) *at all* (Sp, RhPr)? (14) Who (QFocA) takes (+, TrPr; Q, Tr) *the trouble – or the joy –* (Sp, Rh) *to make all these things that are wasted, wasted* (FSp, RhPr)* ... (15) It (B, d, Th) was (+, TrPr; AofQ, Tr) *uncanny* (Q, RhPr).

(25) *Dazzling white* (Q, RhPr) the picotees (B, Th) shone (+, TrPr); (26) the golden-eyed marigold (B, Th) *glittered* (+, TrPr; RhPr); (27) the nasturtiums (B, Th) wreathed (+, TrPr; Q, Tr) *the veranda poles* (Sp, Rh) *in green and gold flame* (FSp, RhPr). (28) If only (TrPro) one (B, d, Th) had (+, TrPr; Q, Tr) *time to look at these flowers long enough* (Sp, Rh)*, *time to get over the sense of novelty and strangeness* (FSp, Rh)**, *time to know them* (FSp, RhPr)***! (29) But (TrPro) as soon as one paused to part the petals, to discover the underside of the leaf (Set, Th)*, along (Set, Th) came (+, TrPr; Pr, Tr) *Life* (Ph, RhPr) (30) and (TrPro) one (B, d, Th) was (+, TrPr) *swept* (+, TrPr; Q, Rh) *away* (Sp, RhPr). (31) And (TrPro), lying in her cane chair (Set, Th)*, Linda (B, Th) felt (+, TrPr; Q, Tr) *so light* (Sp, RhPr); (32) she (B, d, Th) felt (+, TrPr; Set, d, Th) *like a leaf* (Sp, RhPr). (33) Along (Set, Th) came (+, TrPr; Q, d, Th) Life (B, d, Th) *like a wind* (Sp, RhPr) (34) and (TrPro) she (B, d, Th) was (+, TrPr) *seized and shaken* (+, TrPr; RhPr); (35) she (B, d, Th) had (+, TrPr) *to go* (Q, RhPr). (36) Oh dear (TrPro), would (QFocA; +, TrPr) it (B, d, Th) *always* (Sp, RhPr) be (+, TrPr; AofQ, Tr) so (Q, d, Th)? (37) Was (QFocAnt; +, TrPr; Pr, Tr) there (Set, d, Th) *no escape* (NegFocA; Q, RhPr)?

(1)*   [a manuka tree] that (B, d, Th) grew (+, TrPr; Q, Tr) *in the middle of the front grass patch* (Sp, RhPr),

(6)*   if (TrPro) you (B, d, Th) held (+, TrPr; Q, Tr) *one of those flowers* (Sp, Rh) *on the palm of your hand* (FSp, RhPr)

(6)**   and (TrPro) looked (+, TrPr; Q, Tr) at it (Set, d, Th) *closely* (Sp, RhPr),

(7)*   as if (TrPro) each (B, Th) was (+, TrPr; AofQ, Tr) *the careful work of a loving hand* (Q, RhPr).

(9)*   when (TrPro) you (B, d, Th) turned (+, TrPr; Q, Tr) it (Set, d) *over* (Sp, RhPr)

(10)*   as soon as (TrPro) they (B, d, Th) *flowered* (+, TrPr; Q, RhPr),

(11)*   as (TrPro) you (B, d, Th) *talked* (+, TrPr; RhPr);

(14)*   to make (+, TrPr; Q, Tr) *all these things that are wasted, wasted* (Sp, RhPr)**...

(14)** [all these things] that (B, d, Th) are (+, TrPr) *wasted, wasted* (Q, RhPr)...

(28)*   [time] to look (+, TrPr; Q, Tr) at these flowers (Set, d, Th) *long enough* (Sp, RhPr),

(28)** [time] to get (+, TrPr; Q, Tr) *over the sense of novelty and strangeness* (Sp, RhPr),

(28)*** [time] *to know* (+, TrPr; Q, RhPr) them (Set, d)!

(29)*   as soon as (TrPro) one (B, d, Th) paused (+, TrPr; Q, Tr) *to part the petals* (Sp, Rh)**, *to discover the underside of the leaf* (FSp, RhPr)***,

(29)** to part (+, TrPr; Q, Tr) *the petals* (Sp, RhPr),

(29)*** to discover (+, TrPr; Q, Tr) *the underside of the leaf* (Sp, RhPr),

(31)*   lying (+, TrPr; Q, Tr) *in her cane chair* (Sp, RhPr),

The following three sections will bring some more observations on the theme, transition and rheme.

Additional notes on transition
(transition proper oriented elements)

This section offers an explanation of the concept of transition proper oriented (TrPro) elements. The TrPro-function is performed by a transitional element that through its temporal or modal feature comes close to the TMEs. It is in this sense that the former is oriented to the latter. *Oriented to* is not to be regarded as synonymous with *perspectived to* here. The TrPro-function can be performed, for instance, by adverbials of indefinite time and sentence adverbs. When acting as TrPro-elements, they exercise the third dynamic semantic function performed by adverbials (see p. 49).

Speaking of English, such sentence adverbs are meant as normally stand between the subject and the notional component of the verb. They are closely related to the modal indication conveyed by the TMEs. In the presence of one or more successful competitors, they usually retain their close relationship to the TMEs and together with them enter into the development of the communication after the foundation (theme) has been laid. They are then regarded as TrPro, and can retain this status irrespective of sentence position.

> He will naturally be surprised.
> Naturally, he will be surprised.
> He will be surprised, naturally.
>
> He, of course, works very hard.
> Of course, he works very hard.
> He works very hard, of course.

In the absence of competitors, a sentence adverb conveys the information towards which the communication is perspectived. It serves as a specification and functions as RhPr.

> Does he work hard? Of course, he does.
> After all this he felt offended. Naturally.

Naturally represents a separate distributional field, in which no competitors are present.

As for the adverbial of indefinite time, it remains closely related to the temporal indication conveyed by the TMEs and is regarded as TrPro if framed in between the subject and the verbal notional component. If occurring outside this frame, it may loosen its relationship with the TMEs and serve as a setting or perhaps even as a specification. A detailed treatment of its behaviour outside the frame remains pending.

> My friend's family usually (TrPro) stay up half the night watching television.
> For their holidays the Browns generally (TrPro) go to France.
> Peter often (TrPro) worked in the British Museum.
> Sometimes (Set) I work on Saturdays, but usually (Set) I go to town.
> He gets rather angry sometimes (Set).
> This happened sometimes (Sp), not every day (Sp).

It is worth noticing that an English adverb of indefinite time that has been framed in could be more readily rendered into Czech by an aspectual verb form than one that occurs outside the frame, serving as a setting or a specification.

> He usually went for long walks in summer.
> V létě chodíval na dlouhé procházky.
> (In summer he-used-to-go/he-usually-went for long walks.)

In the Czech sentence, the habitual action is expressed by the TMEs of the verb.

It should be added that I owe the concept of the TrPro-element and the interpretation of its function to Aleš Svoboda. I also accept his suggestion that in their ordinary use the conjunctions perform the TrPro-function.

In regard to the information conveyed, a conjunction indeed comes close to the TMEs. It is significant that their implementation may depend on the conjunction used. This is illustrated especially by languages in which the subjunctive and the conditional can assert themselves to a larger extent than in English.

It lies in the nature of the conjunction that it stands in relation not only to the TMEs of the field it introduces, but also to the TMEs of the field with which it establishes contact. In the latter case it performs a function that – after Svoboda – can be described as superclausal transition.

Additional notes on theme (diathematic elements)

Let me now throw some light on the structure of the theme. An analysis of the first paragraph of the Mansfield text will illustrate. The thematic elements have been italicized. Within the paragraph, all the thematic elements form what has been termed the thematic layer of the paragraph. The non-thematic elements, on the other hand, form the non-thematic layer, the rhematic elements within it forming the rhematic layer (see Firbas 1961: 93–5). The thematic elements within the distributional subfields provided by the subordinate clauses have been interpreted separately.

(1) *In a steamer chair* (Set, DTho), *under a manuka tree that grew in the*

middle of the front grass patch (Set, DTho), *Linda Burnell* (B, DTh)
dreamed the morning away. (2) *She* (B, d, ThPr) did nothing. (3) *She* (B,
d, ThPr) looked up at the dark, close, dry leaves of the manuka, at the
chinks of blue between, (4) and *now and again* (Set, DTh) a tiny
yellowish flower dropped *on her* (Set, ThPr). (5) Pretty – (6) yes, *if you
held one of those flowers on the palm of your hand and looked at it closely*
(Set, DTh), *it* (B, d, ThPr) was an exquisite small thing. (7) *Each pale
yellow* (B, DTh) petal shone as if each was the careful work of a loving
hand. (8) *The tiny tongue in the centre* (B, DTh) gave *it* (Set, d, ThPr)
the shape of a bell. (9) And *when you turned it over* (Set, DTh) the
outside was a deep bronze colour. (10) But *as soon as they flowered* (Set,
DTh), *they* (B, d, ThPr) fell and were scattered.

(1)* [tree] *that* (B, d, DTh) grew in the middle of the front grass patch,
– (5)* if *you* (B, d, ThPr) held one of these flowers on the palm of your
hand and looked *at it* (Set, d, DTh) closely, – (7)* as if *each* (B, d, ThPr)
was the careful work of a loving hand. – (9)* when *you* (B, d, ThPr)
turned *it* (Set, d, ThPro) over – (10)* as soon as *they* (B, d, ThPr)
flowered.

A detailed analysis of thematic elements has been undertaken by
Svoboda (1983), who has established a number of thematic functions.
Somewhat simplifying his approach, I find the following features to be
the most relevant.

(i) Some thematic elements convey information that is non-existent
     within, i.e. irretrievable from, the immediately relevant preceding
     context and hence context-independent.
(ii) Other thematic elements convey information that has already
     appeared within this sphere of context, having occurred in the
     immediately relevant section of the non-thematic layer; for instance,
     in the non-theme of the immediately preceding distributional field.
     Such thematic elements convey retrievable and hence context-
     dependent information that has been transferred from the non-
     thematic to the thematic layer.
(iii) Other thematic elements repeat information that has occurred in the
     immediately relevant section of the thematic layer and that now
     becomes more firmly established in this layer.

These different types of thematic element differ in the extent to which they contribute towards the further development of the communication, and hence carry different degrees of CD. Most dynamic are those that convey context-independent information (type (i)), less dynamic those that convey context-dependent information transferred from the non-thematic layer to the thematic layer (type (ii)), and least dynamic those that convey context-dependent information recurring in the thematic layer (type (iii)).

According to Svoboda, elements of types (i) and (ii) perform the function of diatheme (DTh; they are diathematic) and those of type (iii) that of theme proper (ThPr). The interplay of FSP factors makes it necessary to elaborate on this classification. Svoboda has devised a scale of thematic functions reflecting a gradual rise in CD. The bottom end of this scale is taken up by ThPr and the upper end by DTh, theme proper oriented elements (ThPro) and diatheme oriented elements (DTho) ranking between them.

Diathemes occur in the basic distributional fields 1, 4, 6, 7, 8, 9 and 10, and in the subfields 1a and 5a. Themes proper occur in the basic distributional fields 2, 3, 4, 6, 8 and 10, and in the subfields 5a, 7a, 9a and 10a. DTho-elements are to be found in 1 and a ThPro-element in 9a. For further illustration see Svoboda (1983) and Firbas (1989 and this volume pp. 149ff.).

A piece of thematic information shared by two or more distributional fields becomes hyperthematic. In this way hyperthematic strings are formed within the thematic layer. With the exception of the item opening the string, all the other items must be context-dependent. The longer the string, the more distinct its hyperthematicity becomes.

Additional notes on rheme (strings of specifications)

Turning our attention to the rhematic section of the distributional field, we find that a question of particular interest is the mutual relationship between a Sp-element and FSp-elements. For considerations of space I shall only summarize what I have demonstrated in greater detail elsewhere (Firbas 1986b, 1989).

Sp-elements and FSp-elements are always context-independent and take the communication further than Set-, Pr-, B- or Q-elements. They prove to be their successful competitors and exceed them in CD. They are all rhematic. In terms of actual linear arrangement, a Sp-element and one or more FSp-elements occurring together within a distributional field form a (continuous or discontinuous) specification string.

The member closing the string conveys the information towards which the development of the communication within the distributional field is perspectived; it carries the highest degree of CD within the field and serves as RhPr. The other members of the string take the development of the communication step by step towards the information conveyed by the final member. It follows that all the members of the string show a gradual rise in CD in a way that coincides with linear modification; compare the following two sentences quoted from *CEGL* (482) and the three versions of Matthew 14.8b as found in the Authorised Version (AV), the Revised Version (RV) and the Revised Standard Version (RSV).

> The student was *politely* (Sp) assessed *by the teacher* (FSp1) *impressionalistically* (FSp2) *by means of an interview* (FSp3). The patient was *carefully* (Sp) treated *by the nurse* (FSp1) *medically* (FSp2) *with a well-tried drug* (FSp3).
> Give me *here* (Ad1, Sp) *John Baptist's head* (O, FSp1) *in a charger* (Ad2, FSp2). (AV)
> Give me *here* (Ad1, Sp) *in a charger* (Ad2, FSp1) *the head of John the Baptist* (O, FSp2). (RV)
> Give me *the head of John the Baptist* (O, Sp) *here* (Ad1, FSp1) *on a platter* (Ad2, FSp2). (RSV)

The three Matthew sentences show three different orders within a specification string consisting of an object (O) and two adverbials (Ad1, Ad2). But whatever the order (Ad1, Ad2, O; Ad1, O, Ad2; or O, Ad1, Ad2), it shows a gradual rise in communicative importance, that is in CD: Sp, FSp1, FSp2. In each case the last member of the string expresses the information to which the communication within the sentence is perspectived. The first and the second members develop the communication towards this information. In each case the actual linear arrangement coincides with the interpretative arrangement.

It could be argued that the AV belongs to a different period than the other two versions, but the observation concerning the gradual rise in CD within a specification string applies even to the older periods of language. Moreover, an examination of twenty-seven late modern English versions – including the RV, the RSV and the Revised

Authorised Version (RAV) and twenty-four twentieth-century versions – reveals the following:

16 versions have the Ad1 – Ad2 – O order
2 versions have the Ad1 – O   – Ad2 order
2 versions have the [–] – O   – Ad2 order
7 versions have the O   – Ad1 – Ad2 order

The comparison shows that in the English versions the most mobile element within the string is the O. Whereas Ad1 either opens the string or occurs in its middle, but never closes it, Ad2 never opens it, but occurs either in its middle or at its end. In two cases Ad1 is not implemented at all.

The reluctance of Ad1 to move to end position within the string deserves some comment. This reluctance is hardly unrelated to the character of the semantic content of Ad1 and to the character of its semantic relations. Like Ad1, Ad2 is implemented as an adverbial of place. But whereas in the passage under examination Ad1 has strong temporal connotations (in some versions it is expressed, for instance, by *here and now* and *this moment*), Ad2 strongly connotes manner. It indicates the way the head is to be presented to the young woman. Under these circumstances it is rather the strong connotation of manner and the goal of the action, expressed by O, that compete to complete the communication. It should be noted that of the three members of the string it is only Ad1 that in a few cases remains unimplemented.

All this does not dispute the leading role of linear modification in determining the degrees of CD within the specification string, but illustrates how, within limits, semantic structure co-determines the distribution of degrees of CD within the string.

A comparison of languages would show different predilections for certain orders within specification strings consisting of objects and adverbials. Much valuable light has been thrown on such predilections by the investigations of Hajičová and Sgall (see, for example, 1982). They speak of systemic ordering, having in mind that different language systems may require different types of sequencing semantic contents.

The functional perspective of the noun phrase

In order not to overburden the analysis of the Mansfield text with details, I have not taken the attributive element into account. It is possible to do so, because the attributive element does not operate as a separate clause constituent. Although it can be implemented in a variety of ways (as a word, phrase, semiclause or clause), it remains part of an attributive construction, which consists of a headword and one or more attributive elements. Such a construction is regarded as a noun phrase. As the way the noun phrase functions in the act of communication presents interesting problems, I am now turning my attention to them and will come back to them in other places later (see pp. 94–6 and 167–9).

I agree with Svoboda (1968, 1987) that the noun phrase provides a distributional subfield of CD. I also agree with him that if context-independent the attributive element takes the development of the communication a step further than its context-dependent or -independent headword. The attributive element amplifies the meaning of the headword. If context-independent, it is more dynamic than its headword and carries a higher degree of CD. At the moment, suffice it to say that the headword performs the B-function and the attributive element the Q-function. (For further details, see pp. 94–6.) Under these conditions, the semantic relationship between the headword and the attribute asserts itself irrespective of sentence position: if it does not operate in the same direction as linear modification, it overrides it assigning greater communicative importance to the attributive element.

In accordance with Svoboda's (1968) interpretation, I regard a context-independent attributive element as rhematic and its headword, or head constituent, for that matter, as thematic within the distributional field provided by the attributive construction.

Let us compare the following French and English attributive constructions: *peinture abstraite – abstract art*; *peinture mate – matt paint*; *peinture brillante – gloss paint*; *peinture en bâtiment – house painting*; *peinture au pistolet – spray painting*; *peinture au rouleau – roller painting*. If context-independent, the attribute will convey the information towards which the attributive construction is perspectived. This applies no matter whether the headword is context-dependent or -independent. Under these contextual conditions, the attribute proves to be a successful competitor within the distributional field provided by the attributive construction. It carries a higher degree of CD than its headword irrespective of the actual linear arrangement.

For further illustration, let us compare at least the following sentences taken from the English original of the Mansfield text and its French translation.

> (25) Dazzling white the picotees shone; (26) the golden-eyed marigold glittered; (27) the nasturtiums wreathed the veranda poles in green and gold flame. (28) If only one had time to look at these flowers long enough, time to get over the sense of novelty and strangeness, time to know them.
>
> (25) Des fleurettes blanches brillaient éblouissantes; (26) les renoncules aux yeux d'or scintillaient; (27) les capucines enguirlandaient de flammes vertes et dorées les piliers de la véranda. (28) Si seulement on avait le loisir de regarder assez longtemps ces fleurs, le temps de laisser passer le sentiment de leur nouveauté, de leur étrangeté, le temps de les connaître!

The attributive adjectives in the two texts are all context-independent. So are the attributively used noun phrases (*of novelty and strangeness, aux yeux d'or, de la véranda, de leur nouveauté* and *de leur étrangeté*) and the attributively used infinitival semiclauses (for instance, [*time*] *to look at these flowers long enough*, [*time*] *to get over the sense of novelty and strangeness*; [*le temps*] *de regarder assez longtemps ces fleurs*, [*le temps*] *de laisser passer le sentiment de leur nouveauté, de leur étrangeté*). All these attributive elements carry higher degrees of CD than their headwords.

The perspective of the subfield changes if the attributive element is context-dependent and only the head element is context-independent; cf. *He was fond of almost anything that was old – old books, old furniture, old pictures…* The context-dependent attributive element is thematic and the headword rhematic. (For a further discussion of this perspective, see p. 167.)

The examples show that an attributive structure, which provides a distributional subfield of CD, can be quite complex. It can, in fact, contain attributive structures of lower rank, which in their turn provide lower-rank CD subfields.

Languages may differ in their placement of attributive elements, but the CD relationship between the headword and an attributive element remains the same. This observation is not invalidated by the differences in markedness shown by different languages in accordance with their word-order systems. A position that is marked in one system need not be marked in another. Only as markedness serves a communicative purpose, the degree of CD carried by the positionally marked element is intensified.

Dynamic and static

In the preceding discussions I frequently used the designation 'dynamic semantic function'. There is a good reason for using it when dealing with the development of the communication, for a distinction is to be made between two angles from which a semantic and grammatical sentence structure can be viewed: static and dynamic. Viewed from the static angle, the structure is unrelated to any context; it does not operate in an act of communication. Viewed from the dynamic angle, it does operate in an act of communication and is linked with a particular contextual situation.

From the static point of view, verbs and adjectives express characteristics (qualities), the former tending to express transient, the latter permanent characteristics (qualities) (see Mathesius 1975: 58). They continue to do so in and out of context, but viewed from the dynamic point of view, it is not always the quality or some specification of it towards which the communication is perspectived within the sentence. For instance, if in *And then Peter came into the room* the subject *Peter* is context-independent and the adverbial *into the room* context-dependent, the sentence is not perspectived towards the transient quality of coming or its amplification stating the place of arrival, but to the person concerned. If, on the other hand, *Peter* is context-dependent and *into the room* context-independent the sentence is perspectived in the other direction – towards the quality of coming and ultimately towards its amplification. From the dynamic point of view, the two variants serve two different communicative purposes. This makes it necessary to distinguish between the dynamic semantic Pr-function and the dynamic semantic Q-function and between other dynamic semantic functions entailed by this distinction.

Verbs that, from the static point of view, express the characteristic of appearance/existence (e.g., *come*, *appear*, *exist*) are particularly suited to perform the dynamic Pr-function. But they can do so only under certain contextual conditions. Under other conditions, they perform the dynamic Q-function. Statically speaking, they of course continue to express the characteristic of appearance/existence.

On the other hand, verbs that, from the static angle, do not even suggest the characteristic of appearance/existence are not excluded from performing the dynamic Pr-function, although they are particularly suited to perform the dynamic Q-function. For instance, if in *The kettle boils* the subject *kettle* is context-independent, it certainly permits the Ph-perspective, the verb performing the Pr-function. If context-dependent, on the other hand, it prevents the Ph-perspective and permits only the Q-perspective, the verb performing the Q-function. Statically speaking, the verb *boil* is not a verb of appearance/existence.

Let me add a terminological note in this connection. In my earlier writings I spoke of 'the dynamic function of expressing appearance/existence on the scene' (App/Ex) and of 'the dynamic function of expressing a phenomenon that appears or exists on the scene' (Ph). The scale that these functions, together with the Set-function, constitute was referred to by me as 'the Existential Scale'. I have replaced these terms and speak of 'the dynamic semantic function of presenting a phenomenon' (Pr), 'the dynamic semantic function of expressing a phenomenon to be presented' (Ph), and 'the Presentation Scale' instead. The original terms did not cause any difficulty as long as they were understood as expressing concepts of the dynamic approach, and the dynamic notion of existence/appearance on the scene was not confused with the statically viewed semantic content of existence/appearance on the scene. I have replaced the original terms in order to avoid confusion between the static and the dynamic approaches.

6   Some special issues of the theory of functional sentence perspective

The first part of the present chapter will amplify the preceding discussions by concentrating on the FSP function of transition proper in connection with (i) the boundary between theme and non-theme both in verbal and in non-verbal distributional fields and the related question of bipartition, tripartition or pluripartition, and (ii) the FSP of questions, negative sentences and commands. The second part will amplify the preceding discussions by returning to (iii) the concept of CD and (iv) the phenomenon of potentiality, and by dealing with (v) the FSP contextual applicability of a semantic and grammatical sentence structure and (vi) the signals of the distribution of CD degrees.

Boundary between theme and non-theme

1 *In verbal fields*

In the foregoing, emphasis was laid on the different roles played in communication by the notional component of the verb and its categorial exponents. Let me concentrate on the latter and outline their operation at the syntactic, semantic and FSP levels. Doing so, I shall contribute to the question of the boundary – and link, for that matter – between theme and non-theme.

At the syntactic level, the categorial exponents establish a link between the grammatical subject and the grammatical predicate. In this way, they serve as a centre within the sentence viewed as a field of syntactic relations. ('Centre' is not used here as a word order, but as a relational term.)

The syntactic meaning of the categorial exponents is rooted in their semantic content (see, p. 14). By indicating singularity or plurality, temporal relations, the speaker's attitudes, etc., they provide a link between the semantic content of the sentence and the extralinguistic reality. (The term 'extralinguistic reality' is used in its most general sense here. It refers to anything concrete or abstract in relation to which language is employed – the extralinguistic situation; see Crystal (1985: 117). The extralinguistic situation may include even linguistic phenomena that are not used as communicative means, but have become objects referred to in the communication.)

On account of the semantic heterogeneity of the indications that they convey, the categorial exponents can perform different FSP functions. But irrespective of other FSP functions that they may perform, they invariably serve as TrPr. They do so especially through the TMEs (see p. 70). By providing a link, and at the same time a boundary, between the Th (the foundation-laying elements) and the non-Th (the core-constituting elements), the TMEs serve as a centre within the sentence/clause/semiclause viewed as a distributional field of CD. (Once again 'centre' is not used here as a word-order, but as a relational term. It refers to the central position in the interpretative arrangement, which may, but need not, coincide with the central position in the actual linear arrangement.)

The outline just presented points to a case of striking congruence of functions performed by the TMEs: their establishing a link between the subject and the predicate, their establishing a link between the language event and the extralinguistic reality and their establishing a link between the Th and the non-Th. Inconspicuous though they may be, the TMEs perform a central role in the system of language.

Let me illustrate how the semantic heterogeneity of the categorial exponents manifests itself in FSP. If we compare the sentences *He has appeared* and *A problem has emerged in this/that discussion* and assume that *He* and *in this/that discussion* are context-dependent and hence thematic, we find that the *-s* as a PNE (exponent of person and number) points to the thematic *He* in the first sentence, and to the rhematic *A problem* in the second. But it functions simultaneously as a TME, and – like the entire complex of categorial exponents, *has* and *-ed*, which performs the same function – mediates between the thematic section, *He/in this discussion*, on the one hand, and the non-thematic, *appear-/emerg- A problem*, on the other, and serves as TrPr.

If the same contextual conditions apply to the *yes–no*-questions *Has he appeared?*, *Has a problem emerged in this discussion?* and *Did a problem emerge in that discussion?*, the functional perspective of the sentential semantic content remains the same, but the modal and polarity indications show increased communicative importance, in other words, an increase in CD. Let us note the participation of word order, the auxiliary *did* and the question mark in signalling interrogativity. At the same time, however, the TMEs continue to perform their mediatory function. (For a more detailed discussion of the role of the TMEs in questions, see pages 100–2.)

The complex character of the semantic content of the categorial exponents is also borne out, for instance, by cases in which one indication is singled out in contrast and becomes RhPr. For instance, *John/He does go home* can appear in opposition not only to *John doesn't go home*, but also, for instance, to *John can go home*, *John will go home*, etc. In consequence, *Does* becomes bearer of RhPr on account of PosPol, M (mood/modality) and T (tense), respectively. Simultaneously, however, the TMEs perform the function of TrPr. In each case, this means that apart from the establishment of the link between Th and non-Th and the indication singled out as RhPr, the information conveyed by the sentence is context-dependent and therefore thematic.

The context dependence/independence of the indications of M and T raise some interesting problems. It may be argued that the speaker selects his or her communicative role (mood) and decides on the kind of comment or assessment (modality) anew in every act of predication, the same applying to the temporal relation between the language event (the sentence) and the reported extralinguistic event. (This was actually my argument in Firbas 1965.) Nevertheless, from the point of view of the development of the communication, there is a difference between a change of an indication (for instance, that of the speaker's role or that of the temporal relation) and the indication remaining the same as in the preceding sentence. In the latter case, the TMEs become context-dependent in regard to the recurring indication (see Lyons 1968: 336).

But although, on account of one or another indication or other indications, the TMEs – or the entire complex of categorial exponents, for that matter – may become thematic or even rhematic, the link established by the TMEs between the Th and the non-Th is a unique phenomenon *sui generis* owing to which the TMEs invariably perform the function of TrPr. This link ensues from the communicative purpose motivating the language event and is irretrievable from the immediately relevant context (see Adamec 1966: 22–3; Daneš 1974b: 111). It is a new element in the development of the communication and an important contribution towards its further development.

Comparing the FSP function of the notional component of the finite verb and that of its categorial exponents, we find that the categorial exponents show a kind of functional heterogeneity not normally displayed by the notional component. But concurring with the function of TrPr invariably performed by the TMEs, the functional heterogeneity of the complex of the categorial exponents serves a good purpose. The fact that on account of some of its components the complex is thematic, and on account of others transitional and occasionally even rhematic, shows its Janus-faced character. Its capability to point in two directions – in that of the Th and in that of the Rh – and simultaneously to link the Th and the non-Th places it in the centre of the sentence, which serves both as a field of syntactic relations and as a field of FSP relations. On account of its special functions I regard the complex as a separate communicative unit. In consequence, the notional component of the finite verb is regarded as another communicative unit.

It may also be argued that the comparative semantic weakness of the TMEs cannot exceed in CD all the thematic elements, some of which may be context-independent and semantically quite weighty. Paradigmatically speaking, context-independent semantic weightiness is indeed always linked with greater informativity than semantic weakness and therefore carrying a higher degree of CD. Comparing *He was a poor scholar*, *His youngest son was a poor scholar*, *Joe's youngest son was a poor scholar*, and *My good old friend Joe's youngest son was a poor scholar*, we find that provided only *He*, *His* and *My* are context-independent, then the subjects, which perform the B-function, do not convey the same amounts of information and therefore differ in degrees of CD. On the other hand, the subject complements, which perform the Q-function, do not differ in the amount of information they convey and carry the same degree of CD. Paradigmatically speaking, the two last items of the 'subject column' semantically outweigh the item re-occurring in the 'subject complement column'. But applying the syntagmatic view, which takes into account the mutual relationship between the elements, we find that in each sentence it is the subject complement, *a poor scholar*, that completes the communication and therefore carries the highest degree of CD. Under these circumstances, the degree of CD carried by the subject complement as a Q-element is higher than the degree of CD carried by the subject as a B-element. Svoboda has shown (1968: 71–2) that, though expanded and having thereby its CD raised, a thematic subject does not become communicatively more important than the non-thematic rest of the sentence, the latter having its CD raised correspondingly (see also Firbas 1968: 22). It is the development of the communication that is the last court of appeal in determining the degree of CD. The Q-function takes the development of the communication further than the B-function: in other words, it is the place that an element occupies in the development of the communication (reflected by the interpretative arrangement) that ultimately determines its degree of CD.

The fact that the linking function can assert itself only after the foundation has been laid places the TMEs after the foundation-laying (thematic) elements in the interpretative arrangement. It is on the foundation provided by these elements that the TMEs start building up the core (non-Th) of the communication.

Semantic weightiness by itself does not determine the degree of CD. Semantically weighty though it may be, a context-dependent element contributes less towards the further development of the communication and carries a lower degree of CD than any context-independent element. As for the context-independent elements, it is their dynamic semantic function that determines their place in the development of the communication. Semantic weightiness does play an important role in the development of the communication. Its role, however, cannot be assessed from a paradigmatic viewpoint, which proves to be static because it disregards the dynamic semantic functions. The assessment 'contributing more than another element to the further development of the communication' is therefore to be understood as 'taking the communication further than another element on the way towards the completion of the communication'.

I have so far dealt with the finite verb form. Let me now turn to the non-finite form of the verb. Even the non-finite verb form consists of a notional component and a categorial exponent or exponents. The function of the latter is less extensive than in the case of the finite form, but invariably involves the signalling of TrPr within the given subfield.

Reading his book (Set, Th)*, he (d, B, Th) missed (+, TrPr; Q, Tr) the news (Sp, RhPr).
Reading (+, TrPr; Q, RhPr) his book (Sp, RhPr),

The categorial exponent of *reading* is the *ing*-element. Through its relation to the context-dependent subject *he*, it co-expresses the indication of P (person) and N (number) and in this respect it actually conveys a thematic feature. Through its relation to *-ed* of *missed* it co-expresses the indications of T and M. In this way it acts as a TME and performs the function of TrPr within the subfield, and is linked to TrPr of the basic field. In *While reading his book, he missed the news*, it is linked with the conjunction *while*, which Svoboda would regard as TrPro. Owing to its character, a conjunction comes close not only to the TMEs of the field it introduces, but also to the TMEs of the field to which the one introduced is linked on. I accept these interpretations offered by Svoboda. As will be discussed in greater detail presently, Svoboda has also demonstrated that even a subfield provided by a noun phrase has its TrPr.

The link which obtains between a distributional field and the extralinguistic reality and which coincides with the link between Th and non-Th (TrPr) must be implemented in one way or another if the distributional field is to fulfil its communicative purpose. If not explicitly expressed by the TMEs or their formal counterparts in the noun phrase (p. 72), it is expressed at least vicariously or regarded as ellipted (an observation made by Svoboda, 1983: 80). A verbless sentence structure (*Fire! A wonderful achievement.*) is related to the extralinguistic reality by intonation in the spoken language or by punctuation and capitalization, which stake off the sentential distributional field in the written language. It follows that a sentence serving as an utterance is never devoid of TrPr (Svoboda, ibid.). A sentence can be themeless, but cannot be rhemeless or transition-properless. The Th may remain linguistically unexpressed and suggested by an extralinguistic referent, but the Rh must be linked on to it in one way or another. Let me just add one more example.

If in *Rain was falling*, the subject is context-independent, it performs the Ph-function and acts as RhPr, the verbal notional component *fall-* performing the Pr-function and acting as Tr. There is no Set-element present that would act as Th. Serving as TrPr, the TMEs link the non-Th on to the situation present extralinguistically. Seen against the background of the Pr-Scale, the Set-function has not been implemented. Under the contextual condition stipulated, *Rain was falling* is themeless. (This interpretation is a modification of my previous view – see, for example, Firbas (1986a: 51) – according to which I assigned *fall-* the thematic function.)

2 *Boundary between theme and non-theme in non-verbal fields* (*noun phrases*)

I have already dealt with the FSP functions of the headword and its attribute within a noun phrase, which, following Svoboda (1968), I regard as a distributional field of CD. The question arises whether even within such a field the TrPr function is performed.

Answering this question I have to point out that I also agree with Svoboda that even a simple noun phrase (*a girl*) provides a distributional subfield (Svoboda 1987). If context-independent, the noun (or, to be exact, its notional component) performs the Ph-function and acts as RhPr. If present, a determiner and/or its equivalent performs (perform) the Set-function and is (are) thematic. The exponents of case and number, linking the determiner with the noun (or, to be exact, its notional component), perform the function of TrPr. As the exponents are nominal in character, Svoboda speaks of 'nominal TrPr'. (The exponent of case is implemented by endings, including the zero ending, prepositions or grammaticalized word order.)

In this way, Svoboda has extended the notion of TrPr to the noun phrase. I find it a valuable contribution to the study of the microstructures of functional syntax (Svoboda 1989). As in the case of the verb, even in that of the noun, the notional component and the categorial exponents perform different FSP functions. This should be borne in mind even if this fact is not explicitly recalled in the following discussion.

Let me recall that the structure of a noun phrase may become quite complex, because an attribute may be implemented by a noun phrase or a clause or a semiclause and provide a distributional subfield of its own; and that, if context-independent, the attribute is assigned the Q-function while the headword performs the B-function. This is not at variance with Svoboda's interpretation that was adduced above, according to which a context-independent headword performs the Ph-function. Under the contextual conditions stipulated, the headword performs both the Ph-function and the B-function, participating in the implementation of the Combined Scale (see p. 67). On condition that the attribute is context-independent, Svoboda interprets the complex noun phrase *a girl standing in the corner* as: *a* (Set) *girl* (Ph & B) *standing* (Q) *in the corner* (Sp).

As for the distribution of the thematic, transitional and rhematic functions, Svoboda finds that the TrPr effect of the exponents of case and number extends over the entire complex phrase and offers the following interpretation: *a* (Set, Th) *girl* (Ph & B, Tr) *standing* (Q, Tr) *in the corner* (Sp, RhPr). This interpretation reckons with an extensive transitional section.

Proceeding in this way, Svoboda adopts another solution than that arrived at in Svoboda 1968, where under the conditions stipulated he interprets the headword as thematic and the attribute as rhematic (see this volume, p. 84). He modifies his original solution because he finds a parallel between the communicative function of the verb in a clause and that of a headword in a complex noun phrase. For particulars, the reader is referred to Svoboda (1987).

I agree with Svoboda's interpretation of the complex noun phrase implementing the Combined Scale, but I prefer his original thematic interpretation of the headword (1968). As for his concept of nominal TrPr, I find it a valuable contribution to the theory of FSP, and – in accordance with his idea of microstructures in functional syntax – even extend its application (see below).

As I see it, the noun-phrase headword simultaneously performing the Ph-function and the B-function is reminiscent of the subject in the *A young king ruled his country capriciously and despotically* sentence type commented on earlier (page 67). *A young king* performs the Ph-function, but in regard to the further development of the communication it simultaneously performs the B-function. This function renders it thematic. I find that with due alterations the same applies to the headword which under the same contextual conditions operates in the complex noun phrase *a girl standing in the corner*.

In the next step, I assume the formal exponents of attributiveness to establish a separate nominal TrPr between the headword and its attribute. Like the verbal TrPr, this nominal TrPr is not affected by the different perspectives the noun phrase may appear in. This induces me to offer the following interpretation. On condition that the attribute is context-independent, the noun phrase *a girl standing in the corner* functions in the perspective: *a girl* (Ph & B, Th) *standing in the corner* (Q, Rh).

Like Svoboda's, this interpretation regards the noun phrase as implementing the Combined Scale. It assumes, however, that apart from a nominal TrPr linking *a* and *girl*, there is another nominal TrPr (of lower rank) linking *a girl* and *standing in the corner*. Being a semiclause, *standing in the corner* provides a subfield. It has its own semiverbal TrPr: *standing* (Q, Tr) *in the corner* (Sp, Rh). It follows that the suffix *-ing* acts as nominal TrPr in two ways. On the one hand, it acts as a link between *a girl* and *standing in the corner*; and on the other hand, between *standing* and *in the corner*.

Continuing Svoboda's functional microanalysis, I interpret the noun phrase *in the corner* as providing a distributional subfield, in which *the* is thematic and *corner* rhematic; the preposition *in* is an exponent of case serving as nominal TrPr.

3 Bipartition, tripartition and pluripartition

The establishment of a Tr between a Th and a Rh suggests tripartition. (Needless to say, 'between' applies to the interpretative arrangement, which may but need not coincide with the actual linear arrangement.) The establishment of a ThPr and the rest of the Th, a TrPr and the rest of the Tr, and a Rh to the exclusion of RhPr and a RhPr – or (with greater delicacy, after Svoboda) the establishment of a ThPr, a ThPro-element, a DTho-element and a DTh; a TrPr, a TrPro-element and the rest of the Tr; and a Rh to the exclusion of RhPr and the RhPr – suggests pluripartition. ('Pluripartition' is to be understood here as pertaining to more than three parts; compare the term 'pluriliteral' employed by Hebraists in the sense of 'having more than 3 letters in the root'; see the *Concise Oxford Dictionary*, 7th edn, entry *pluri-*.)

The division into Th and non-Th suggests bipartition. Needless to say, with the exception of RhPr and TrPr not all the FSP functions enumerated must necessarily be implemented (see p. 93).

Is my approach bipartitional, tripartitional or pluripartitional? In the literature, my approach is often presented as tripartitional (see, for example, Bogusławski 1977: 203). Szwedek tells his readers that 'in his most recent paper Firbas (1983) seems to withdraw from his earlier rigid, sexpartition approach' (1986: 64).

In an earlier work (Firbas 1974: 25), I state that 'the delicacy of segmentation depends on the purpose of the investigation', but at the same time (pp. 25–6) emphasize the importance of the concept of TrPr, which, if it proves correct, points to 'a boundary between the thematic and the non-thematic section'. The paramount importance of this boundary has been one of my main concerns ever since 1965, when my paper on TrPr appeared (Firbas 1965). My emphasis on the boundary role of TrPr shows that in essence my approach is not tripartitional or pluripartitional, but bipartitional.

In the light of these facts it cannot be said that in 1983 I withdrew from an earlier, more rigid, sexpartition approach. The FSP functions enumerated above have been gradually established in the course of empirical investigations unhampered by any rigidity. As for the expression 'sexpartition', I have not used it in my writings, but have preferred the expression 'pluripartition' (Firbas 1983a). Svoboda's enquiries into the thematic and transitional functions have in fact expanded the gamut into a scale of more than six items.

Speaking of the tripartitional division (Th–Tr–Rh), Szwedek finds that it involves 'a fundamental methodological fault', because it 'is not based on one, uniform criterion' (1986: 64). He argues that I quite explicitly link Th and Rh to the preceding context (context-bound versus context-unbound), while regarding Tr as a relation between the two and identifying it as such without recourse to the context. This argument is based on the assumption that I delimit the Th and the Rh on the grounds that they convey context-bound and context-unbound information, respectively; but this assumption is incorrect. Some scholars indeed delimit the Th and the Rh in this way, but this is not my solution of the problem. Context dependence/independence is certainly a factor involved in the delimitation of any of the functions constituting the gamut of FSP functions; it is, however, only one factor in an interplay of factors.

The functional sentence perspective of questions, negative sentences and commands

The preceding sections have demonstrated the important FSP roles performed by the categorial exponents of the verb as well as by those of such nominal elements as the noun and the adjective. It is not without interest to examine the FSP roles played by these elements in questions, negative sentences and commands. Let me first concentrate on the FSP of the question.

The question performs two functions: (i) it announces that the questioner is in want of some knowledge and it appeals to the interlocutor to supply it; and (ii) it informs the interlocutor of what the questioner would like to know and of the perspective from which he wishes the missing knowledge to be approached (see Firbas 1957: 91).

The first function is performed by the means capable of signalling interrogativity, such as the interrogative words (e.g., *who, where*), the modal exponent of the finite verb, word order and – in the spoken language – intonation. The second function is performed by the semantic contents of the elements making up the question, the perspective being the outcome of the interplay of FSP factors.

The pieces of information towards which the question is perspectived serves as the RhPr of the question. Adopting Quirk *et al.*'s term 'question focus' (*GCE*, 52), I use it synonymously with 'RhPr of the question'. According to contextual conditions, a question structure functions in different perspectives. (In the examples below, the rhemes proper or question foci have been italicized.)

> When will Father go with Peter *to London*?
> When will Father go *with Peter* to London?
> When will Father *go* with Peter to London?
> When will *Father* go with Peter to London?
> When *will* Father go with Peter to London?
> *When* will Father go with Peter to London?
> Will Father go with Peter *to London*?
> Will Father go *with Peter* to London?
> Will Father *go* with Peter to London?
> Will *Father* go with Peter to London?
> *Will* Father go with Peter to London?

The FSP of a question is determined by the same laws of interplay as the FSP of a declarative sentence. Any element of the question can convey the RhPr (question focus) provided it is not prevented from doing so by a successful competitor.

But other solutions than the one just outlined have been offered. For instance, in Mathesius' view (1941, 1942), subscribed to by Křížková (1972), it is the *wh*-word in the *wh*-question of the finite verb in the *yes–no*-question that expresses the Rh; the rest of the question expresses the Th. While the 'rest' conveys information known to the questioner, the *wh*-word in the *wh*-question or the finite verb in the *yes–no*-question indicates what is unknown to him or her. The *wh*-word substitutes for a piece of knowledge to be disclosed and the finite verb asks for confirmation or denial of information the questioner is already familiar with.

This view does not take the addressee into account, who must be told what information he or she is expected to complete, or to confirm or deny. Such information or part of it usually remains irretrievable from the immediately relevant context. For instance, the forms *Who?* or *Does he?* cannot be used if the addressee is incapable of completing them by information retrievable from this context. If the speaker/writer and not the immediately relevant context were the criterion of known information, then every declarative sentence would have to be interpreted as conveying known information and as being entirely thematic.

In this connection Halliday's approach to the question should be mentioned (1967b: part 5). In essence, Halliday ascribes the question the same two functions as my interpretation: (i) that of conveying the message that there is something the speaker does not know and wants to know; and (ii) that of conveying explanatory comment about his or her demand. But Halliday's approach is not the same as mine. It has to be remembered that Halliday links the Th invariably with the beginning, and the Rh with the rest, of the sentence. In his interpretation the unmarked, most frequent Th of the *wh*-question is the *wh*-element, and the unmarked, most frequent Th of the *yes–no*-question the finite verbal element. In either case, the rest of the question is rhematic. The Th then performs function (i). The explanatory comment (function (ii)) is predominantly a matter of what is termed by Halliday 'information structure', constituted by recoverable (old) and non-recoverable (new) information. The recoverability or non-recoverability of the information, i.e. its derivability or non-derivability from the preceding context, is decided by the speaker, who presents the information as recoverable or non-recoverable by indicating the latter – to the exclusion of the former – with nuclear stress.

In my approach the FSP of the question is determined by the distribution of CD over its elements. As this distribution is an outcome of an interplay of factors, thematicity or rhematicity is not determined solely by sentence position. Linear modification is only one of the factors. The last arbiter of retrievability or irretrievability is not the speaker, but the immediately relevant context, which is binding both for the speaker and for the addressee. As for intonation, I do not regard it as a means of the written language. Its operation in FSP – also in questions – will be discussed in the part dealing with FSP in the spoken communication (pp. 189–91).

In consequence, the functional perspectives of the question structures adduced above would be interpreted by me as follows. First the relationship of the question to the immediately relevant context is examined and the context-dependent elements are established. Then the operation of linear modification and semantics within the context-independent section of the question is analysed and the relationship between the context-independent elements assessed. In doing so, it is convenient to start by asking whether the question contains any successful competitors of the verb.

Let us assume that *Father* is context-dependent and that in the *wh*-question as well as in the *yes–no*-question the other elements are context-independent. These contextual conditions lead to the interpretation given below. (Different contextual conditions necessarily alter this interpretation. These alterations will be discussed later.) Apart from being context-dependent, *Father* is thematic also on account of the B-function it performs.

Within the context-independent section, the verb – or rather its notional component – acts as a Q-element and is transitional. It has two successful competitors: the two adverbials following it, which serve as specifications and are rhematic. The one that comes last serves as a FSp and RhPr (see p. 82); it conveys the information towards which the question is perspectived, and is therefore the question focus.

The interrogative *when* in the *wh*-question cannot be looked upon as a successful competitor of the verb. This is because of its vicarious character. It substitutes for an adverbial element that is to be expressed in the reply. On account of its weak semantic character it does not serve as a temporal specification, but acts as a context-independent temporal setting. Hence it is thematic, but carries a higher degree of CD than the context-dependent *Father*. It will be further commented upon below.

Coming back to the context-independent verb, we find that it carries the lowest degrees of CD within the context-independent section of the question. The plural 'degrees' is justified, for the verb consists of the notional component and the categorial exponents, the former acting as a successful competitor of the latter.

As we already know, the semantic content of the categorial exponents is fairly complex. On account of the semantic features of person and number the categorial exponents act as PNEs; under the circumstances, these features relate to the Th and are thematic. Through the features of tense and mood, the categorial exponents act as TMEs and perform the function of TrPr, providing a link between the Th and the non-Th.

In the *yes–no*-question the ME indicates unsolved *yes–no*-polarity. In this way it points forward to the solution to be given in the reply. Within the question itself it points to the element towards which the question is perspectived, i.e. to the question focus. Not conveying itself the missing information, but vicariously pointing to it via the question focus, it acts as the question focus anticipator (QFocA) within the *yes–no*-question. In this way, the TMEs continue to serve as TrPr, but simultaneously point through the *yes–no*-polarity feature to RhPr and in this way are rhematic.

The term 'anticipator' is used in regard to the further development of the communication. Strictly speaking, it is a term of the interpretative arrangement. In the actual linear arrangement, it may occasionally happen that the focus precedes the element conveying the anticipator; cf., for example, *My father was late yesterday?* in which the focus precedes the anticipator if 'being late yesterday' is context-dependent information.

In the *wh*-question, interrogativity is co-expressed by the *wh*-word. Like the ME in the *yes–no*-question, it points forward to the reply. It does so via the question focus and therefore acts as a QFocA. In consequence, its FSP function is quite a complex one, too. For reasons given above, it performs a thematic function, but simultaneously its interrogativity feature perspectives it towards TrPr, and its capacity as a QFocA perspectives it towards RhPr, inducing it to perform a rhematic function.

The interpretations just offered apply to the two of the question structures that were adduced above, in which *Father* is the only context-dependent element. The other question structures function under different contextual conditions. What changes under these conditions? The answer is a simple one. The moment it becomes context-dependent, an element becomes thematic. As for the context-independent elements, they behave in the way discussed above. The one that proves to be without a successful competitor carries the highest degree of CD and takes over the role of the question focus (RhPr of the question). It should be borne in mind that even the *wh*-word or the ME of the finite verb can carry the highest degree of CD, cease to act as QFocA and itself perform the role of focus if the rest of the question (with the exception of the context-independent function of TrPr performed by the TMEs and the context-independent TrPro feature borne by the *wh*-word) is context-dependent. But though becoming focus within the question, the *wh*-word does not cease pointing beyond the question to the information to be disclosed in the reply. It comes even closer to this information in one rather special use that undoubtedly pertains to the periphery of the language system.

A question is meant to imitate and in this way anticipate the declarative structure of the reply. The *wh*-word is then placed in the position where the element disclosing the missing information would occur; cf. *And then he went where and met who?* These imitative structures perspective their communication towards the *wh*-words. In fact, the question anticipates and imitates the FSP of the reply.

Like the question, even the negative sentence has its focus anticipator. It is the negative particle *not* or another element conveying negation that assumes the role of the anticipator of RhPr (focus) in the negative sentence. For instance, the structure *Father will not go with Peter to London* can function in different perspectives according to different contextual conditions. (See Firbas (1976: 49). An important study of the contextual conditions linked with negation has been offered by Hajičová (1975).) With one exception (see below), *not* is always perspectived to the element that carries the highest degree of CD and serves as RhPr (focus) of the negative sentence. The particle *not* serves as the negation focus anticipator (NegFocA).

> Father will not go with Peter *to London.*
> Father will not go *with Peter* to London.
> Father will not *go* with Peter to London.
> *Father* will not go with Peter to London.
> Father *will* not go with Peter to London.
> Father will *not* go with Peter to London.

The particle *not* can carry the highest degree of CD, cease to act as NegFocA and itself perform the role of focus if all the other elements (with the exception of the TMEs that remain context-independent on account of its function of TrPr) are context-dependent.

A NegFocA can occur in a sentence together with a QFocA. If this is the case, they relate to the same element in the sentence, which performs a double function; it simultaneously serves as a question focus and as a negation focus.

> Will not Father go with Peter *to London?*
> Will not Father go *with Peter* to London?
> Will not Father *go* with Peter to London?
> Will not *Father* go with Peter to London?

> *Will* not Father go with Peter to London?
> Will *not* Father go with Peter to London?

As for the CD relationship between the two anticipators, the NegFocA exceeds in CD the QFocA as long as they both remain context-independent, which is the usual case. Exceptionally, however, either focus anticipator can take over the role of focus under the special contextual conditions stipulated above and carry the highest degree of CD within the sentence.

A focus anticipator is also to be found in commands. In the verbal type of command it is implemented by the MEs and PNE(s) of the verb. These exponents, which are frequently implemented by one and the same overt signal, indicate the role of the speaker (issuing a command) and the appeal to the listener (for the execution of the command).

A comparison of French *bois, buvons, buvez* and English *drink, let us drink, drink* reveals different signalling devices. English *drink* does not indicate whether one or more persons are appealed to. A signalling device is provided even by the 'bareness' of the English verb stem, the jussive role and the appeal being signalled by the absence of an ending and an accompanying pronominal form.

In the absence of successful competitors the notional component of the verb expresses RhPr and acts as the command focus. If present, a successful competitor takes over this function and perspectives the command away from the notional component of the verb. The verbal categorial exponent conveys the focus if all elements that could perform this function are context-dependent and can therefore no longer serve as successful competitors.

> Go with Peter *to London*.
> Go with *Peter* to London.
> *Go* with Peter to London.
> *Do* go with Peter to London.

In the last sentence it is the indication of the appeal to the listener that itself becomes focus.

Once again, the categorial exponent(s) of the verb simultaneously performs (perform) more than one function in FSP. Apart from invariably performing the function of TrPr, the M-feature points in an anticipatory fashion to the RhPr (focus) and under special conditions (see above) can even come to convey the RhPr (focus) itself; on account of the PN-feature the categorial exponent(s) refers (refer) to the addressee and is (are) thematic. In verbless commands (*Silence!*), the TrPr function can be vicariously performed by the exclamation mark (see p. 93).

Let me add a note on the term 'focus'. In the present study I have so far combined it with 'question', 'negation' and 'command' in reference to the rhemes proper of questions, negative sentences and commands, respectively. But by analogy with these terms we can also speak of, for instance, the 'declarative focus' in reference to the RhPr of the declarative sentence (positive or negative) and the 'emotive focus' in reference to the RhPr of a re-perspectived spoken sentence.

The concept of communicative dynamism revisited

The foregoing has demonstrated what an important role the phenomenon of CD plays in the theory of FSP as presented in this study. For years it has been studied by me and my colleagues attached to the Brno Department of English. (See the writings of Aleš Svoboda, Helga Chládková, Eva Golková, Josef Hladký, Eva Horová, Jiří Hruška, Jana Chamonikolasová, Ludmila Urbanová and myself, published mostly in *Brno Studies in English*; see also Firbas and Golková (1975).) We cannot claim to have discovered it. Scholars before us were aware of its existence in one form or another. But we may perhaps claim to have been investigating it in a consistent manner and on a truly extensive scale.

As to the work of the scholars before us, let me recall, for instance, Hermann Paul's concept of communicative value (1920), Karl Boost's concept of the same name (1955), Vaclav Ertl's concept of content weightiness and importance (1926, par. 552), František Trávníček's concept of importance (1937), Mukařovský's concept of content accumulation (1941: 129–30), K. G. Krushel'nitskaya's concept of communicative load (1961), Dwight L. Bolinger's concept of the gradation of meaning (1952: 1125), and last but not least Vilém Mathesius' concept of the relative shading of the importance of sentence elements (1947: 218; for Mathesius' evaluation of Trávníček's concept of importance, see Mathesius 1947: 335; cf. Firbas 1983: 68). I believe I was the first to use the term 'communicative dynamism' in the literature (1956: 107); the credit for coining it, however, goes to Josef Vachek, who suggested it to me in a private communication. It is gratifying to find that the term and concept of communicative dynamism have been used in *CGEL*.

It can be said that the degree of CD carried by a linguistic element is the relative informational (communicative) value the element acquires in the development of the communication. Informational (communicative) value or importance can, of course, be judged from various viewpoints. The viewpoint applied in my approach to FSP is the place an element takes up in the development of the communication, the completion of this development coinciding with the fulfilment of the communicative purpose. The closer an element comes to this completion, the greater its informational (communicative) value or importance. It is from this viewpoint that 'informational (communicative) value' or 'importance' is to be understood in the present study. It serves as an explanatory concept synonymous with 'communicative dynamism'.

A context-independent element comes closer to the fulfilment of the communicative purpose, in other words, to the completion of the communication, than a context-dependent element; it is therefore communicatively more important and carries a higher degree of CD. Context-dependent elements that are more firmly established within the thematic layer contribute less to the further development of the communication than those context-dependent elements that are not so well established in it; in regard to the fulfilment of the communicative purpose the former are less important than the latter; they carry lower degrees of CD. As has also been shown, even within the context-independent sphere elements differ in their proximity to the completion of the communication; even context-independent elements differ in communicative importance and hence in degrees of CD. The degrees of communicative importance and hence of CD are also borne out by the phenomenon of competitorship.

In the spoken language, the degrees of CD are borne out by their relationship to the degrees of prosodic prominence (PP). The problem of this relationship will be taken up in the second part of the present study (pp. 143–224). The problem of the number of degrees of CD displayed by a sentence has been dealt with on pages 16–19, where a distinction between a carrier of CD and a communicative unit has been drawn. Needless to say, the existence of the phenomenon of CD is also corroborated by the work of our predecessors referred to above.

In this connection it is worth mentioning that Chafe (1974, 1976) has expressed the view that he cannot think of more degrees of CD than two. He holds that a piece of information can be assumed to be either present in or absent from the addressee's consciousness. In his approach, the presence in or the absence from the addressee's consciousness is the criterion of the givenness or the newness of a piece of information. Since this criterion offers only these alternatives, an element can only be established as conveying either given or new information; a piece of information cannot be assumed to be partly but not completely present in the addressee's consciousness; an element cannot therefore be partly given and partly new. This induces Chafe to say that 'it is hard to see from the Czech writings that the notion of degrees of consciousness, or a gamut of communicative dynamism, is supported by linguistic evidence' (1974: 120). Likewise, in his 1976 paper Chafe says:

it appears from the examples provided by Czech linguists that CD has more in common with the given–new distinction than with the other statuses we will consider. That being the case, it is interesting that CD is said to be a matter of degree, and not a binary distinction. If we identify a low degree of CD with givenness and a high degree with newness, the question arises as to whether there are intermediate degrees of given and new. The implication would be that the speaker can assume something to be in the addressee's consciousness to a greater or lesser degree. This psychological implication would be of considerable importance if it could be established. For the moment, however, it is necessary to say that it has not been demonstrated that given vs. new is anything more than a discrete dichotomy. (Chafe 1976: 33)

It is important to note that Chafe is actually inclined to equate three dichotomies: (i) that of given vs. new; (ii) that of being assumed to be present in vs. being absent from the addressee's consciousness; and (iii) that of low degree of CD vs. high degree of CD.

It has already been emphasized (p. 37) that according to my approach givenness, i.e. context dependence, is conditioned by the presence of the information and/or its referent in the immediately relevant context, whereas according to Chafe's approach it is conditioned by the assumption of the speaker that the information is present in the addressee's consciousness. Chafe's criterion of givenness cannot therefore be equated with my criterion of context dependence. Moreover, the distribution of degrees of CD is not determined solely by the dichotomy of context dependence and context independence, but by an interplay of factors. My analyses of this interplay, which are based on linguistic facts offered by the text and extralinguistic facts present in the immediately relevant situational context, testify to a CD gamut constituted by more degrees of CD than two.

My analyses nevertheless do not do away with the dichotomy of context dependence and context independence, but demonstrate that this dichotomy does not invariably coincide with that of thematicity and non-thematicity. Even elements that convey information that is partly context-dependent and partly context-independent (see pp. 36–7) do not disprove the dichotomy of context dependence and context independence, because they are either predominantly context-dependent or predominantly context-independent and accordingly prove to operate as if they were entirely one or entirely the other.

I have not studied the relationship between degrees of CD and their counterparts in the mind of the language user, but I do not think that the language user is unaware of the development of the communication. As early as 1844 Henri Weil aptly spoke of the point of departure and the goal of the communication and the movement of thought from the former to the latter. I hold that such movement does not consist in two steps only, one being the starting point and the other the goal. Other steps leading from the starting point to the departure can occur between the two. This observation corroborates the existence of a gamut of CD conceived of as a reflection of the development of the communication.

Chafe's interpretation of the degrees of CD is, for instance, accepted – without any mention of my enquiry into the interplay of factors determining the degrees of CD – by Helas Contreras in his valuable monograph on Spanish word order (Contreras 1976: 16). It is, however, gratifying to find that Contreras' observations and analyses corroborate the interplay of (i) linear modification, (ii) the semantic character of the sentence elements and the character of the semantic relations into which they enter, and (iii) context dependence/independence; that is, the three FSP factors operating in the written language. Nevertheless, it is disappointing that he tells his reader nothing of my enquiries into this interplay, nor of my enquiries into the relationship between the distribution of degrees of CD as determined by this non-prosodic interplay and the distribution of prosodic prominence. In this way, the reader is in fact deprived of references to linguistic evidence bearing out the gamut of degrees of CD.

As the foregoing discussions have demonstrated and the following will continue to demonstrate, the distribution of degrees of CD is determined by an interplay of factors. In this connection, however, an objection must be dealt with – the objection that the FSP factors are heterogeneous. This objection, raised by Bogusławski at the conference on text linguistics in Warsaw in October 1983, is not justified, but proves very stimulating, for it prompts me to underline an essential fact that lies at the basis of the interplay of the FSP factors – a fact constituting a common denominator to which the FSP factors can be brought.

As has been shown, the character of the semantic content (together with the character of its semantic relations) lends the content a certain communicative value. In the development of the communication, however, this value is lowered if affected by context dependence. If unaffected by context dependence, then – in accordance with the character of the content (and the character of its semantic relations) – it changes with changes in sentence position (in other words, is affected by linear modification) or remains unchanged irrespective of sentence position (in other words, is unaffected by linear modification). The communicative value is assessed here in regard to the closeness to the completion of the development of the communication. The closer the semantic content comes to it, the more it contributes to the development of the communication; in other words, the higher its degree of CD.

In the written language, all this involves the interplay of three factors: the semantic factor, the contextual factor and that of linear modification. In the spoken language, this interplay is joined by the factor of intonation. In the interplay, each factor concerns the operation of a semantic phenomenon in the development of the communication. This is the common denominator to which the FSP factors can be brought. This common denominator clears them of the imputation of heterogeneity.

More thoughts on potentiality

Amplifying the discussions of the preceding chapters, I propose to continue the enquiry into the phenomenon of potentiality, which occurs when the interplay of FSP factors permit of more than one interpretation. Let me examine the following three sentences, paying special attention to the function of the verb *gather* and its accompanying subject. The sentences are taken from Moffatt's translation of the New Testament.

> (1)   [...but,] as great crowds gathered to him, [he entered a boat and sat down, while all the crowd stood on the beach.] (Matt. 13.2)
>
> (2)   [At that time they had a notorious prisoner called Jesus Bar-Abbas; so] when they had gathered, [Pilate said to them...] (Matt. 22.16)

(3) [...; but those who had seized Jesus took him away to the house of Caiaphas the high priest,] where the scribes and elders had gathered. (Matt. 26.57)

In (1) the presence of context-dependent *to him* and context-independent *great crowds* induces the notional component of *gather* to carry the meaning of appearance and to perform the Pr-function; *to him* and *great crowds* perform the Set-function and the Ph-function, respectively. The zero plural variant of the non-generic indefinite article co-signals the context independence of the subject *great crowds*, to which the field is perspectived, implementing the Pr-scale. In (2) the notional component of *gather* has no competitor. It performs the Q-function. The field implements the Q-scale. This time, the communication is perspectived towards the act of assembling, not at the assembling crowd. The notion of crowd is retrievable from the immediately relevant context (see Matt. 27.15). The interpretation of (3) is not so straightforward. Both *the scribes and elders* and *gathered* are context-independent. As the notional component of *gather* does not explicitly express 'appearance', it may induce the field to be perspectived to the act of gathering and to implement the Q-scale. On the other hand, the context independence of the subject, the absence of other competitors and the tendency of the verb to act as an introductory element may perspective the field to the persons assembling and induce it to implement the Pr-scale. The latter interpretation is the likelier of the two. The correctness of this estimate is supported by languages in which the sentence position of the subject is not so fixed as in English. Such languages can render the interplay unequivocal by placing the context-independent subject in end position. The following French version will illustrate.

[Ceux qui avaient arrêté Jésus l'emmenèrent chez Caïphe le Grand Prêtre,] où se réunirent les scribes et les anciens. (La Bible de Jérusalem)

Another example of potentiality is offered by the following passage:

The breeze of morning lifted in the bush and the smell of leaves and wet black earth mingled with the sharp smell of the sea. Myriads of birds were singing. A goldfinch flew over the shepherd's head. (M 10.13)

The passage is taken from the introductory chapter of Katherine Mansfield's story 'At the bay'. The chapter offers a description of the bay in the early morning. The subjects *The breeze of morning*, *Myriads of birds* and *A goldfinch* undoubtedly act as Ph-elements, their verbs performing the Pr-function. The elements *in the bush* and *over the shepherd's head* serve as settings that express information reminding the reader of the general setting of the introductory chapter. The description of this setting speaks of 'bush-covered hills at the back' and a substantial part of the narration following it and preceding the passage under examination is devoted to the shepherd and his flock. Another feature of the general setting is the presence of the sea. If in consequence even *with the sharp smell of the sea* is interpreted as a setting, the subject *the smell of leaves and wet black earth* is to be regarded as a Ph-element. Together with the other three subjects, it then forms a rhematic layer stating what features appeared on the morning bay scene.

The thread of suggestive semantic clues (see pp. 56–8) producing the rhematic layer described is present in the text. But it is not signalled in a way excluding another interpretation potentially present. In the second sentence, *the sharp smell of the sea* is context-independent and interpretable as a specification. If this interpretation is chosen, the notional component of *mingled* is assigned the Q-function and perspectives the communication away from the information conveyed by the subject. In this case, the most important piece of information presented is not the emergence of the smell of the leaves and wet black earth, but the merger of this smell (coming from the bush) with the sharp smell of the sea.

I shall return to the potentiality linked with the FSP function of the subject in the part devoted to the spoken communication (pp. 183–6).

The contextual applicability of functional sentence perspective

The preceding discussions, including those of the phenomenon of potentiality, have demonstrated that as a rule a semantic and grammatical sentence structure can be used under various contextual conditions created by the immediately relevant context. In actual use, a sentence structure may be either entirely context-independent, or through some of its elements context-dependent and through others context-independent. All its possible uses stake out its contextual applicability.

An extreme case of context dependence occurs when the sentence structure is repeated in order to put one of its semantic contents or one of its semantic features in heavy contrast, the information put in heavy contrast, and the link between it and the rest of the information, being the only context-independent items. Adopting a term coined by Bolinger (1952: 1123), I regard such second use of a sentence structure as a case of 'second instance'. Let me first illustrate the second and then the first instance.

> He said:
> 'Yes, Madame. It was a phrase – a chance phrase of yours the other day which roused my attention.'
> Christine, her eyes still on Patrick, said:
> 'Yes? What did I say?'
> 'It was in answer to a question from the Chief Constable. You described how you went in Miss Linda Marshall's room on the morning of the crime and how you found her absent from it and how she returned there, and it was then that the Chief Constable asked you where she had been.'
> Christine said rather impatiently:
> 'And I said she had been bathing? Is that it?'
> 'Ah, but you did not say quite that. You did not say "she had been bathing." Your words were, "she said she had been bathing."
> Christine said:
> 'It's the same thing, surely.'
> 'No, it is not the same! The form of your answer suggests a certain attitude of mind on your part. Linda Marshall came into the room – she was wearing a bathing-wrap and yet – for some reason – you did not at once assume she had been bathing. That is shown by your words, "she *said* she had been bathing." What was there about her appearance – was it her manner, or something that she was wearing or something she said – that led you to feel surprised when she said she had been bathing? (Chr 174–5)

A case of second instance is the sentence 'she *said* she had been bathing' (the italics are original). The structure 'she said she had been bathing' is repeated in order to throw special emphasis on the information conveyed by the notional component of the verb. The repetitions of the structure 'she had been bathing', occurring earlier and in the closing sentence of the quotation, are not cases of second instance, for the purpose of repetition is not to throw one particular item into special relief. Note the italics used by the written language to ensure the second-instance effect. The spoken language would place the intonation centre, i.e. the most prominent prosodic feature borne by the structure, on the item to be thrown into conspicuous relief and effectively reduce the prosodic prominence of the rest. (For the delimitation of contextual applicability in the spoken language, see pages 214–15.)

In the second-instance sentence the semantic item to be singled out for particular attention serves as RhPr. The rest of the sentence is diathematic, with the exception of the TrPr linking feature conveyed by the TMEs. Since a second-instance sentence is a repetition of a structure that has just been used, it may be asked what has become of the original distribution of degrees of CD within the non-rhematic (diathematic) part of the sentence. It has not been totally obliterated, but its vestiges have been efficiently backgrounded. This means that within second instance it is the contextual factor that almost exclusively determines the distribution of CD, the operations of the semantic factor and linear modification being reduced to a minimum.

Cases of second instance are extremely rare, but they occupy a pole of a scale extending from complete context independence to maximum context dependence. Let me now turn to the first instance. Within its sphere, I distinguish between a basic instance level and ordinary instance levels.

On the basic instance level, a semantic and grammatical sentence structure is entirely context-independent. This assessment does not mean that the sentence structure operates outside any context; nor does it preclude possible dependence on contextual spheres beyond that delimited as the immediately relevant preceding context, verbal or situational. It states that the sentence structure does not convey a piece of information retrievable from this immediately relevant sphere. As in other places in the present study, it is in relation to this sphere of context that the designation 'context-independence' is to be understood (see p. 31). On the basic instance level, where none of the information conveyed is dedynamized by the contextual factor, the distribution of CD is determined by an interaction of the semantic factor and linear modification.

Within first instance it is on the ordinary instance levels that a sentence structure is affected by contextual dedynamization. I speak of levels because the number of elements dedynamized may vary. The higher their number, the greater the distance from the basic instance level. On the ordinary instance levels the distribution of CD is determined by a full interplay of the three factors, the contextual, the semantic and linear modification.

A sentence structure may show a predilection for a particular instance level, but in principle a sentence structure is not restricted to one instance level in its application. For instance, the most natural application of *A hunter killed a lion* is on the basic instance level, but contextual conditions could be thought of that would place it on other instance levels, first or second. Or the structure *She said she had been bathing* most naturally operates in an ordinary instance level; but I have demonstrated its application on a second-instance level (where any sentence structure may appear) and it is not difficult to imagine that it could also operate on the basic instance level. It could occur, for instance, at the beginning of a story where it would convey only irretrievable information. As a personal pronoun is 'predilected' for carrying context-dependent information, its occurrence on the basic instance level would, of course, create a special effect (see p. 40).

Wide contextual applicability is shown, for instance, by the *Peter/the young teacher greeted Eve/the old lady* type. It can, for example, open a text and be entirely context-independent, but it can also occur within it and be context-dependent through one or more of its elements; cf. *Peter/he greeted Eve*, *Peter greeted Eve/her*, *Peter/he greeted Eve/her*, (*Richard greeted Marion*) *and Peter greeted Eve/and Peter Eve*. Finally, its second-instance uses must be taken into account as well.

The discussion of contextual applicability can be amplified by the following four notes.

1 Establishing the two poles of contextual applicability, I have not chosen entire context dependence as the opposite pole to entire context independence. This is because entire context dependence means mere repetition unmotivated by any communicative purpose. Mere senseless repetition, i.e. nothing but a copy of what has been uttered, is a pathological phenomenon. Purposeful repetition, on the other hand, can take place for a wide variety of reasons (see pp. 175–6). The purpose a sentence serves induces it to convey an irretrievable message *sui generis* and prevents it from being entirely context-dependent.

2 Acquainting her reader with my instance levels, Lutz links the basic instance level with what I have termed the basic distribution of CD (Lutz 1981: 57). But the basic distribution of CD cannot be invariably linked with the basic instance level (see Firbas 1979: 50–2). Nor is it the

only distribution of CD realized at this level: for instance, if entirely context-independent, i.e. if functioning at the basic instance level, the structure *A boy met a girl one morning* does not realize the basic distribution of CD; it is not perspectived to *one morning*, but to *a girl*.

3 It could be argued that *Peter* and *the young teacher* in the example sentences quoted above may be linked with different degrees of familiarity in regard to a definite situation. This may well be the case, but in spite of it they operate on the basic instance level as long as they appear in sentences that are entirely context-independent – in regard to the immediately relevant context, that is. But borderline cases occur and uncertainty may arise, for instance, as to whether a sentence is entirely context-independent, or context-dependent through one of its elements. Such uncertainty, however, need not necessarily affect the distribution of CD, which may be unequivocally determined by the interplay of factors.

4 A hierarchical ordering of the applications within the sphere of the ordinary instance levels remains pending. It could be based on the differences in the aptitude for successful competitorship as displayed by the elements of a semantic and grammatical sentence structure.

Signals of the distribution of communicative dynamism

The fact that a written semantic and grammatical sentence structure operates on different instance levels without any formal change may induce the critic to refuse to recognize the accompanying changes in CD distribution resulting from these different applications. But the phenomena employed by the FSP factors and implementing the CD distributions are objectively present in the immediately relevant context, verbal and situational. Context dependence is effected and signalled through the actual retrievability of a piece of information. The link that is so established between the immediately relevant context and the sentence structure is an objective fact. Objective facts are also the position of an element in the actual linear arrangement, and the character of its semantic content and the character of its semantic relations. In the spoken language, another important objective fact is the prosodic feature borne by the element. All these facts play their roles in implementing the distribution of CD. Their signalling power must be taken into account: the signals offered need not of course be simple in character; more often than not they are complex.

As has already been pointed out, an efficient simple signal *par excellence* is provided by the TMEs in that they invariably indicate TrPr. An investigator may also regard the indefinite article as a simple signal of rhematicity. But the indefinite article performs this function only under certain conditions. It cannot signal rhematicity on its own, but only in co-operation with other phenomena. Together with them, it can constitute a complex signal of rhematicity. (For a more detailed discussion of the operations of the articles in FSP, see Firbas 1966.) For instance, in *A boy came into the room*, the indefinite article *a* co-signals rhematicity if (i) *boy* conveys irretrievable information (signalled by the absence of the information from the immediately relevant context), (ii) *the room* conveys retrievable information (signalled by the presence of the notion in the immediately relevant context), and (iii) the notional component of the verb conveys the meaning of appearance (signalled by the semantic character of the component). All these concurring phenomena are objective facts and join the indefinite article in co-forming a complex signal. If under the same contextual conditions, the order *Into the room came a boy* were used, the end position of the subject would be another co-signal of the rhematicity of the subject. In the spoken language, the IC occurring on *boy* is in full agreement with this FSP status of the subject. In fact, by enquiring into the concurrence of phenomena conditioning FSP functions, the preceding discussions as well as those that are to follow aim at establishing simple and complex signals of these functions.

The phenomena that serve as simple signals or that co-constitute complex signals are the means of FSP. This raises the question of the relationship between FSP factors and FSP means/signals (prompted to me by Daneš in a private communication). By 'factors' (linear modification, the contextual factor and the semantic factor, and in addition intonation in the spoken language) I mean the formative forces co-implementing the distribution of degrees of CD. Particularizing the operations of a factor, I specify the phenomena involved (e.g., the position in the actual linear arrangement, the objective presence of a piece of information within the immediately relevant context, a definite semantic character linked with a grammatical form, and a prosodic feature in the spoken language). These phenomena become the means/signals of FSP.

It must, of course, be remembered that the interpreter may approach FSP either from the encoder's or the decoder's point of view. After all, the language user constantly exchanges the role of the encoder for that of the decoder and vice versa. Nevertheless, the cause–effect direction remains the same: for instance, linear modification determines or co-determines the degrees of CD; it is not the other way round. Bearing these facts in mind, one can speak not only of an interplay of factors but also of an interplay of means/signals.

A means that serves as an FSP signal or constitutes such a signal as a rule simultaneously performs another function or other functions in the system of language. This raises the question of the congruence of functions. The degrees of congruence between the functions vary and come into existence under certain conditions. A remarkably high degree of functional congruence is displayed by the TMEs (cf. p. 89). This is what induces them to serve as a simple FSP signal.

Nosek has posed the question of the role of the parts of speech in FSP (1985a, 1985b). Even this question concerns the congruence of functions. I have taken the problem up elsewhere (Firbas 1988), attempting to show how my previous writings on FSP have contributed to it.

7 Word order and functional sentence perspective

Word order as a system

The preceding chapters have demonstrated that in the interplay of the FSP factors determining the distribution of CD over the written sentence, linear modification manifests itself – if not worked counter to by the contextual factor and/or the semantic factor – through the actual linear arrangement of the elements. In this way it asserts itself as an important factor (principle) of word order. This raises the problem of the relationship between word order and FSP. This problem will be taken up by the present chapter. Let me first offer a few thoughts on word order in general and word-order principles in particular.

The literature on word order is extensive, but of specific relevance to my research is Mathesius' view that word order is a system constituted by the mutual relations of word-order principles (Mathesius 1942; 1975; 153–63). These principles are essentially valid for all Indo-European languages and possibly even for languages outside the Indo-European sphere, but may differ in the extent of their operation from language to language, or even from one period to another in the development of one particular language. Like other systems of language, the system of word order is not viewed as closed and perfectly balanced. Mathesius emphasizes that the word-order system of a language can be understood in a more comprehensive way if it is compared with that of another language, preferably one of different structure. He refers to this approach as the method of analytical comparison (Mathesius 1936: 95).

Mathesius deals with the following word-order principles, regarding them as the most important ones: the principle of grammatical function, the principle of coherence of members, the principle of FSP, the principle of emphasis and the principle of sentence rhythm. Other principles of minor importance could be thought of, but are not dealt with.

I shall now characterize the principles named and comment on the ways they operate in English and in Czech, applying Mathesius' method of analytical comparison. (I shall not offer exhaustive treatments of Czech and English word order. Such treatments can be found in *CGEL* and the comprehensive grammar of Czech prepared by the Czechoslovak Academy of Sciences (See Daneš *et al.* 1987), respectively.) In the comments I shall point out in what respect I modify both Mathesius' concepts of the principles and his view of their mutual relations.

The principle of grammatical function manifests itself in that the sentence position of an element is determined by its syntactic function (Mathesius 1942: 182). In accordance with it English puts the subject before the predicative verb and the latter before the object. As for the principle of coherence of members, it manifests itself not only in a negative way, not permitting the insertion of another item between the two members, but also in a positive way, making the change in the position of one entail a change in the position of the other so that the two may remain contiguous (ibid.: 183). For the present purposes it is possible to merge these two closely related principles, i.e. that of grammatical function and that of coherence of members, into one – the grammatical principle. This is also the procedure adopted by Mathesius (1975: 153).

The principle of FSP arranges the sentence elements in a Th–Tr–Rh sequence. If asserting itself to the full extent, it even orders the elements within the Th, the Tr and the Rh in accordance with a gradual rise in CD, and induces the sentence to display what has been termed 'the basic distribution of CD'. (See p. 10. The concepts of CD, a gradual rise in CD and the basic distribution of CD have been introduced by me.) For reasons to be given below, I have modified the name of this principle to 'the FSP linearity principle'.

The principle of emphasis orders the words in a way that strikes the recipient as more or less out of the ordinary. This is due to the fact that the same words can appear in an order that does not create such an impression of unusualness. The unusual order fulfils an additional communicative purpose not served by the usual order, and is in this sense marked; cf. the pairs *Dostal pětku i ze čtení* ('He-got five even from reading' i.e. 'He got the worst mark even in reading'), *I ze čtení pětku dostal* ('Even from reading five he-got'); *We trust that we know how to*

prize these great men, These great men we trust that we know how to prize.
In each pair, the second sentence conveys an additional piece of
information that is not purely factual and may be somewhat loosely
termed 'emotive'. In the first pair, the unusual order underlines the
language user's (speaker's or writer's) negative attitude to the boy's
school report (a five being the worst mark). In the second pair, the
unusual order imparts a solemn ring to the sentence, or at least
intensifies it if one finds that the words *trust*, *prize* and *great* suggest a
degree of solemnity even in the usual order. In any case, the unusual
placement of *these great men* itself conveys a non-factual kind of
information that stylistically colours the sentence. I should add that
instead of 'the principle of emphasis' I speak of 'the emotive principle'.
This is because I find that the latter designation suggests the non-factual
information more forcibly.

The principle of sentence rhythm produces a certain pattern of heavy
and light elements (which are respectively stressed and unstressed in the
spoken language). These patterns may differ from language to language.
Whereas the Czech sentence cannot open with a rhythmically light
element, the English sentence can. It can even open with a string of light
elements. As has been pointed out by Mathesius, a special stylistic effect
is achieved in English if both the beginning and the end of the sentence
are made rhythmically heavy. Thus instead of the sentence *He no sooner
began to speak than every one was silent*, with a rhythmically weak
beginning, it is possible to use the variant *No sooner did he begin to speak
than every one was silent*, with a beginning made rhythmically heavy
(Mathesius 1942: 305).

It is worth noticing that the stylistically coloured word order reflects
the co-operation between the rhythmical and the emotive principles.
This brings us to the question of the mutual relationship of word-order
principles. Mathesius has convincingly shown that while in English the
dominant role in the system of word order is played by the grammatical
principle, in Czech it is played by the FSP linearity principle. The
following discussion is to bear out the importance of this observation.

In comparison with Czech, English is less ready to observe the
Th–Tr–Rh sequence. This is because the grammatical principle renders
English word order less flexible. In spite of it, English shows a strong
tendency to render the grammatical subject thematic and in this way to
avoid or mitigate a 'clash' between the grammatical and the FSP
linearity principles. Mathesius has established a number of constructions

employed by English to arrange the sentence elements in a Th–Tr–Rh sequence: the passive construction with a subject directly affected by the action (*The book is being read*); the passive construction with a subject indirectly affected (*I have been given the advice*); the so-called possessive passive (*Everywhere he had crowds hanging on his lips*); or the so-called perceptive passive (*Upon examination of these, I found a certain boldness of temper growing in me*), etc.

Nevertheless, the fact that English is less ready than Czech to observe the Th–Tr–Rh order has led Mathesius to draw the conclusion that 'English differs from Czech in being *so little susceptible* to the requirements of FSP as to *frequently disregard them altogether*' (Mathesius 1942: 187; translation and italics mine). He even goes the length of speaking of 'comparative English *heedlessness* of FSP' (ibid., translation and italics mine).

It can be gathered from these formulations that – at least in respect of the written language – Mathesius regards word order as the only means of FSP. Challenged by these formulations, I have set out to enquire into the problem of the means of FSP and have come to the conclusion that apart from word order there are other means in the written language that are capable of signalling FSP. The fact that unmarked word order deviates from, or does not reflect, the Th–Tr–Rh sequence does not testify to the insusceptibility of the sentence to FSP.

As FSP exceeds the sphere of word order (linear modification being only one of the FSP factors and FSP being signalled also by other means than word order), the mere designation 'FSP principle' suggests too wide a connotation. Wishing to restrict the connotation to word order, I prefer to use the designation 'FSP linearity principle'.

Let me now discuss the relationship obtaining between the emotive principle, on the one hand, and the FSP linearity principle and the grammatical principle, on the other. Mathesius has demonstrated that in Czech the Th–Rh order conveys the information in an unagitated, unemphatic, non-emotive way, whereas the reverse, i.e. Rh–Th, order does so in an agitated, emphatic, emotive way; cf. *Dostal pětku i ze čtení* and *I ze čtení pětku dostal*. (Needless to say, word order is only one of the means through which emotive colouring can be added to a sentence; see pp. 186–8.) Mathesius concludes that the emotive principle constitutes a counterpart of, or rather a complement to, the FSP linearity principle. The Th–Rh order and the Rh–Th order are regarded by Mathesius as objective and subjective, respectively. He evaluates the objective order as unmarked and the subjective order as marked. He applies this evaluation both to Czech and to English. This view deserves some comment.

First a note on the word order of questions. Mathesius holds that the questions are emotive in character and that their normal word order is subjective (see Mathesius 1942: 302). This order is reflected by the *yes–no*-questions opening with the verb *to be* or *to have* (either principal or auxiliary) or a modal verb; cf. *Is that your coat?*, *Had the man no friends*, *Have you seen that*, *Could he hear you?* (ibid.). But Mathesius finds that the *yes–no*-questions opening with a non-auxiliary form of *to be* or *to have* show a 'clash' between the grammatical principle, which for English requires that the subject should precede the verb, and the emotive principle, which requires that the Rh should precede the Th. This 'clash' is removed in the questions that open with an auxiliary, for their subject precedes the notional component of the verb; cf. *Did you get there in time?*

My interpretation of the FSP of the question is different (see pp. 97–103). In the presence of successful competitors, the *wh*-word in the *wh*-question or the verbal exponent of *yes–no*-polarity in the *yes–no*-questions cannot convey the RhPr (focus) of the question (see p. 101). If in the structures re-adduced below only *the man* and the pronouns express context-dependent information, their rhemes proper are conveyed by the elements italicized, occurring in end or penultimate position. (The element *your coat* of the first question is not RhPr on account of *your*, but *coat*.)

> Is that *your coat?*
> Had the man *no friends?*
> Have you *seen* that?
> Could he *hear* you?
> Did you get there *in time?*

As these questions do not show the Rh–Th arrangement, their word order cannot be regarded as subjective. Moreover, the positions of the subject and the verb forms in the interrogative sentences are fixed and perform a grammatical function: they signal, or at least co-signal, the interrogativity of the sentence. They are therefore to be interpreted as required by the grammatical principle.

Mathesius' examples of declarative sentences with subjective word order are drawn from the grammars by Curme, Wendt and Deutschbein as well as from his own material.

> Men there are yet living who have seen him, on many a day in the early seventies, riding his horse up Main Street, clad in the colourful garb of the past.
> This lesson time will teach to all alike.
> These great men we trust that we know how to prize; and one of these was Milton.
> One misconception at least he has removed.
> Colonel Lawrence gives an account of his expedition and a thrilling story it is.
> Therefore have we linked ourselves to the only Party that promises us the boon we seek.
> Little you care about my health.
> Murmur she may, but it is in her sleep.

As I see it, all the word orders used produce a marked effect; but they do not invariably open with a rhematic element. Although the preceding contexts have not been given, one can well assume that it is most natural to interpret the initial elements *This lesson*, *These great men*, *one of these*, *Therefore* and *Murmur* as thematic (on account of their context dependence and/or their performing the B- or the Set-function). This means that rhematicity of the initial element is not the common denominator to which the orders used can be brought. There is, however, another feature that serves as a common denominator.

The words could be re-arranged into orders not creating the impression of markedness; cf., for instance, *There are men yet living...'* *Time will teach this lesson to all alike, We trust that we know how to prize these great men, It is a thrilling story, We have therefore linked ourselves to...* In contrast with these orders, all the original deviate from syntactic patterns regarded as normal. In this way they all deviate from the requirements of the grammatical principle. It is this deviation that acts as the common denominator.

It follows that English and Czech marked word orders differ in the principle from which they deviate. Whereas Czech marked word order deviates from the FSP linearity principle, English, or to be exact modern English, marked word order deviates from the grammatical principle (see p. 118). Whereas in Czech the emotive principle is a counterpart of, or rather a complement to, the FSP linearity principle, in English it is a counterpart of, or rather a complement to, the grammatical principle. It is significant that in both languages it is the dominant word-order principle that determines the marked or unmarked character of word order. Though accounting for marked modern English word order in a different way than Mathesius, I uphold his idea of the dominant word-order principle. In fact, my account substantiates his idea.

The present discussion of the mutual relationship of word-order principles has been initiated by a note on the relationship between the rhythmic principle and the emotive principle. Continuing the enquiry into this relationship, let me first analyse the FSP of the two English variant sentences adduced above (p. 119).

> He (B, d, ThPr) no sooner (TrPro) began (+, TrPr; Q, Tr) to speak (Sp, Rh) than every one was silent (FSp, RhPr).
>
> No sooner (TrPro) did (+, TrPr) he (B, d, ThPr) begin (+, TrPr; Q, Tr) to speak (Sp, Rh) than every one was silent (Sp, RhPr).
>
> than (TrPro) every one (B, DTh) was (+, TrPr; AofQ, Tr) silent (Q, RhPr).

The re-arrangement of the weak and the heavy elements does not bring about a change in FSP. The weak elements carry their weak degrees of CD irrespective of the sentence positions in which they occur. The re-arrangement does not change the CD relationship between the weak and the other elements.

Different rhythmic patterns are also shown by these four Czech variants, in which a string of weak elements is formed by *se na to*: *Nemohu se na to ani podívat* ('I-cannot *refl. pr.* at it not-even look'), *Ani se na to nemohu podívat* ('Not-even *refl. pr.* at it I-cannot look'), *Ani podívat se na to nemohu* ('Not-even look *refl. pr.* at it I-cannot'), *Ani se na to podívat nemohu* ('Not-even *refl. pr.* at it look I-cannot').

> Nemohu (B, d, ThPr; +, TrPr; NegFocA) se (ThPro) na to (Set, d, DTh) ani (NegFocA) podívat (Sp, RhPr).
>
> Ani (NegFocA) se (ThPro) na to (Set, d, DTh) nemohu (B, d, ThPr; +, TrPr; NegFocA; Q, Tr) podívat (Sp, RhPr).
>
> Ani (NegFocA) se (ThPro) na to (Set, d, DTh) podívat (Sp, RhPr) nemohu (B, d, ThPr; +, TrPr; NegFocA; Q, Tr).
>
> Ani (negFocA) podívat (Sp, RhPr) se (ThPro) na to (Set, d, DTh) nemohu (B, d, ThPr; +, Tr; NegFocA; Q, Tr).

The first version, closing with NegFocA and RhPr, is unmarked; the fourth, opening with NegFocA and RhPr, is marked. Both the second and the third versions show some degree of markedness, the second coming closer to the first and the third coming closer to the fourth. Noting all this, we find that neither the positional change of the rhythmically weak string *se na to*, nor the positional changes of *ani*, *nemohu* and *podívat* alter the mutual relations of the degrees of CD, which remain the same in all the four variants.

Neither the re-arrangements caused by the rhythmical principle nor those caused by the emotive principle affect the interpretative arrangements, i.e. the functional perspectives of the sentences involved. The interpretative arrangement remains the same; but though leaving the mutual relations between the degrees of CD unaffected, the emotive principle effects an overall rise in (intensification of) CD, which is evidently most intensive within the Rh. Against the background of the unmarked order, the attitudinal information signalled by the employment of the marked order is additional, and hence entails a rise in CD.

It follows from what has been demonstrated that the objective and the subjective word orders do not necessarily produce the same effect in English and Czech. This is due to the different positions of the English and the Czech emotive principles in their respective word-order systems. Two languages may use the same word order, but the effects produced need not necessarily be the same.

My interpretation of the operation of the emotive principle in English differs from that offered by Mathesius; but though differing from his interpretation, it bears out the usefulness of his concept of the dominant word-order principle. By regarding the emotive principle in English as a counterpart of, and complement to, the grammatical principle, my interpretation underlines the dominant character of the latter.

I have shown that the susceptibility of a sentence to FSP cannot be judged by the extent to which its distribution of CD coincides with a gradual rise in CD, i.e. with what has been termed the basic distribution of CD. This is because word order is not the only means employed by FSP. FSP is not merely a matter of word order in the written language, nor merely a matter of word order and intonation in the spoken language. It has been demonstrated that both word order and FSP constitute systems that are interrelated. As in the act of communication the entire sentence structure is put in a definite kind of perspective and as word order forms part of that structure, the system of FSP is hierarchically superior to that of word order. Word order is only one of the means of FSP and acts as such only under certain conditions.

Mathesius does not conceive of FSP as a system, but his idea of factors (principles) operating within the system of word order has proved applicable to FSP phenomena as well. The interrelatedness of the system of word order and the system of FSP bears out Vachek's conception of language as a system of systems (1958). Needless to say, neither the system of language nor its subsystems are regarded as rigidly closed spheres. If it were so, potentiality – operating on the periphery of the system – would have no place in language. (On the relation of centre and periphery in the system of language, see Daneš 1966.)

Topicalization

A good deal of Mathesius' English examples of emotive word order show the phenomenon that is referred to by *CGEL* as 'fronting'. It consists in moving into initial position an item that is otherwise unusual there (*CGEL* 1377). By returning to this phenomenon I wish to illustrate further the character of the relationship obtaining between the system of word order and that of FSP.

Let me comment on two groups of examples quoted from *CGEL* (ibid.) and showing the phenomenon of fronting. Comparing these English sentences with their Czech counterparts preserving the English order, we shall once again find that an order that is regarded as unusual in one language need not appear so in another.

(1) Wilson his name is.
An utter fool she made me feel.
Really good meals they serve at that hotel.
(2) That much the jury had thoroughly appreciated.
Most of these problems a computer could take in its stride.
This latter topic we have examined in chapter 3 and need not reconsider.
To this list may be added ten further items of importance.

Whereas the sentences of the first group are perspectived towards the information conveyed by their initial elements, the sentences of the second group are perspectived towards the information conveyed by their final elements. In other words, whereas the former open with rhematic and close with thematic elements, the latter open with thematic and close with rhematic elements. Idiomatic Czech translations could be offered that retain the order of ideas as well as their perspective. The following two sentences respectively represent the first and the second group.

Skutečně dobrá jídla podávají v tom hotelu.
('Really good meals they-serve in that hotel')
S většinou problémů by si počítač
('With most problems it-would *refl. pr.* computer
hravě poradil.
with-great-ease it-cope.)

It is only the word order of the Cezch sentence representing the first group that is marked. The word order of the Czech sentence representing the second group is unmarked. (This is because the first sentence shows the Rh–Th, and the second the Th–Rh, order.) The fronting effect produced by the English sentences of the second group is not rendered by the Czech unmarked order.

This means that in the second group the information conveyed by the fronted diathematic elements (e.g. *That much, Most of these problems*) is opposed to the rhematic message (e.g. 'the thorough appreciation', 'the easy accomplishment') more forcefully in English than in Czech. The communicative effect of the Czech translations is about the same as that produced by the English versions with unmarked word order, cf. *The jury had thoroughly appreciated that much, A computer could take most of these problems in its stride.*

Summing up my observations in terms of actual linear arrangement and interpretative arrangement, I find that the English and the Czech sentences under examination tally with each other in regard to both arrangements. They do not, however, tally in all cases in regard to the unmarkedness/markedness of their actual linear arrangements (word orders).

It is perhaps not out of place to recall at this point that, in my approach, Th is not a position-bound concept. (The same applies to my concepts of Tr and Rh.) Some scholars link the Th invariably with the beginning of the sentence: see e.g. *CGEL*, Halliday (1985), Grzegorek (1984). The fronted element is referred to by some as topic and the process of fronting as topicalization (see Crystal 1985: 311; Grzegorek

1984: 71; on the other hand, Sgall, Hajičová and Panevová (1986) link the topic with context-bound information and do not regard it as a position-bound phenomenon). Commenting on topicalization, Crystal makes the interesting remark that 'the topic/comment contrast is sometimes difficult to establish, owing to the effects of INTONATION (which has a "competing" INFORMATION-signalling function), and in many types of sentence the analysis is more problematic, such as in COMMANDS and QUESTIONS' (Crystal 1985: 311; capitals are his). As I see it, the difficulty of establishing a topic/comment contrast will certainly arise if topic and comment are interpreted as communicative roles in the orientation (FSP) of the sentence and at the same time invariably linked with sentence positions.

As for the FSP of commands and questions, the following can be said. Regarding FSP as signalled by an interplay of means, of which word order is one, we can account not only for declarative sentences, but also for commands and questions (see pp. 97–103, 103–4).

As for intonation, it will be shown in the second part of my study that intonation does not operate independently of the non-prosodic means in signalling FSP. In the sphere of the spoken language it joins the interplay of FSP factors/means. In this manner it does not really perform a 'competing information-signalling function' in the sense that it clashes with the interplay of non-prosodic FSP factors. In joining the interplay, it co-operates with them. By way of illustration let me just add that in the example sentences discussed above the IC (intonation centre) occurs on the element serving as RhPr. If the RhPr changes its place, the IC follows it. But for a detailed discussion of the relationship between the distribution of degrees of CD as determined by the interplay of non-prosodic factors and the distribution of degrees of prosodic prominence (PP), which is implemented in the spoken language, the reader has to be referred to the second part of the present study.

Notes on Old English and present-day English word orders

The method of analytical comparison which has just been applied in a comparison of the word-order systems of present-day English and present-day Czech can equally be applied in a comparison of the word-order systems of Old and present-day English.

It is well known that in contrast with present-day English, Old English has a comparatively free word order. The grammatical principle requires the observation of a number of patterns in Old English (see Quirk and Wren 1955: paras. 144–7; Firbas 1957: 80), but it is the FSP linearity principle that plays the leading role in the Old English word-order system (Firbas 1957). It determines word-order markedness or unmarkedness (ibid. 78). Four case studies are given to illustrate the relationship between the FSP linearity, grammatical and emotive principles in the word-order systems of Old and present-day English. The cases examined are sentences taken from the West Saxon translation of the gospel according to Matthew (edited by Grünberg 1967) and their counterparts in present-day English. The first case study follows.

> On ðam dagum com iohannes se   fulluhtere and
> in those days   came John   the Baptist   and
> bodode   on þam westene   iudee (Matt. 3.1)
> preached in the   wilderness Judean

This is the first mention of John the Baptist in the gospel. In consequence, the subject 'John the Baptist' conveys context-independent information. In the presence of the temporal adverbial and the verb of appearance, which perform the Set-function and the Pr-function, respectively, it performs the Ph-function and acts in the first part of the compound sentence as RhPr. Its rhematicity is also signalled by its final position. In this way, the word order observes the FSP linearity principle, making the thematic adverbial and the transitional verb precede the rhematic subject. Leaving aside the question of the text from which the West Saxon gospel has been translated, let me add that this is also the order of the Greek version, the Vulgate and its recent revision. Also the Authorised Version and two of its revisions, the Revised Version and the Revised Standard Version, retain this order.

> In those days came John the Baptist, preaching in the wilderness of Judaea, … (AV)

But all the twenty-one other modern English versions available to me place the subject before the verb. (Nineteen are twentieth-century translations or revisions of such translations; two are twentieth-century revisions of early modern English texts: the Revised Authorised Version (RAV) and the revised version of the Challoner–Rheims New Testament (Ch–Rh). In all these versions it is the grammatical principle that asserts itself in this way. The types of translation offered by them are the following.

At that time John the Baptist came and started preaching in the desert of Judea. (GN, 3rd edn)
In due course John the Baptist arrived, preaching in the Judean desert:... (Phillips)
About that time John the Baptist made his appearance, preaching in the Desert of Judea. (Weymouth)
In those days John the Baptist came on the scene, preaching in the desert of Judaea. (Moffatt)
In those days John the Baptist came preaching in the wilderness of Judea. (RAV)
About that time John the Baptist appeared as a preacher in the Judean wilderness;... (NEB)
At that time John the Baptist came to the desert of Judea and started preaching. (GN, 4th edn)
When John the Baptizer made his appearance as a preacher in the desert of Judea, this was his theme:... (NAB)
It was in those days that John the Baptist began his mission. (Rieu)

In the presence of an adverbial performing the Set-function and of a verb of appearance performing the Pr-function, the subject of the first version (GN, 3rd edn) performs the Ph-function. In spite of its initial position, it therefore acts as RhPr.

The subject performs the Ph-function and is rhematic even if the verb of appearance is followed by a participial semiclause (see Phillips), which conveys the same message as the second parts of the Old English and the GN compound sentences. Introduced by a comma, the semiclause performs a Sp-function and becomes RhPr. Realizing the Set, Pr, Ph and Sp functions, the sentence is then an implementation of the Combined Scale. (The Combined Scale is also implemented by the group of versions represented by the AV, quoted above, in which the subject follows the verb of appearance.) The Pr-function can also be performed by a phrase metaphorically expressing appearance, the subject continuing to perform the Ph-function; cf. *made his appearance* in Weymouth (Moffatt's translation has *came on the scene*).

It could, of course, be argued that the metaphorical phrase operates less forcefully against linear modification than the simple verb of appearance and that the verb of the phrase may assume the Q-function and perspective the sentence away from the subject, which would perform the B-function and became thematic. The sentence would then implement the Quality Scale. This interpretation cannot be rejected outright and the phenomenon of potentiality completely ruled out, but the meaning of appearance expressed by the metaphorical phrase and the absence of John the Baptist from the preceding context are strong indicators of the Ph-function of the subject. A rhematic subject is therefore a more probable interpretation.

In Rieu's sentence, *John the Baptist* functions as subject within the subfield provided by the *that*-clause. Unlike the phrase *made his appearance*, the phrase *began his mission* linked with the subject does not express appearance explicitly and serves the Pr-function less readily. If assigned the Q-function by the interpreter, it perspectives the *that*-clause away from the subject. Once again potentiality cannot be entirely ruled out. But Rieu's version differs from the others by employing the cleft construction, which by operating counter to linear modification turns *in those days* into the RhPr of the entire sentence.

In the RAV, NEB and GN (4th edn) sentences, the verbs *came* and *appeared* are closely linked with amplifications that serve as specifications. This induces the verbs *came* and *appeared* to perform the Q-function and the specifications to act as rhemes proper. In consequence, the sentences are perspectived away from the subjects, which perform the thematic B-function. With due alterations, the same applies to the subfield provided by the *when*-clause of the NAB version. In the RAV the close link between the verb and its amplification, *preaching*, is established through the absence of a comma before the latter. (Just compare the different effect produced by the presence of the comma before *preaching* in Phillips, AV and Moffatt.)

The comments show that not all the present-day English translations are perspectived to the subject, *John the Baptist*. This raises the question which translation comes closest to the Greek original,

> En de   tais hēmerais ekeinais paraginetai Iōannēs ho
> in now the days   those   came   John   the
> baptistēs kērussōn en tē erēmoi tēs   Ioudaias, ...
> Baptist   preaching in the desert of-the Judea, ...

It is evident that it is a translation that by implementing the Combined Scale makes the subject rhematic and the element expressing the preaching in the desert RrPr. This is the perspective that is unequivocally signalled by the Greek original. It is important to note that the rhematic subject introduces the notion of 'John the Baptist' into the narration a good deal more effectively than its thematic counterpart. As this notion remains in the thematic layer throughout the entire rest of the chapter, such an effective introduction of it into the narration is certainly justified.

As for the sentence position of the rhematic subject, its final position in the Old English sentence is unmarked. This is because it is in agreement with the principle dominant in the Old English system of word order – the FSP linearity principle. But the initial position of the rhematic subject in the present-day English sentences is unmarked as well. This is because it is in agreement with the principle dominant in present-day English word order – the principle of grammatical function.

The second contrastive case study can now follow.

> ... butan intingan hig   me   weorþiað and lærað manna
> in   vain   they me worship and teach men's
> lara. (Matt 15.9)
> lore

This is the FSP of the first clause of the OE compound sentence: *butan intingan* (Sp, RhPr) *hig* (B, d, ThPro) *me* (Set, d, ThPr) *weorþiað* (+ ; Q, Tr). The rhematic opening of the sentence is a deviation from the requirements of the FSP linearity principle and renders the word order marked.

The same order is found in the Greek original, in the Vulgate, its recent revision, the AV and its revised versions, the RV, RSV and RAV. Some of the twentieth-century translations retain the original order of notions, but the majority of them avoid it.

> But in vain do they worship me,... (Phillips)
> ...vain is their worship of me,... (Moffatt)
> They worship me in vain;... (NIV)
> But their worship of me is all in vain,... (Goodspeed)
> ...; their worship of me is in vain,... (NEB)
> Their worship of me is vain,... (Knox)
> But their worship is to no purpose,... (BBE)
> They do me empty reverence,... (NAB)
> It is in vain that they keep worshipping me,... (NWT)
> Uselessly, they worship Me with their teaching of human commands. (MLB)

The word orders of the twentieth-century versions opening with RhPr are marked. But this is not because of their rhematic opening, but because of their deviation from the grammatical principle: the finite verb occurring before the subject of a declarative sentence. The majority of the twentieth-century versions, however, do not show such a deviation. In contrast with the word order of the Old English version, their word orders are unmarked. The MLB is the only twentieth-century version not perspectiving the message to the notion of vainness.

The third contrastive case study can be opened now.

> Witodlice be þam wæstme byð þæt treow
> verily   by the fruit   is   the tree
> oncnawen. (Matt 12.33)
> known
> ...; for by the fruit the tree is known. (Ch–Rh)
> For by its fruit the tree is known. (Rieu)
> ...; for by its fruit the tree is known. (NWT)
> ...; for by its fruit you will get knowledge of the tree. (BBE)
> ...: for the tree is known by his fruit. (AV)
> ...; for the tree is known by its fruit. (RSV, Weymouth, Moffatt)
> ...; a tree is judged by its fruit. (Goodspeed)
> A tree is identified by its fruit. (MLB)
> ...; for a tree is recognised by its fruit. (NIV)
> ...; the test of the tree is in its fruit. (Knox)
> ...; for you can tell a tree by its fruit. (NAB)
> For a tree is known by the kind of fruit it bears. (GN, 3rd edn)
> You can tell a tree by its fruit. (Beck)
> ...; you can tell a tree by its fruit. (NEB)
> ...; since it is by its fruit that a tree is known. (TCNT)

The sentence presents a conclusion drawn from facts adduced in the immediately relevant preceding context (*Either make the tree good and its fruit good, or make the tree bad and its fruit bad* (NEB)). The notion of 'the tree' remains within the thematic layer of the paragraph (see p. 79), becoming a hypertheme (see p. 81). The notion of 'the fruit', on the other hand, has been rhematized owing to the conclusion-drawing character of the message. (Under the circumstances, the effect produced by the conclusion resembles that produced by a recapitulation; see page

173. The rhematized element is heterogeneous in regard to context dependence/independence – see page 32 – for the notion of 'fruit' has already occurred in the immediately relevant context.)

The Old English uses the same order of ideas as the Greek original, the Vulgate and its recent revision. The same order also appears in the revised Ch–Rh version, but not in the AV and its revisions. Like the AV, a majority of the twentieth-century versions avoid placing the adverbial *by its fruit* in front position. For different reasons, such placement renders both the Old English and the present-day English word orders marked. In Old English it is the deviation from the FSP linearity principle, but in present-day English the deviation from the grammatical principle, that renders the word order marked.

The avoidance by the majority of the twentieth-century English versions of the marked placement is a noteworthy fact. As a comparison of the Old English version of Matthew with a twentieth-century counterpart shows, present-day English word order shows lesser flexibility, which reduces its applicability as a vehicle of emotion (see Firbas 1957). The fourth case study is another illustration of this observation.

> [Gang bæftan me, Satanas.] Wyðerræde þu eart
> go behind me Satan hostile you are
> me,... (Matt. 16.23)
> to-me
> [Get thee behind me, Satan:] thou art an offence unto me;...
> (AV)
> [Get behind me, Satan!] You are a hindrance to me;...
> (RSV)
> [Out of my sight, Satan!] You are a temptation to me;...
> (Williams)
> [Back, Satan;] thou art a stone in my path;... (Knox)
> [Away with you, Satan;] you are a stumbling block to me.
> (NEB)
> [Out of my way, Satan!]...you stand right in my path,...
> (Phillips)
> [Get away from me, Satan!] You are an obstacle in my
> way,... (GN, 4th edn)
> [Get out of my sight, you Satan!] You hinder me,...
> (Goodspeed)

[Get out of my sight, you Satan!] You are trying to make me trip and fall. (NAB)

[Get behind Me, devil!] You're tempting Me to sin,... (Beck)

The Old English version has the same word order as those of the Greek original, the Vulgate and its recent revision. It is significant that all the modern English versions accessible to me, twenty-four in number, including those of the AV and its revisions and the revised Ch–Rh version, open with *you* and do not deviate from the grammatical principle. In all these versions the emotive principle has been prevented from asserting itself.

Examples of Old and present-day English sentences differing in regard to word-order emotiveness could be multiplied. Conclusions identical with those presented here follow also from a comparison of the Old English poem *The Battle of Maldon* with its present-day English translations (see Kuchařová-Blažková 1980).

A comparison of Old with present-day English word order reveals that in the course of historical development a change has taken place in the relationship between the FSP linearity principle and the grammatical principle, the latter replacing the former in the role of the dominant principle. The lesser mobility of elements within a present-day English sentence limits the use of present-day English word order as a vehicle of emotion. The exact assessment of the extent to which this observation applies must be left to further research.

Basic instance-level implementations

Let me further illustrate the relationship between word order and FSP by a discussion of the most common grammatical realizations of the Presentation Scale (Set–Pr–Ph) and the Quality Scale (Set–B–Q–Sp) on what has been termed the basic instance level. These realizations (in the interpretative arrangement) respectively are:

Adverbial (Set), Verb (Pr), Subject (Ph);
Adverbial (Set), Subject (B), Verb (Q), Adverbial (Sp).

It will be remembered that sentences operating on the basic instance level are entirely context-independent, which permits the interplay of linear modification and the semantic factor to fully assert itself. It will also be remembered that the arrangement of the items of the scales, which reflects a gradual rise in CD, is interpretative. This arrangement may, but need not, coincide with the actual linear arrangements employed. The example sentences will be English, German, French and Czech. Their word orders will be unmarked. (As will be demonstrated, marked word orders are not excluded from the basic instance. They do not, however, represent the most common types.)

Presentation Scale
(Pr1) An accident occurred yesterday. (Pr2) Gestern geschah ein Unglück. (Pr3) Gestern ist ein Unglück geschehen. (Pr4) Es geschah gestern ein Unglück. (Pr5) Es ist gestern ein Unglück geschehen. (Pr6) Hier un malheur est arrivé. (Pr7) Hier il est arrivé un malheur. (Pr8) Včera se stalo neštěstí. (Yesterday *refl. pr.* it-happened accident.)

The interpretative arrangements of these sentences are the same. The temporal adverbial performs the Set-function and is diathematic; the TMEs serve as TrPr; the notional component of the verb performs the Pr-function and is transitional; and the subject performs the Ph-function and serves as RhPr.

Although, strictly speaking, the sentences Pr4, Pr5 and Pr7, containing an anticipatory subject (*es, il*), are not basic instance sentences, they have been added, because they come very close to the basic instance. As has been explained, the pronominal anticipatory subject *it/es/il* is considered to convey context-dependent information (see p. 24). In the examples quoted, they perform the Set-function and serve as themes proper.

Quality Scale
(Q1) A boy made a mistake through inattentiveness yesterday. (Q2) Ein Knabe machte gestern einen Fehler aus Unaufmerksamkeit. (Q3) Ein Knabe hat gestern einen Fehler aus Unaufmerksamkeit gemacht. (Q4) Gestern machte ein Knabe einen Fehler aus Unaufmerksamkeit. (Q5) Gestern hat ein Knabe einen Fehler aus Unaufmerksamkeit gemacht. (Q6) Hier un garçon a fait une faute par inattention. (Q7) Včera nějaký chlapec udělal chybu z nepozornosti. (Yesterday some boy he-made mistake out-of inattentiveness.) (Q8) Nějaký chlapec udělal včera chybu z nepozornosti.

All these sentences share the same interpretative arrangement. The temporal adverbial performs the Set-function and is diatheme oriented; the subject performs the B-function and is diathematic; the TMEs serve as TrPr; the notional component of the verb performs the Q-function and is transitional; the object performs the Sp-function and is rhematic; and the adverbial of cause performs the FSp-function and serves as RhPr.

Let me first offer a few comments on the FSP interplay of the semantic factor and linear modification and on its impact on word-order markedness or unmarkedness. In the presence of a Ph-subject and/or a Sp-object and/or a FSp-adverbial of cause, the adverbial meaning 'the day before this one' (e.g. *yesterday*) performs the Set-function. It does so irrespective of sentence position. But a change in its position may effect or co-effect a marked word order, markedness depending on the word-order system employed. For instance, the German and the Czech orders *Ein Unglück ist gestern geschehen* and *Neštěstí se stalo včera* would be marked. In contrast with the German and Czech Set-adverbials *gestern* and *včera*, the English counterpart *yesterday* becomes somewhat foregrounded if shifted from end to front position; cf. *Yesterday an accident occurred, Yesterday a boy made a mistake through inattentiveness.*

The context-independent adverbial of cause *through inattentiveness/ aus Unaufmerksamkeit/par inattention/z nepozornosti* behaves differently. It has its degree of CD affected by linear modification and loses its FSp-status if shifted to front position. Such a shift entails a considerable change in CD relations: it turns a specification, towards which the communication is perspectived, into a setting, which merely states a concomitant circumstance.

The CD relation between the context-independent subject *an accident/ein Unglück/un malheur/neštěstí*, performing the Ph-function, and the notional verbal component of *occurred/geschah/geschehen/ arrive/stalo*, performing the Pr-function, remains the same irrespective of sentence position. In German and Czech, however, the shift of the subject to front position is marked (see above).

As for the verb *made*/etc. and the object *mistake*/etc. in the sentences of the second group, the former performs the Q-function and the latter the Sp-function irrespective of position. This holds good with one proviso. It remains open what happens if the object occurs in front position. A context-independent object would then precede a context-independent subject (*Einen Fehler hat gestern ein Knabe aus Unaufmerksamkeit gemacht*). As has been discussed earlier (p. 46), this configuration opens the door to potentiality. Owing to linear modification the context-independent object in front position may lose its rhematic status and becomes thematic.

Having made all these comments, I can now offer the following evaluation of the unmarked word orders of the basic instance sentences adduced above under (Pr1)–(Pr8) and (Q1)–(Q8). Let me first turn to the Presentation Scale.

The German sentence Pr2, the French sentence Q6 and the Czech sentences Pr8 and Q7 realize the basic distribution of CD. The English sentence Pr1, on the other hand, deviates from it to such an extent as to produce its mirror image. (The sequence of its elements shows a gradual fall in CD.) But the English Q1 sentence shows a high degree of conformity with the basic distribution of CD, the final temporal setting being the only deviation from it (see Q1). With the exception of Pr1, all the sentences put the element carrying the highest degree of CD either in end position or at least in penultimate position.

In implementing the Quality Scale, all the four languages preserve the order B–Sp–FSp. In addition to this, the TMEs occur either in their entirety or in part between B and Sp. This means that in implementing the Quality Scale, all the four languages in fact preserve the order B–TMEs–Sp–FSp. But for the German sentences that place the notional verbal component in end position (Q3 and Q5), all the sentences (including the German sentences Q2 and Q4) preserve the order B–TMEs, Q–Sp–FSp. In the sentences under discussion, the dynamic functions B, Q, Sp and FSp are performed by the semantic contents 'agent' (Ag), 'action' (Act), 'goal' (G), 'cause' (C). The observations concerning the word order of the Q-sentences just discussed are shown in table 7.1 in regard to semantic structure, grammatical structure and FSP.

On the other instance levels the relations between the semantic and grammatical structure, on the one hand, and FSP, on the other, will change. But let me briefly comment on the structure *The boy made a mistake through inattentiveness yesterday*, which differs in one point from the structure *A boy made a mistake through inattentiveness yesterday*: *The boy* replaces *A boy*. Corresponding replacements – *der Knabe*, *le garçon* and *chlapec* – can be made in the German, French and Czech versions.

In their most natural use, these structures are context-dependent through their B-elements. They operate on an ordinary instance level that comes perhaps closest to the basic instance level and they can be

Table 7.1 *Word order of the Q-sentences under discussion*

Semantic structure	Ag	Act	G	C	*or*	Ag		G	C	Act
Grammatical structure										
English	S	V+	O	Ad						
German	S	V+	O	Ad	*or*	S	v+	O	Ad	V+
French	S	V+	O	Ad						
Czech	S	V+	O	Ad						
FSP										
Dynamic semantic functions	B	Q+	Sp	FSp	*or*	B	+	Sp	FSp	Q+
CD distribution	Gradual rise in CD: a display of the basic distribution of CD					A gradual rise in CD ending on the penultimate element, after which a fall in CD takes place				

Note: + = TMEs; v = auxiliary verb.

looked upon as representing the most common type of implementation of the Quality Scale on this ordinary instance level. It is remarkable that the observations tabulated in regard to basic instance are applicable to them as well.

This holds good in spite of the fact that the relations between the semantic and grammatical structure, on the one hand, and FSP, on the other, do not remain the same on the two levels involved. The difference concerns the CD relationship between the adverb meaning 'the day before' and the subject. Whereas on the basic instance level this adverb is exceeded in CD by the subject, on the ordinary instance level it is the other way round. This difference, however, is irrelevant to the present argument, for the adverb meaning 'the day before' occurs in different positions and is not covered by table 7.1. (Only those elements have been tabulated that are ordered in the same way in all the structures commented on.)

The same word order in English, German, French and Czech as revealed by the most common implementations of the Quality Scale on the basic instance level and on the ordinary instance level standing closest to it is a striking phenomenon. It should not pass unnoticed that this word order is in harmony with the 'natural order' (*ordo naturalis*) advocated by the ancient grammarians. Let me briefly add some comment on the concept of *ordo naturalis*.

A detailed survey of the application throughout the centuries of this concept has been offered by Jellinek (1913–14: paras. 563–78). From his survey it can be gathered that the medieval grammarians agreed that the natural order consisted in the sequence SUBJECT, PREDICATIVE VERB, ITEMS OF VERBAL COMPLEMENTATION (para. 565). Basically the same order was prescribed by the ancient grammarian Dionysius of Halicarnassus. He maintained that it reflected the natural order of the phenomena in nature itself. In his view, word order was a *physei* phenomenon (para. 568).

The order SVO linked with the meanings 'agent', 'action' and 'goal', and the order VS linked with the meanings 'appearing' and '(appearing) phenomenon', indeed tally with orders established through our experience of the extralinguistic reality. They may therefore be regarded as iconic. But language does not invariably follow the orders of the extralinguistic reality. It is not a slave to this reality. Owing to an interplay of means, controlled by the immediate communicative concern and purpose of the speaker, language is capable of approaching the extralinguistic reality from different angles and viewing it in different perspectives. For instance, instead of starting the communication, the 'agent' can be presented as the piece of information towards which the communication is perspectived; cf. *A boy was praised by a teacher*. In their most frequent uses, both the structures *A teacher praises a boy* and *A boy was praised by a teacher* implement the Quality Scale, but only the first displays an actual linear arrangement tallying with the 'natural' order in the extralinguistic reality. (The absence of correspondence is in fact linked with the passive, which in relation to the active is marked. It is the unmarked form that reflects the extralinguistic order.)

Viewing order from the abstraction level of the Scales, we find that the positions allotted by the Scales to the dynamic functions in the interpretative arrangement are not at variance with the language user's experience of the extralinguistic reality either (cf. Enkvist's felicitous concept of 'experiential iconicism'; Enkvist 1981). In terms of this experience it is natural that the Set-function (conveying the scene) should precede the Pr-function (conveying appearance) and that in its turn the Pr-function should precede the Ph-function (conveying the appearing phenomenon). With due alterations the same applies to the order of the B, AofQ, Q, Sp and FSp functions. The ascription of a quality, permanent or transient, assumes the existence of a quality bearer. A specification requires as a necessary antecedent the phenomenon to be specified. These interpretative arrangements, however, need not coincide with the actual linear arrangements.

All this necessitates some comment on the sense in which we use the expression 'natural word order' when remaining within the system of language. In this connection it must be borne in mind that what is a natural – normal, usual or ordinary – order in one language need not appear to be so in another. Seen in this light, naturalness or unnaturalness of a word order is determined by the word-order system of the language involved. From this point of view one could even speak of natural unmarked orders and natural marked orders and orders that are unnatural and therefore unacceptable.

In any case, language does not disregard the order established through our experience of the extralinguistic reality. But the relationship between the extralinguistic order, its reflection in our minds through our experience and its presentation by the language we use cannot be assessed in the straightforward manner adopted by the ancient and the medieval grammarians. Viewing word order as a *physei* phenomenon in the ancient sense of the word ends in a failure to appreciate duly the flexibility of language in general and word order in particular. But the structuralist and functionalist linguist cannot avoid the challenge of the ancient and the medieval grammarians' problem of natural order. His awareness of the necessity to relate structure to function, however, enables him to study the problem in a more appropriate setting. Appreciating the grains of truth in the observations of the ancients and the medievals, he can reiterate the question of natural order and deal with it in the light of the complex interplay of factors determining naturalness in language.

These observations close the first part of my study, in which I have concentrated on the operation of FSP in written communication. I can now turn to the second part, in which I propose to discuss the operation of FSP in spoken communication.

Part II
Functional sentence perspective in spoken communication

8   Non-prosodic distribution of degrees of communicative dynamism and degrees of prosodic prominence

Degrees of prosodic prominence

How does the spoken language react to the distribution of the degrees of CD as determined by the interplay of the non-prosodic factors of FSP? Is there a relationship between this distribution and the distribution of degrees of prosodic prominence? But can we speak of degrees of PP? For instance, O'Connor and Arnold's treatment of the English system of intonation and their system of tonetic notation (O'Connor and Arnold 1973) permit the conclusion that the configuration of prosodic features within what is termed by them 'tune' and here 'tone unit' ('a stretch of speech containing one intonation nucleus'; *CGEL* 1356) displays a hierarchy of PP.

Within the tone unit, the section constituted by the head and the nucleus shows greater PP than the sections serving as pre-head and tail. The most prominent feature of the entire tone unit is the nucleus. On the other hand, the lightest feature, occurring either outside or inside the head, is absence of stress. As the head and the nucleus exceed in PP the pre-head and the tail, O'Connor and Arnold regard the stresses inside the head as well as the nucleus as accented, and the stresses occurring in the pre-head and tail as unaccented (1973: 31–6). All this suggests at least four degrees of PP: (i) absence of stress (occurring inside or outside the head); (ii) stress not combined with accent (occurring on stressed syllables in the pre-head or the tail); (iii) stress combined with accent (occurring on stressed syllables inside the head); and (iv) nuclear stress, or for short, nucleus (see also Gimson's (1970: 267) four degrees of accentuation). It is significant that O'Connor and Arnold link the variation in PP to the variation in communicative importance (1973: 5).

Within the tone unit, a salient part, made up by the head with the nucleus, and a non-salient part, made up by the pre-head and tail, are also distinguished by Crystal (1969: 208). He also speaks of 'pre-head', 'head', 'nucleus' and 'tail', referring to the beginning of the head as 'onset'. Salience and non-salience of the same type are also reflected by the texts tonetically transcribed in *CGEL* and in Svartvik and Quirk's *A corpus of English conversation* (Svartvik and Quirk 1980; referred to also as *Corpus*). It is also significant that *CGEL* endorses the relationship between PP and CD (*CGEL*: 1356).

It should only be pointed out in this connection that whereas, in addition to unstressed elements, the pre-head as marked out by O'Connor and Arnold can contain elements bearing unaccented stress, the pre-onset section as marked out in the *Corpus* consists only of unstressed elements. This means that the two approaches occasionally differ in the interpretation of the first stressed syllable of the tone unit. While according to O'Connor and Arnold this syllable still operates within rank (ii), the *Corpus* in fact interprets it as already operating within rank (iii). But the cases in which the two approaches coincide heavily outnumber those in which they do not. Moreover, the difference between the two, if present, does not necessarily affect the interpretation of the relative degrees of PP within the distributional field. In any case, even the tonetic transcription used in the *Corpus* suggests at least four degrees of PP. These four degrees can be presented as follows (the terms 'pre-head' and 'head' are not used in this presentation because they are not normally employed by *CGEL* in its discussion of intonational phenomena): (i) absence of stress (occurring inside and outside the section between the onset and the nucleus); (ii) stress occurring in the tail after the nucleus; (iii) stress occurring in the pre-nuclear section beginning with the onset; and (iv) nuclear stress, or for short, nucleus.

All this points to a gamut of degrees of PP. As I shall demonstrate later, this gamut is not limited to four degrees only, but can be substantially expanded. Let me here point out at least that not only in the written language, but also in the spoken language linear modification manifests itself. It is assumed that prosodic features of the same rank (i, ii, iii or iv) gain in PP in the direction from the beginning to the end of the distributional field. In consequence, it is legitimate to speak of a distribution of degrees of PP over a distributional field and to enquire into the relationship between the distribution of degrees of CD as determined by the non-prosodic factors of FSP and the distribution of degrees of PP.

My enquiry into this relationship will be based on texts tonetically transcribed according to O'Connor and Arnold and on texts tonetically transcribed by the *Corpus*. As for the purposes of my enquiry the above-discussed interpretational difference between the two tonetic notations is a comparatively minor one, I might be justified in adopting one tonetic notation in the examples to be adduced. But wishing to avoid any distortion, I will quote the examples from their sources without replacing the tonetic notation originally employed. I take it that the reader is acquainted both with O'Connor and Arnold's system of tonetic notation and with that employed in the *Corpus*. I shall, however, mention at least those features of the two systems that are most relevant to the present analysis. The following symbols (numbered by me) occur in the examples tonetically transcribed according to O'Connor and Arnold

1 ₀m,	2 'm,	3 ‚m,	4 ˇm,	5 ⌁m,
6 ˎm,	7 ˋm,	8 ^m,	9 ‚m,	10 ′m,
11 ˇm,	12 ˃m,	13 ¯m,	14 /.	

Let me remind the reader that (i) with one exception (see below) absence of stress is left unmarked. (ii) Stressed syllables occurring within the pre-head or within the tail are preceded by a small circle placed high or low in accordance with the pitch movement (see no. 1). (iii) The first syllable of the head, which is regarded as accented, is marked by one of the following symbols: no. 2, indicating a high head; no. 3, a low head; no. 4, a falling head; and no. 5, a rising head. Like stressed syllables within the pre-head and the tail, even the stressed syllables within the head are marked by the small circle (see no. 1); but as they occur within the head, they are to be regarded as accented. (iv) A nucleus is marked by one of the following symbols: no. 6, indicating a low fall; no. 7, a high fall; no. 8, a rise–fall; no. 9, a low rise; no. 10, a high rise; no. 11, a fall–rise; and no. 12, a mid-level tone. The exception mentioned under (i) is no. 13, indicating a high pre-head, which is unstressed. Instead of the vertical stroke used by O'Connor and Arnold, I use a slanting one (no. 14). It indicates the end of one tone unit, and the beginning of another. But a full stop closing a sentence and a capital letter opening it can be regarded as performing the same demarcation role and the slanting stroke is not used in such cases. For a more detailed explanation of the significance of the symbols adduced, the reader is referred to O'Connor and Arnold (1973).

As for the material taken from the *Corpus*, the tonetic symbols adopted by me are – with one exception – those applied by the *Corpus*.

Table 8.1 Symbols occurring in the *Corpus* material

Tone unit		End of tone unit
	‖	Onset
	[yes]	Subordinate tone unit
Nucleus	yès	Fall
	yés	Rise
	yēs	Level
	yẻs	Fall–rise
	yês	Rise–fall
	yès yés	Fall-plus-rise
	yés yès	Rise-plus-fall
Booster	▷ yes	Continuance
	△ yes	Higher than preceding syllable
	△ yes	Higher than preceding pitch-prominent syllable
	△ yes	Very high
Stress	'yes	Normal
	"yes	Heavy
Pause	yes . yes	Brief pause (of one light syllable)
	yes – yes	Unit pause (of one stress unit or 'foot')

The exception is the indication of the end of a tone unit, /, a symbol used by me for this purpose also in the material taken from texts tonetically transcribed according to O'Connor and Arnold. At the present stage of enquiry, I do not take into consideration non-linguistic activity, for instance laughing or coughing, nor simultaneous talk (see Svartvik and Quirk 1980: 21–2). I accept the substitutes offered in the *Corpus* for the 'incomprehensible words', i.e. such as have proved to be uncertain in the tape-recording (see ibid.: 24). The symbols adopted by me in the material taken from the *Corpus* are displayed in table 8.1 (see ibid.: 22).

Before opening the enquiry into the relationship between the distribution of degrees of CD as determined by the non-prosodic FSP factors and the distribution of degrees of PP, and before establishing the gamut of degrees of PP, let me make the following general remarks. The degrees of PP are considered to be realized through a combination of intensity and pitch, a combination that according to Daneš constitutes the phenomenon of intonation (Daneš 1957: 141). It may be argued that PP is co-produced by rhythm, tempo, pauses and features that may be referred to as paralinguisitic (see Crystal and Quirk 1964; Crystal 1969: ch. 4). I agree, but in principle all these features are regarded as secondary and will not be covered by the enquiry at the present stage of research.

Following Mathesius, Daneš has further developed the conception of three functional spheres of sentence intonation: (i) that of the structuration function; (ii) that of FSP; (iii) that within which 'intonation represents a steady subjective commentary on the utterance, mostly with an emotive or emotional colouring' (Daneš 1987: 19–20). The present enquiry concentrates mainly on sphere (ii) and sphere (iii), investigating the relation between the two.

The subjective commentary is a special type of information. In fact, it is an integral part of oral communication (see Uhlenbeck 1983: 17). In consequence it affects the degrees of CD carried by the sentence elements and their distribution over the sentence – in other words, the FSP of a sentence.

As for a delimitation of the emotive component of an utterance, i.e. a semantic and grammatical sentence structure serving a definite communicative purpose in the act of communication, I am in essence adopting Grepl's definition (Grepl 1967: 9; Bauer and Grepl 1980: 20). By the emotive component of an utterance I understand the emotional attitude that is taken up by the speaker in regard to the reality conveyed and that is expressed by him with linguistic means. (The expression 'linguistic means' is meant to cover both the devices of the written language and those of the spoken language.) I wish to emphasize that I shall not cover the vast field of problems connected with emotiveness in language, but merely open an enquiry into the ways the distribution of degrees of CD is affected by emotiveness in spoken English.

The preceding observations have indicated that the degrees of PP can be expected either merely to reflect the distribution of degrees of CD as determined by the non-prosodic FSP factors or additionally to reflect an intensification of these degrees of CD owing to the information also conveyed at the level of the spoken language.

We are therefore justified in regarding intonation (viewed with Daneš as a combination of intensity and pitch) as a factor that joins the interplay of FSP factors at the level of the spoken language. It operates as a factor, because – as will become clear – apart from merely reflecting the distribution of degrees of CD as determined by the interplay of non-prosodic FSP factors, it is capable not only of disambiguating this interplay, but of affecting it in a significant way. But it will also be demonstrated that as a participant in the interplay, it cannot operate independently of the non-prosodic factors.

It follows that an enquiry into the relationship between the distribution of degrees of CD as determined by the non-prosodic FSP factors and the distribution of degrees of PP cannot identify the two distributions, i.e. treat them as if they were one and the same phenomenon (see pp. 216–18). It must be borne in mind that the latter of the two distributions does not necessarily merely reflect the former, but is capable of creating additional degrees of CD.

In the spoken language, the interplay of FSP factors is participated in by (i) the semantic factor (see pp. 41–65), (ii) the contextual factor (see pp. 21–40), (iii) linear modification and (iv) intonation.

Let me now start my enquiry into the relationship between the distribution of the degree of CD as determined by the non-prosodic FSP factors (or non-prosodic CD distribution, for short) and the distribution of the degrees of PP (or PP distribution). In the course of the enquiry I shall gradually establish the gamut of degrees of PP. Instead of using the full designations 'distribution of degrees of CD as determined by the interplay of non-prosodic factors' and the 'distribution of degrees of PP', I shall occasionally merely speak of 'the two distributions'.

Perfect correspondence between the non-prosodic distribution of communicative dynamism and distribution of prosodic prominence

Let me take a simple example first. (The numbers after 'AT' (Arnold and Tooley 1972) indicate the page and line where the example sentence begins.) The sentence

It should be ˇgood.   (AT 11.04)

contains a nucleus and a pre-head. As for the non-prosodic CD distribution, the highest degree of CD is carried by *good*, the lowest by *it*; *should* and *be* rank between the two. *It* is thematic, serving as ThPr; *good* is rhematic, serving as RhPr; *should be* serves as TrPr through its TMEs, the weak notional component of *be* serving as a weak transition. As for the PP distribution, we find that, though in an inconspicuous way, the three unstressed elements show a gradual rise in PP. (It applies here that prosodic features of the same rank are subject to linear modification: they gain in PP in the direction from the beginning to the end of the distributional field.) The highest degree of PP is borne by *good*. The non-prosodic CD distribution is not at variance with the PP distribution. The correspondence between the two distributions is perfect.

It should   be ˋgood.
ThPr   + +;TrˋRhPr.

In addition to a pre-head and a nucleus, the following sentence also contains a head:

... he was 'coming by °plane to ˋLuton.   (AT 93.34)
ThPr + ' +;Tr   °Rh   ˋRhPr.

The two distributions are in perfect correspondence.

The following example contains not only a pre-head, a head and a nucleus, but also a tail. Once again, the two distributions are in perfect correspondence.

You   'keep such a °lot of ˋrubbish in your ₒbag.   (AT 31.1)
ThPr ' +;Tr   °ˋRhPr   ₒDTh.

The first sentence below contains only a nucleus, *Sorry* serving as RhPr. TrPr is vicariously indicated by intonation (see p. 93). The second sentence is another implementation of the pre-head, head and nucleus configuration. Both sentences show perfect correspondence between the two distributions.

ˇSorry. You're 'getting ˋsoft.   (AT 49.18)
[+]ˇRhPr. Th + 'Tr; + ˋRhPr.

The examples just adduced demonstrate the basic pattern of the relation between the non-prosodic CD distribution and the PP distribution. Against this background seemingly more complex relational patterns can be accounted for, as well as patterns displaying a certain amount of lack of perfect correspondence.

Apparent complexity may be due to a communicative unit that displays more than one prosodic feature; cf. *Such a lot of rubbish* in AT 31.1 above. In such a case, it is the most prominent of these features that determines the PP of the unit and represents it in relation to the PP of the other units occurring within the same distributional field. Here is another example.

I'll   'play my °new ˇSquallies ₒrecord .   (AT 7.09)
ThPr+   ' + ;Tr   °ˇₒRhPr

The object *my new Squallies record* constitutes one communicative unit, but displays four degrees of PP: absence of stress (*my*), unaccented stress (*record*, in the tail), accented stress (*new*) and nucleus (*Squallies*). It is the nucleus that serves as the representative feature of the communicative unit. In terms of representative features, the sentence displays perfect correspondence between the two distributions.

As a distributional field of PP, the sentence may contain more tone units than one. Interpreting such a sentence, one has to take into account the representative features and the operation of linear modification in the spoken language (see p. 144). In consequence, out of the two nuclei in each of the two sentences below, the one occurring later is considered to be more prominent. (An important proviso concerning the sequence of two nuclei will be discussed on page 152.)

I'll be ˇtaking the ˇentrance eₒxam / in No ˇvember.
ThPr + ˇ + ;Tr   ˇₒRh /   ˇRhPr
    So   I shall 'stay on at ˇschool / at ˇleast until
TrPr ThPr   +   ' + ;Tr   ˇRh /
ˇChristmas.   (AT 11.26)
    ˇˇRhPr.

In each sentence, the nuclei accompany members of a specification string. The nucleus occurring last accompanies a temporal specification serving as RhPr. In these terms, the correspondence between the two distributions is again perfect.

Special mention must be made of distributional subfields, which are provided by subordinate clauses, semiclauses and noun phrases and which function as communicative units within superordinate fields. Let me comment on subfields provided by subordinate clauses and semiclauses. Subfields provided by noun phrases will be dealt with later (see pp. 167–9). In the interpretations, the non–prosodic CD distribution within a subfield is presented within parentheses.

He'll   come 'round with ˇMarjory,   he
(ThPr+   ' + ;Tr   ˇRhPr)ˇRhPr ThPr
    ₒsays.   (AT 5.27)
    ₒ+ ;Tr.

The nucleus on *Marjory* performs a double function: it signals the RhPr within the subfield, and in its representative function the RhPr of the entire basic distributional field.

It should be recalled that 'subfield' has been suggested by 'subordination' and motivated by the fact that within a superordinate field a structure constituting a subfield operates as a communicative unit. This does not mean, however, that a subfield cannot serve as RhPr, i.e. the rhematic unit towards which the superordinate field is perspectived.

The following sentence contains two subfields provided by semiclauses realized by expanded infinitives.

> I'm   'hoping   to go to `Cambridge /
> ThPr +   ' + ;Tr (+ ;Tr   `RhPr)`Rh /
> to read `chemistry.   (AT 11.25)
> (+ ;Tr   `RhPr)`RhPr.

Each subfield has its RhPr, signalled by a nucleus, the infinitive serving as Tr. It contains no explicitly stated thematic element. It may, of course, be assumed that the Th is at least implicitly present. (The use of the infinitive presupposes a subject identical with that of the principle clause.) Within the basic (principle) field, both subfields are rhematic, forming a specification string. The subfield coming last serves as RhPr of the basic field.

In the following sentence, the expanded infinitive forms a subfield within a subfield.

> I could 'help to re°organize the °school `library
>   '°°`RhPr
>   he   ₀says.   (AT 11.31)
> ThPr ₀ + ;Tr.
> (I could 'help to re°organize the °school `library)
> (ThPr   + ' + ;Tr   °°`RhPr)
> [to re°organize the °school `library]
> [° + ;Tr   °`RhPr]

In fact, the nucleus on *library* performs a treble function: it also signals the RhPr of the subfield superordinate to it; and eventually the latter in its entirety as RhPr of the basic field.

It appears appropriate at this point to insert a modification of the basic observation that the last nucleus within a distributional field is the most prominent prosodic feature within this field. (In this capacity it acts as the representative feature of the field and could be referred to as its 'intonation centre'. If not specified, this term will be used here in reference to the basic distributional field. It has been introduced into the literature by Daneš; see e.g., 1957, 1960.)

It has been known for some time that within a distributional field a low rise (together with its low head if present) that occurs after a fall does not exceed the fall in PP (see, e.g., Halliday 1970: 38; O'Connor and Arnold 1973: 82; *CGEL* 1601). Though occurring after the fall, such a low rise (together with its low head if present) appears in the prosodic shade cast by the fall. All the elements so shaded have their PP prominence lowered. I agree with Chamonikolasová (1985: 52), who, in the gamut of PP, places such a low rise between accented stress assigned to rank (iii) (see p. 144) and the nucleus assigned to rank (iv)

Likewise, the stresses occurring in the low head preceding such a low rise do not exceed in PP the stresses normally occurring in heads. On the other hand, they remain more prominent than stresses occurring in tails.

> It'll   be   ʼon / in a ˌfew ˌminutes.   (AT 9.32)
> ThPr+   +;Tr ˋRhPr /   ˌˌDTh.
>
>   I was ʼtalking to Mrs ˋJones / at the ˋpaper ₀shop /
> ThPr   +   ʼ+;Tr   ˋRh /   ˋ₀RhPr
> the ˌother ˌday.   (AT 19.14)
>   ˌˌDTh.
>
> Mum   was ʼwriting to Cousin ˋJeannie / ˌlast ˌnight.
> ThPr + ;TrPr   ʼ+ ;Tr   ˋRhPr /   ˌˌDTh.
>   (AT 41.10)

None of the three word groups occurring after a high fall acts as a rhematic element; each is an adverbial element serving as a temporal setting. It is diathematic, and it is the communicative unit preceding it that serves as RhPr. All this is in harmony with the distribution of PP. RhPr bears the IC, and the diathematic adverbial following it occurs in the post-IC prosodic shade.

The note just presented expresses perhaps the most important modification to the basic observation that within a distributional field the most prominent (and functionally weightiest) prosodic feature is the last nucleus. Further research can be expected to add further modifications. For instance, if a fall–rise is followed by a low rise – or, to be more exact, if a tone unit with a 'switch-back' feature is followed by a tone unit with a 'take-off' feature (see O'Connor and Arnold 1973: 143 and 170), it is the fall–rise that bears the IC of the distributional field.

> [ˏThat's the ˋtrouble. I ˏdon't really ˋknow. – ˋDon't say
> you °wanted to be an ˇair-₀hostess.]
> ˋThat' s what °girls ˇusually ₀want / when they ˏsay
> ˋDTho + ;Tr °ˇ₀RhPr /
> they ₀don't ˏknow. (AT 63.35)
> ₁₀ˏDTh.

The information conveyed by the *when*-clause is context-dependent. The clause expresses a setting.

In regard to the gamut of PP, the final nucleus once again occurs in a configuration that places it in the prosodic shade cast by the nucleus preceding it. I shall take this into consideration when summarizing the observations concerning the gamut of PP.

Let me close this section by illustrating perfect correspondence between the two distributions with examples taken from the *Corpus*, text S.1.4. The numbers following the examples are those of the tone units.

> we ‖do . △seize the CHÀNCE / of ‖stopping
> ThPr ‖ + . △ + ;Tr /
>
> LÈCTURES / (668–9)
> ˋ‖ ˋRhPr /
>
> you ‖just △STÌCK that on the BACḰ / (820)
> ThPr ‖△ ˋRhPr ThPro ˊDTh /
>
> We' ve ‖had it on △PÌCNICS / (940)
> ThPr + ‖ + ;Tr ThPro △ ˋRhPr /
>
> there' s a ‖poor little FÉLLOW / who's . ‖trying to 'get
> ThPr + ;Tr /
>
> through FÍNALS / for the ‖third "TÌME / (970–2)
> / ‖ˊ‖ˈˊ"ˇRhPr /

In the last example, let us note the multiple function of the nucleus on *for the third TIME.* It occurs on the RhPr of the subfield provided by the semiclause

to 'get through FĬNALS / FOR THE ‖third "TĬME /
' + ;Tr   ′Rh /   ‖"ᵛRhPr /

which serves as RhPr within the subfield provided by the relative clause

who' s . ‖trying to 'get through FĬNALS /
DTh+ . ‖ + ;Tr

for the ‖third TĬME /
'ᐟ‖ᵛRhPr /

This relative clause serves as RhPr within the distributional field provided by the attributive structure

a ‖poor little FĔLLOW / who ...for the ‖third "TĬME /
‖′DTh /   ‖"ᵛRhPr /

The nucleus on *for the third TIME* performs a treble representative function. Twice it represents the prosodically most prominent communicative unit in a subfield and once in the basic distributional field. In terms of communicative units, the non-prosodic CD distribution and the PP distribution are in perfect correspondence.

The observations on the gamut of PP may now be summarized as follows.

Each of the four basic ranks of prominence – (i), (ii), (iii), (iv) – can be expanded owing to the operation of linear modification (see p. 144).
Between (iii) and (iv) come final nuclei which occur in configurations lowering their PP in relation to the last but one nucleus in the field.
Between (i) and (iii) come stressed elements occurring in a head that together with a final nucleus appears in the prosodic shade cast by the last but one nucleus of the field.

Prosodic intensification imposed upon perfect correspondence between the two distributions

Looking for presence or absence of perfect correspondence between the two distributions, I have so far not paid attention to the type of tune used. But the type of tune may convey additional meaning to, or rather emotively colour, or give special emphasis to, the meaning conveyed by non-prosodic means. The meanings of the tunes, or rather the meanings conveyed by them in co-operation with non-prosodic meanings, are described, for instance, in O'Connor and Arnold 1973 and in a number of other monographs on English intonation (e.g., Palmer 1924; Schubiger 1935, 1958; Kingdon 1958a, b; Bolinger 1965; Halliday 1967a, 1970; Crystal 1969; Crystal and Davy 1975). For the purposes of the present discussion, I shall confine myself to the following observations.

The additional meaning, the emotive colouring, or the special emphasis supplied by a tune is an amplification of the meaning (information) conveyed by written, non-prosodic means. Such prosodic intensification naturally entails a rise (rises) in CD. It follows that, under the circumstances, the total amount of CD carried by the spoken sentence is higher than that of its written counterpart. This effect is produced by intonation acting as an FSP factor at the level of the spoken language. As – in terms of relations between the degrees – the PP distribution corresponds to the non-prosodic CD distribution, I speak of prosodic intensification imposed upon perfect correspondence between the two distributions.

The prosodic intensification of perfect correspondence between the two distributions consists in the use of an evidently marked tune, in other words, an evidently marked configuration of prosodic features. As presence or absence of perfect correspondence between the two distributions is the main concern of the present study, I shall not attempt to draw a clear-cut distinction between unmarked and marked tunes, but shall concentrate on cases of evident markedness.

[We'd have been ˈmuch too ₒlate / for the ˌlast ˏferry.]
    It ˋleaves the ˅mainland / about ˋeight.   (AT 53.25)
DTh ˋ + ;Tr   ˅Rh /   ˋRhPr.
['Even ^Andrew was ₒpleased. And 'he's ^difficult to ₒplease.]
    He'   s 'such a per^fectionist.   (AT 59.17)
ThPr + ;Tr   '^RhPr.
[Your 'old °banger ˋdid colₒlapse under ₒFrank's ₒweight. -
ˌNo, it ˏdidn't.] It be ˏhaved very ˋwell.
        ThPr   ˏ + ;Tr   ˋRhPr.

[It was ˋour ₀silly ₀fault.] We   ⸜ran out of ˋpetrol.   (AT 53.08)
          ThPr ⸜ + ;Tr   ˋRhPr.

The nuclei duly occur on elements (*mainland, perfectionist, very well* and *petrol*) marked out by the interplay of non-prosodic factors of FSP as rhemes proper. But the chosen tunes, namely the 'jackknife', the 'take-off' and the 'long jump', convey in addition that the speaker is impressed by another person's reaction (see O'Connor and Arnold 1973: 78, 274), that he resentfully contradicts the interlocutor's statement (ibid.: 58) and voices his protest (ibid.: 73, 191), respectively.

Selective non-reevaluating intensification

The cases discussed so far show perfect correspondence between the non-prosodic CD distribution and the distribution of PP. I will now turn to types that do not show such perfect correspondence.

Well,   ˋI' m going to ˅scout ₀camp.   ˋJoan'll
TrPro ˋThPr + + ;Tr   ˅₀RhPr.   ˋDTh +
         be in ˅Skye. And ˋMum and ˅Dad / are 'talking about
       + ;Tr   ˅RhPr.   ˋ˅DTh / + '+ ;Tr
        ₀going to ˋPlymouth, / to 'see Aunt ˋSusan.   (AT 45.06)
           ₀ˋRh /   'ˋRhPr.

In the examples adduced, the interplay of the non-prosodic FSP factors does not permit the verb to carry the highest degree of CD. The verb cannot do so because of the presence of a context-independent goal of motion (*to scout camp*), a context-independent localization (*in Skye*), a context-independent particularization of the content of the talk (*about going to Plymouth*), and a context-independent purpose (*to see Aunt Susan*). In each case it performs the Q-function and carries a lower degree of CD than its successful competitor, which performs the Sp-function. The verb is transitional and its successful competitor serves as RhPr. On the other hand, being context-independent, the verb exceeds in CD the subject, which, expressing an agent (*I*, *Mum and Dad*) or a bearer of a state (*Joan*), performs the B-function and is thematic.

    As for the correspondence between the two distributions, it is perfect in the Tr–Rh direction, but imperfect in the Tr–Th direction (direction to be understood in terms of interpretative arrangement). The thematic subject bears a more prominent prosodic feature (cf. the stresses on *I* and *Joan* and the fall–rise on *Mum and Dad*) than the transitional verb. In this way the thematic subject becomes prosodically intensified (see Firbas 1968: 21–3).

It is important to note that in the examples adduced the prosodic intensification of the Th has not affected the perfect correspondence between the two distributions in regard to the Th–Rh relationship. In spite of its prosodic intensification, the Th is exceeded in PP by the Rh. In other words, the distribution of PP continues to reflect the perspective as determined by the interplay of the non-prosodic FSP factors.

Paradigmatically speaking, a prosodically intensified thematic subject carries a higher degree of CD than a thematic subject that has not been prosodically intensified. But syntagmatically speaking, a rise in CD affecting a thematic subject entails a corresponding rise throughout the non-thematic section of the sentence. On a foundation (provided by the theme) carrying an intensified degree of CD, the essential information (conveyed by the non-thematic section) is built up and shows a rise (rises) in CD in accordance with its position in the interpretative arrangement (see Svoboda 1968: 71–2; Firbas 1968: 21; and this volume, p. 91).

Returning to the string of sentences under discussion and examining their immediately preceding context (part of which is adduced below), we find that the prosodic intensification of the thematic subjects (especially the accent on *I* and the fall–rise on *Mum and Dad*) has been resorted to for good reasons.

> ˉCouldn't 'Frank go as ˌwell? He'd be 'here on his ˋown /
> ˌotherwise. – ˏHow d'you ˋmean?   (AT 45.03)

Prompted by the tone of puzzlement and surprise conveyed by the question *How d'you mean?* (see O'Connor and Arnold 1973: 73), the speaker explains that Frank will be *on his own* because the others (*I, Joan, Mum* and *Dad*) will be away. The prosodic intensification of the subjects, enumerating those who will be absent, participates in bringing out the loneliness Frank might experience.

Prosodically weak transitional verbal elements are by no means a rare phenomenon. This applies not only to the TMEs implemented as auxiliaries and serving as TrPr, but also to the notional component of the finite verb form functioning in the rest of the Tr, although the latter is subjected to prosodic weakening far less often than the former (see

Firbas 1968, 1975). Let me add a few examples to illustrate further this point.

> ˋAll this ˇtravelling / makes me ˋravenous. (AT 25.17)
>   ˋˇDTh / + ;Tr ThPr ˋRhPr.
> ['Don't be ˎrude, young ₒSimon.] The ˋtrouble with ˇyou
>   ˋˇDTh
>
>   ₒis / you've got 'no re°spect for your ˋelders.
> ₒ+ ;Tr /   '°ˋRhPr.
>   (AT 47.22)
> [No.] Oh, ˎthis is ˋdreadful. (AT 31.07)
>   ˎDTh + ;Tr ˋRhPr.
> And the ˇhospital ₒthinks / I 'need to catch °up on
>   ˇDTh ₒ+ ;Tr /
> my ˋsleep. (AT 85.04)
> '°ˋRhPr.
> The ˋpoor old ˇbanger / will col'lapse under the
>   ˋˇDTh / + '+ ;Tr
> ˋstrain. (AT 51.30)
> ˋRhPr.

All the subjects show prosodic intensification, which may be quite conspicuous. It is worth noticing that the prosodic weakening of the notional component of the verb and the prosodic weakness of the TMEs are not at variance with their transitional function. This is in harmony with a tendency to underline the Th–Rh relationship by giving relative prominence to the DTh (which carries the highest degree of CD within the Th) and RhPr (which carries the highest degree of CD within the Rh). (This observation was first made by Aleš Svoboda in a private communication.) The extent to which this tendency can assert itself will have to be determined by further research.

A diathematic subject is not the only element that may show greater prosodic prominence than a transitional verb, although in colloquial English it may represent the most frequent case of prosodic intensification of a thematic element occurring together with a prosodically less prominent transitional verb. Various adverbials acting as diathemes can be adduced in illustration.

> ˋTalking of ˇcamps, / have you 'got all the
>   ˋˇDTh / QFocAnt; + ThPr '+ ;Tr

°things you'll ˏneed, you °two?   (AT 49.29)
     °ˏRhPr   °ThPro.
ˇWhen we °got to ˇGlasgow, / we 'seemed to have
                    ˇ°ˇDTho   / ThPr   ' + ;Tr
°quite a ˋlot in ₒhand.   (AT 53.13)
     °ˇRhPr   ₒDTh.
so to ˇbe on the ˇsafe ₒside /   he 'rang the ˃depot /
                    ˇˇₒDTh / ThPr ' + ;Tr   ˃Rh /
'yesterday ˋmorning.   (AT 55.01)
     'ˇRhPr.
And ˇone ₒday / Cousin Jeannie 'borrowed some ˋhorses.
     ˇₒDTh /   ThPr   ' + ;Tr   ˋRhPr.
                                                   (AT 57.17)

Neither the prosodic intensification discussed in the preceding section nor that discussed in the present section affects the Th–Rh relation. In other words, neither affects the perspective of the field concerned, i.e. the communicative orientation towards the carrier of the highest degree of CD as determined by the non-prosodic FSP factors. This is why the two types of intensification are regarded as non-reevaluating. (Re-evaluating prosodic intensification will be discussed and illustrated in the following section.)

The difference between the two types is the following. Whereas one reflects the non-prosodic distribution of CD in a perfect manner, the other prosodically strengthens some non-rhematic element at the expense of another (cf. the prosodic intensification of the DTh at the expense of the Tr discussed above). In this way, it selects some non-rhematic communicative unit(s) for greater prominence, simultaneously prosodically weakening another (others) within the non-rhematic sphere. This is why this type can be characterized as selective non-reevaluating prosodic intensification.

Re-evaluating prosodic intensification

The re-evaluation procedure and re-evaluated pronouns

It has been demonstrated how perfect correspondence between the non-prosodic CD distribution and the PP distribution provides a background against which the participation of intonation in the interplay of FSP factors is assessed. Seen in this light, a special type is represented by a distributional field in which an element that according to the non-prosodic CD distribution is non-rhematic (thematic or transitional) comes to bear the IC, whereas elements that according to this distribution are rhematic appear in the post-IC prosodic shade. Let me adduce three simple examples first.

ˇThat's a ₒlaugh.   (AT 7.16)

Now, ˋthere's a coₒincidence!   (AT 43.26)

[ˋGoodness!] ˇYou've been ₒquick, Simon.   (AT 15.06)

In the light of the interplay of the non-prosodic factors of FSP, *a laugh*, *a coincidence* and *quick* are context-independent, act as carriers of the highest degree of CD and hence as rhemes proper. Yet none bear the IC; on the contrary, they appear in the post-IC prosodic shade. In each sentence, the IC has been shifted onto an element that in the light of the interplay of the non-prosodic FSP factors is context-dependent and hence thematic.

It may be argued that such an absence of perfect correspondence between the two distributions is a discrepancy disproving an interrelation between them. The shift causing this discrepancy, however, renders the sentences highly emotive, forcibly intensifying the emotive colouring already conveyed or adding some new nuance to this colouring. In this way, the first sentence underlines the strongly depreciatory character of the speaker's remark, the third his appreciative astonishment. The second emphasizes the importance of the concurrence of circumstances for the matter under discussion. The shift causing the discrepancy proves to be highly functional. It is a vehicle of an important and weighty part of the information conveyed. It is significant that this information is transmitted through prosodic intensification which emotively reperspectives the distributional field. As it affects the Th–Rh relation, such intensification is referred to as 're-evaluating prosodic intensification'.

Coming to bear the IC, an element that, owing to the non-prosodic CD distribution is non-rhematic, is re-evaluated to RhPr. On the other hand, the element that, owing to the non-prosodic CD distribution becomes RhPr but appears in the post-IC prosodic shade, is re-evaluated to a thematic element of diathematic status. The ever-present function of TrPr is unaffected by re-evaluation. All the other elements appearing in the shade – unless they are thematic already – are re-evaluated to thematic elements of DTho status. Additional characteristics of the re-evaluation process will be adduced below.

```
ˇThat'        s a ₒlaugh.
DTh   +;Tr  RhPr.  >
ˇRhPr +;DTho  ₒDTh.
Now, 'there'      s a coₒincidence!
TrPro ThPr  +;Tr    RhPr.  >
TrPro ˇRhPr +;DTho      ₒDTh.
ˇYou've   been ₒquick, Simon.
ThPr +    +;Tr RhPr ThPro.  >
ˇRhPr + +;DTho ₒDTh ThPr.
```

The re-evaluation does not obliterate the distribution of degrees of CD as determined by the non-prosodic FSP factors. On the contrary, it can be understood only against the background of perfect correspondence between the two distributions. This fact corroborates the existence of the non-prosodic CD distribution. Seen in this light, re-evaluating prosodic intensification cannot be looked upon as a discrepancy, but must be regarded as a fully systemic phenomenon. It has its place within the language system. As the non-prosodic CD distribution has not been obliterated and as the re-evaluation conveys additional information, the latter entails a rise in CD.

In the examples above, the IC occurs on the grammatical (formal) subject implemented by a pronoun or the existential proadverb *there*. It may, of course, appear on another sentence element as well. In each of the three following sentences the re-evaluating IC is placed on a pronominal object.

```
'He   gave   ^us a ₒconcert ₒlast ₒnight.  (AT 19.33)
ThPr +;Tr ThPro   RhPr    DTh.  >
'ThPr +;Tr ^RhPr  ₒDTh  ₀₀DTho.
[Oh, here's ˇFrank.]
   'Let's   ask  ˇhim about ₒRobert's ₒpresent.
                          (AT 23.08)
+;ThPr +;RhPr ThPro      DTh.  >
'+;ThPr  +;Tr ˇRhPr        ₀₀DTh.
↗What's brought ˇyou round  ₒhere so  ₒearly? (AT 39.20)
QFocA +  +;Tr ThPr  Rh DTh RhPr.  >
↗QFocA +  +;Tr ˇRhPr DTho ₒDTho ₒDTh.
```

Once, again, the IC bearer and the elements occurring in the post-IC prosodic shade reflect re-evaluation. Though re-evaluated, the shaded elements proportionally preserve the original differences in degrees of CD. After the re-evaluation, the element that according to the interplay of non-prosodic FSP factors carries the highest degree of CD within the Rh and serves as RhPr (*a concert, about Robert's present, so early*) now carries the highest degree of CD within the Th and serves as DTh.

As for the elements occurring before the IC bearer, they are not affected by the re-evaluation if they are thematic or transitional. If rhematic, they cannot serve as RhPr. They can become transitional (cf. *ask* in the second of the three sentences above).

Let me add that negation focus anticipators and question focus anticipators retain the rhematic feature (pp. 101 and 102), which perspectives them to and links them with their respective rhemes proper (foci). Re-evaluation changes the perspective, but does not obliterate the rhematic feature of the focus anticipator. Whereas in the non-reevaluated third sentence above *What* is perspectived towards *so early*, after re-evaluation it is perspectived towards *you*. Similarly, whereas in the non-reevaluated sentence below, *-nt* is perspectived towards *see*, after re-evaluation it is reperspectived towards *He*. At the same time both anticipators retain their relation to TrPr and are in this respect TrPro.

> ['Robert's ₒcoming.]
> ˅He   mustn't ₒsee   it   yet.   (AT 39.07)
> DTh + ; NegFocA RhPr ThPr TrPro.   >
> ˅RhPr + ; NegFocA ₒDTh ThPr DTho.

I shall continue the discussion of re-evaluating prosodic intensification in the following sections. But rather than on sentence types I shall concentrate on various groups of elements affected by prosodic re-evaluation. My treatment will not be exhaustive, the main purpose of the present discussion being the establishment of the phenomenon.

The wide variety of elements that can be affected by re-evaluating prosodic intensification may create the wrong impression as to the relative frequencies of cases of perfect correspondence between the non-prosodic CD distribution and PP distribution, cases of non-reevaluating prosodic intensification and cases of re-evaluating prosodic intensification. The frequency problem will therefore be taken up in a special section (pp. 193–206). Another section (pp. 173–4) will demonstrate that emotiveness is not the only motivation for re-evaluating prosodic intensification.

Re-evaluated adverbs of indefinite time

Another group of elements that can be re-evaluated to RhPr by bearing
the IC is formed by adverbs of indefinite time, such as *always, ever, soon,
still*. In their unmarked use, they occur in the *not*-position and are
TrPro.

> It'll ʽsoon get to ₀number ₀one in the ₍charts. [ʽI bet.]
>
> (AT 9.10)
>
> So there are ʽstill some ₀honest ₀people a₀bout, thank
> ₀goodness. (AT 37.31)
>
> They're ʽalways ₀ready to ₀start an ₍argument. (AT 61.15)

The shaded elements are context-independent. But for the re-evaluation,
in the charts, honest people and *to start an argument* would carry the
highest degrees of CD and function as rhemes proper; in consequence
of re-evaluation, they have become diathematic.

Re-evaluated auxiliaries

Another group of elements that are usually non-rhematic and as such can
come to bear the re-evaluating IC is formed by the auxiliaries.

> You ʽare ₀mean, ₀Simon. (AT 23.07)
>
> Oh, ʽMarjorie, you ʽare a ₀dear! (AT 33.23)
>
> [ʹLet's ask the °manager ʽfirst.] We ᵛmight be ₀lucky.
>
> (AT 35.06)
>
> ⁻You ₍were ₀lucky. (AT 37.32)
>
> [ʹPoor old ʽRobert!] He ʽwill have a ₀shock! (AT 27.23)
>
> It ʽwon't take ₍long / to put the ₍table ₀up in the ₍garage.
>
> (AT 7.05)
>
> Joan, ʽdo have a ₀bit of ₍sense. You ʽcan't lose ₀money / by
> ₍sneezing. (AT 37.02)
>
> You know, that ʽdoes make me ₍envious. (AT 45.31)

As has been demonstrated (see p. 90), the semantic content of the
auxiliary, serving as a categorial exponent, is rather complex, which
contributes to its heterogeneity in regard to degrees of CD. It is on
account of the semantic feature of positive/negative polarity that the re-
evaluating IC is placed on the auxiliaries in the sentences above. The
speaker utters either an emphatic assertion or an emphatic denial, the
particular emotive colouring depending on the meaning of the co-text.

In this way the polarity feature serves as RhPr after the re-evaluation; but in its capacity of a TME, the auxiliary continues to perform the function of TrPr.

The sentences under discussion have not entered the second-instance sphere. Let me recall that a second-instance sentence stands in sharp contrast on account of one semantic feature, all the rest of the sentence – to the exclusion of the linking effect of the TMEs – being context-dependent (see p. 164). This does not apply to the above sentences. In none of them is the information conveyed by the shaded elements entirely context-dependent. A second-instance sentence must show a maximum degree of context dependence; consider, for example, [*I am not saying that you were mean, Simon.*] *You ARE mean.* [*Right now. At this very moment.*], which, however, only comes close to genuine second instance, not being an exact repetition.

Re-evaluated notional components of the finite verb

As has been established elsewhere (Firbas 1968, 1975, 1987c) and in the present study (see p. 70), the notional component of the finite verb shows an unmistakable tendency to perform the transitional function. The cases in which it serves as RhPr are comparatively rare; also rare are the cases in which it bears the re-evaluating IC. The unusualness of the phenomenon heightens the effect of re-evaluation.

> [It's 'such an at`tractive ₒcity. They a`ˇdored the ˇcathedral.
> – Yes, it ˇis ₒbeautiful, / `isn't it?] 'I'd `love to ₒsee it
> a₀gain.   (AT 87.06)
> [Oh, `come on, / ‚somebody.] `Come and help ₒfind the ‚ball.
> [It's the 'last °decent one we've `got.]   (AT 13.13)
> [But it's `rather disapˇpointing, / `isn't it?] I was looking
> `forward to a ₒswim in the ₒMediter‚ranean.   (AT 41.04)

The first and the third sentences contain elements that at the non-prosodic level operate as successful competitors of the verbs. Nevertheless, it is not the competitors, but the verb forms *love* and *look forward* that are the IC bearers. The ICs are re-evaluating. (It could also be argued that the verb *love* of the first sentence has a synonymic predecessor – the verb form *adored* – in the immediately relevant context. If this is correct, *love*, or rather its notional component, is context-dependent and at the non-prosodic level thematic.) In the second sentence, *Come*, together with *and*, introduces information that at the non-prosodic level completes the communication. Nevertheless, *Come* is the IC bearer. The IC is re-evaluating. (It could also be argued that *Come* has a synonymic predecessor – *Come on* – in the immediately preceding context. If this is correct, *Come*, or rather its notional component, is context-dependent and at the non-prosodic level thematic.) The intensified emotive values are a desire to see something beautiful (first sentence), a plea for assistance (second sentence) and disappointment in one's expectations (third sentence).

A special group is represented by such verbs as *wish*, *hope* and such predicative adjectives as *sure*, *sorry*, *glad*, which all express some attitude of the speaker and are attitudinal words *par excellence*. At the non-prosodic level, they are exceeded in CD by the context-independent section of the sentence specifying what the attitude relates to. Under such contextual conditions, the shift of the IC onto the attitudinal word causes emotive re-evaluation of the sentence perspective, throwing into relief the very attitude the speaker has assumed.

ˋHope I haven't deˏpressed you too °much.   (AT 73.13)

ˋSorry we're ₀later than we ˏplanned.   (AT 53.06)

Re-evaluated subjects

A pronominal subject that is rendered thematic by the interplay of non-prosodic factors undoubtedly becomes re-evaluated if it bears the IC (cf. the subjects *That*, *there*, *You* and *He* in the examples adduced on pp. 161–2).

A problem, however, is posed by the following group of sentences.

[But there 'must have been °something ˋwrong / with the ˋpetrol ₀gauge, / because the ˇnext we ₀knew, /] the ˋengine had ₀stopped.   (AT 53.15)

The ˇball's making a ₀very ₀queer ₀sound, / ˋisn't it?

(AT 15.20)

The ˇsound is all ₀right.   (AT 15.29)

[You ˋknow you °said] the ˇtube was giving ₀trouble, [Dad]?

(AT 17.22)

And the ˋscreen's so ₀small.   (AT 19.02)

ˋThat one on the ˇcounter isn't ₀bad.   (AT 29.18)

Intonation unequivocally perspectives the sentences towards their subjects. The problem concerns the relationship between the non-prosodic CD distribution and the PP distribution. In the first sentence, the perspective towards the subject is suggested by the verb *stopped*. Under the circumstances, it implicitly expresses non-existence/disappearance and therefore performs the Pr-function in the presence of a context-independent subject as a successful competitor. Intonation reflects this interplay of non-prosodic means.

As for the verbs in the other sentences, they do not express either implicitly nor explictly appearance/existence or disappearance/non-existence for that matter. In the presence of a more dynamic competitor than the context-independent subject, they perform the Q-function and perspective the sentence away from the subject towards the more dynamic competitor. But intonation does not reflect this perspective.

It is worth noticing, however, that in each case a distinctly positive or a distinctly negative feature is ascribed to the notion expressed by the subject. The emotive colouring of this positive or negative assessment has been forcibly enhanced by the re-evaluating shift of the IC, taking place against the background of the perspective suggested by the non-prosodic means and re-evaluating the original thematicity of the subject into rhematicity.

At this point the observation must be recalled that under certain conditions sentences that are entirely context-independent are perspectived towards their subjects, the Ph-function asserting itself before the B-function (see p. 67). Should the tendency to implement the Ph-function before the B-function play the decisive role within the above five sentences, the verb of these sentences would not perform the Q-function, but the Pr-function. The rhematicity of the subject would then be original, i.e. not due to re-evaluating prosodic intensification, as in the case of the subject of the sentence discussed first (*the engine had stopped*).

I believe that, within the system presented and at the present state of knowledge, the interpretation ascribing primary rhematicity to *engine* and the interpretation ascribing secondary rhematicity to the other subjects are the interpretations to be adopted. The discussion, of course, indicates that it may occasionally be difficult to draw a distinct line between primary rhematicity and secondary rhematicity (i.e. such as results from prosodic re-evaluation), the difficulty pointing to the phenomenon of potentiality. In regard to the FSP function of the subject, this phenomenon will be taken up again on pages 183–6 and 222–3.

Intensives

A very important group of elements that frequently bear prosodic intensification is formed by adjectives, adverbs and nouns that in various ways express a high grade of a quality or a high frequency of a phenomenon. They will be referred to as 'intensives' here. I shall deal with them only summarily, not attempting a detailed enumeration and classification. My main concern will be to demonstrate when they become involved in non-reevaluating. and when in re-evaluating, prosodic intensification.

Let me first concentrate on the intensive realized as an adjective which precedes a noun and forms a noun phrase with it. As a clause constituent a noun phrase functions as a communicative unit within a distributional field of CD and in its turn provides a distributional field of CD of lower order. The attributive adjective serves as a communicative unit within this subfield. Let me also recall that, if context-independent, the adjective carries a higher degree of CD than its headword (see p. 84). How does the PP distribution over such a noun phrase react to the non-prosodic CD distribution?

Leaving aside the noun phrase, the most prominent prosodic feature of which – apart from very exceptional contexts – remains linked with one element (cf. the invariable occurrence of stress on *French* in *French teacher* meaning 'teacher of French'; *CGEL* 1040), we find the following relations between the two distributions examined. Within the noun phrase under discussion, a context-dependent adjective bears a less prominent prosodic feature than its context-independent headword; and vice versa, a context-dependent headword bears a less prominent prosodic feature than a context-independent adjective. These are cases of perfect correspondence between the two distributions examined.

> [OK... 'Play that one a`gain ₒFrank. It was a 'net `ball I ₒthink...] Oh `excellent ₒservice. [I 'didn't stand a `chance.]
>
> (AT 15.17)
>
> [The 'students are `excellent,] but we 'also need °excellent `teachers.

Whereas in the first sentence the attributive *excellent* is context-independent and its headword context-dependent (owing to the operation of the immediately relevant situational context), in the second the reverse is true. While in the first sentence the attributive *excellent* exceeds its headword in PP, in the second it is the other way round. The PP distribution within the subfields provided by the noun phrases reflects the non-prosodic CD distribution. In each case the context-dependent element recedes into the backgound.

The situation is not so straightforward if both the attributive adjective and the headword are context-independent. This is the case of *great fun* in the sentences below, in which only *Doubles* is regarded as context-dependent.

> 'Doubles is °always `great ₒfun.   (AT 7.07)
> 'Doubles is °always °great `fun.

Both the adjective and its headword are context-independent, but their prosodic implementations are not the same in the two sentences. The implementation with the nucleus on the adjective is marked; but the marked nucleus does not violate the correspondence between the two distributions.

> Doubles is   always great fun.
> DTh   + ;Tr TrPro   RhPr.

The non-prosodic FSP factors induce the context-independent adjective to exceed its headword in CD. The marked nucleus linked with additional attitudinal information only raises the CD of the adjective at the level of the spoken language. It produces an effective prosodic intensification, but does not re-evaluate the perspective of the noun phrase. The perfect correspondence between the two distributions is preserved.

Let me turn to what has been characterized as the unmarked distribution of PP taking place over a context-independent headword and a context-independent adjective.

> 'Doubles   is °always °great `fun.
> 'DTh + ;Tr °TrPro   °`RhPr.

The distribution of PP over the noun phrase is out of correspondence with the non-prosodic CD distribution. The headword is prosodically more prominent than the context-independent attributive adjective. This 'discrepancy', however, does not have a re-evaluating effect. Why is this so? In the first place, the non-prosodic CD distribution is not obliterated by intonation. Prosodic re-evaluation can only add a new dimension to a distribution that is already in existence. Under the circumstances, no new dimension is added, because the prosodic distribution has lost its re-evaluating force on account of its unmarked character. The function of the most prominent prosodic feature of the noun phrase is primarily representative (see pp. 149–50).

The representative function is, of course, also performed by the most prominent feature of the attributive structure in the first version. Moreover, in each version this feature acts as the IC of the basic distributional field. It occurs on the unit that has been selected by the non-prosodic interplay to serve as RhPr of this field.

Under special conditions the representative feature occurring on an intensive and acting as IC can cause re-evaluating prosodic intensification. This is the case of the nucleus on *great* if the sentence structure *It's always great fun playing doubles* conveys context-independent information.

> It’ s ˈalways °great °fun playing ˋdoubles.
> ThPr + ;Tr ˈTrPro   °°Rh   ˋRhPr.
> It’ s ˈalways ˋgreat $_{o}$fun playing ˏdoubles.
> ThPr + :Tr ˈTrPro Rh > ˋ$_{o}$RhPr   RhPr > ˏDTh.

Within the noun phrase *great fun*, its representative feature behaves in the same way as accounted for above; but in regard to the other communicative units, it produces a re-evaluating effect if implemented as a marked nucleus that acts as the IC. It puts *playing doubles in* post-IC prosodic shade and reperspectives the sentence to the noun phrase *great fun* and ultimately to the intensive *great*.

What has been said about the representative feature of the noun phrase applies to that of a communicative unit containing an adverbial intensive. Without going into detail about the degrees of CD within such a unit, let me point out that it is once again in marked use that the adverbial intensive bears the representative feature.

> They were ˈawfully disap°pointed with ˋMary.
> ThPr + ;Tr   ˈ°Rh   ˋRhPr.
> They were ˋawfully disap$_{o}$pointed   with ˏMary.
> ThPr + ;Tr   Rh > ˋ$_{o}$RhPrRhPr > ˏDTh.
> It ˈdries °much °quicker in the ˋsun.
> ThPr ˈ+ ;Tr   °°Rh   ˋRhPr.
> It ˈdries ˋmuch $_{o}$quicker   in the ˏsun.
> ThPr ˈ+ ;Tr   Rh > ˋ$_{o}$RhPr RhPr > ˏDTh.

If only *It*, *us* and *They* are treated as context-dependent, the following interpretation applies. In terms of communicative units operating in the basic distributional field, the first sentence of each pair shows perfect correspondence between the two distributions examined, whereas the second displays re-evaluating prosodic intensification. Re-evaluation has been brought about by inducing the intensive to bear a nucleus acting as the IC of the sentence. In consequence, the elements *with Mary*, *in the sun* appear in post-IC prosodic shades.

The following pair of sentences demonstrates an intensifying shift of a nucleus (acting as a representative feature and simultaneously as IC) onto the intensive *very*. In either sentence, the nucleus occurs on a final communicative unit non-prosodically signalled as RhPr. It is not shifted from one communicative unit onto another. In this respect, it does not produce re-evaluating prosodic intensification. As for the shift inside the unit, I tentatively interpret it as producing non-reevaluating intensification for the same reasons as given on page 168.

$$\text{He' s made 'very }^{\circ}\text{quick 'time.}$$
$$\text{ThPr + +;Tr} \qquad ^{\text{I}\circ\backslash}\text{RhPr.}$$
$$\text{He' s made 'very }_{\circ}\text{quick }_{\circ}\text{time.}$$
$$\text{ThPr + +;Tr} \qquad \backslash_{\circ\circ}\text{RhPr.}$$

Let me now exemplify the operation of substantival intensives.

$$\text{I' ve still got 'loads of re'vision to }_{\circ}\text{do.}$$
$$\text{ThPr + TrPro +;Tr} \qquad ^{\text{I}\backslash}_{\circ}\text{RhPr.}$$
$$\text{I' ve still got 'loads of re}_{\circ}\text{vision to }_{\circ}\text{do. (AT 9.24)}$$
$$\text{ThPr + TrPro +;Tr} \qquad \backslash_{\circ\circ}\text{RhPr.}$$

The substantival intensive *loads* occurs in a complex noun phrase acting as a communicative unit and providing a distributional subfield. In regard to the further development of the communication, the relationship between *to do* and *loads of revision* is the same as that displayed by the corresponding verb–object combination. The context-independent elements expressing the effected goal of the action exceed in CD those expressing the action. Within *loads of revision*, the qualification expressed by *of revision* exceeds in CD the phenomenon to be qualified, *loads*. This points to *of revision* as the carrier of the highest degree of CD within the complex noun phrase at the non-prosodic level. This designates the qualification of revision to bear the non-marked representative prosodic feature of the noun phrase.

Seen in this light, the shift of the nucleus onto *loads* is a case of re-evaluating prosodic intensification. This re-evaluation, however, affects only the noun phrase. In regard to the other units within the distributional field, the shifted nucleus continues to act as the representative feature of the noun phrase and the IC of the sentence, but does not reperspective the sentence to another unit.

In the following sentence, on the other hand, the intensifying nucleus on the noun phrase *miles* produces a re-evaluating effect on the sentence.

> And of `course,  / it    was        `miles /
>   `TrPro ThPr + ;Tr  Rh > `RhPr /
> to the ,nearest ,filling   °station.   (AT 53.20)
>   RhPr > ,°DTh.

The final adverbial, which serves as RhPr (performing the rhematic Sp-function) at the non-prosodic level, appears in the post-IC prosodic shade and is re-evaluated into a diathematic element. Note the non-reevaluating intensification of the TrPro *of course*.

The operation of an intensive can be summed up in the following scale.

1   The intensive does not bear the representative prosodic feature of the unit in which it occurs.

(a) It remains unstressed; or

(b) shows non-reevaluating intensification.

2   The intensive bears the representative prosodic feature, which

(a) produces non-reevaluating intensification; or

(b) causes re-evaluating intensification within the unit, but does not affect other units (creating no re-evaluating post-IC prosodic shades); or

(c) causes re-evaluation within its unit and simultaneously affects other units, putting them into re-evaluating post-IC prosodic shade.

Let me end the section on intensives with a handful of additional examples.

> (1a)   only   it ˘dries much ˅quicker / if you 'spin
>   TrPro ThPr ˘ + ;Tr   ˅Rh /
>   dry it `first.   (AT 63.12)
>   '`RhPr.
>   It   was   ,still quite `dark.   (AT 59.06)
>   ThPr + ;Tr ,TrPro   `RhPr.

(1b) [Oh, `don't be ,hard on the °lad.] 'After `all, /
                                    '`TrPro /
      he' s been `very ˅helpful.   (AT 47.24)
      ThPr + +;Tr   ˅˅RhPr.
      That'   s `quite an i˅dea.   (AT 47.10)
      DTh +:Tr   ˅˅RhPr.
      He'   s 'such a per^fectionist.   (AT 59.18)
      ThPr +;Tr   '^RhPr.
      [The 'masters at ˃school / 'told me how `wonderful
      it would ₒbe.] 'Excellent `prospects. ... 'Splendid
                                    '`RhPr.
      `jobs.   (AT 71.32)
      '`RhPr.

(2a) The `London ˅Symphony ₒOrchestra /   was
                                ˅˅ₒDTh / +;Tr
      in `splendid ₒform.   (AT 17.19)
             `ₒRhPr.
      We 'had to get ˃up / at some un`earthly ₒhour.
      ThPr '+   ˃Tr   `ₒRhPr.
                                          (AT 59.05)

(2b) She   was 'much too ₒquick ₒfor me. (AT 57.05)
      ThPr +:Tr   `ₒRhPr ₒDTh.
         It   `isn't ˅quite ₒright, [but it's
      ThPr ˅+ ; NegFocA;Tr   ˅ₒRhPr.
      the `best I can ˅see].   (AT 29.18)

(2c)   It was 'such   a re,lief / to ,get your
      ThPr +;Tr   Rh > `,RhPr /   RhPr
      ,telegram, °Mum.   (AT 59.14)
      > ,,DTh °ThPro.
         We' d have been 'much too ₒlate / for the ,last
      ThPr +   +:Tr   Rh > `ₒRhPr /
             ,ferry.   (AT 53.25)
      RhPr > ,,DTh.
      They' ll   be   `miles a ₒhead of me / by the
      ThPr + +;Tr Rh > `RhPrDTh > ₒDTho
      ,time I ,graduate.   (AT 73.06)
      RhPr > ,,DTh.

9 Some more observations on the relationship between the non-prosodic distribution of communicative dynamism and that of prosodic prominence

Deshading

The preceding discussion has demonstrated the role played by the post-IC prosodic shade in re-evaluating prosodic intensification. An element singled out by the non-prosodic FSP factors as RhPr does not bear the IC (which is shifted onto another element), but is shaded, i.e. put in the post-IC prosodic shade. It lies in the nature of the re-evaluating process that the reverse is also possible. Through re-evaluation, an element that, owing to the interplay of non-prosodic FSP factors, is non-rhematic and is to appear in the post-IC prosodic shade becomes IC bearer: it becomes deshaded and is re-evaluated to RhPr.

Like re-evaluating shading, re-evaluating deshading is due to various emotive attitudes, but like the former it also produces specific communicative effects that are not necessarily emotively motivated. A fairly frequent cause of deshading is what may be termed the 'recapitulatory' or 'summarizing effect'. For instance, in the following conversation,

> [ᵛFrank, / 'what shall we give °Robert for his ˋbirthday? –
> 'What about a cigaˋrette-₀lighter? –
> ᵛThat's no ₀good.] He' s   'given up
>   ThPr + + ;RhPr > ' + ;Tr
> ˋsmoking.
> DTh > ˋRhPr.
> – [I'd forˋgotten. 'So he ˋhas. – We must 'think of something
> ˋelse, ₀then.]   (AT 23.09)

Smoking is context-dependent, *cigarette-lighter* being its implicative predecessor. This justifies the placement of the IC on the verb: *He's GIVEN UP smoking*. But by placing the IC on *smoking* the speaker as it were sums up the case, implying: 'In consequence, it is necessary to think of something else.' This conclusion is explicitly stated by the interlocutor.

A summarizing effect is also produced by the ICs on *an electric guitar* and *bag* in the following two examples. The two elements have genuine predecessors in the immediately relevant preceding context and yet become IC bearers.

> [Yes, but I can ˈsee some eˋlectric gui˳tars...
> Well, ˈyou three go ˋon.] ˇI' m going to ˳try /
> ˇThPr + + RhPr > ˳Tr /
> ˉan e↗lectric guiˋtar. (AT 27.31)
> ThPro > ˉ↗ˋRhPr.

In the omitted part of the conversation (replaced by the three dots), the other three interlocutors voice their disagreement with the speaker's enthusiasm for electric guitars. In the sentence under discussion, the deshaded *an electric guitar* becomes part of a resolute decision arrived at and uttered by the speaker. Note the prosodic intensification both of *I* and of *an electric guitar*. The speaker continues:

> I ˌshan't get a˳nother ˳chance like ↗this / for ˋages.

Similarly, conclusiveness is achieved by deshading *my bag* in the following example.

> [You ˈkeep such a °lot of ˋrubbish in your ˳bag... – But ˈthis is ˋserious. I really ˋcan't find my ˳notecase.]
> It ↘isn't
> ThPr + ;NegFocAnt;RhPr > ↘ + ;NegFocAnt;Tr
> in my ˇbag, [I'm ˋsure]. (AT 31.02)
> ThPro > ˇRhPr

The speaker announces the result of her search. The conclusiveness of the statement is further underlined by the words *I'm sure*.

In the dialogue adduced below, the deshading of the first *then* (which in unmarked use would function here as a temporal setting) and of *Cup Final* forcefully underlines the speaker's firm conviction that the TV set must be in good order on the particular day.

> [ˈAfter ˋall, / we've ↘got to have a reˇliable set / for ↘next °Saturday ˇweek. ↘Mustn't have the °service inter°rupted ˇthen, / ˋmust we? – ˈWhy not °then in parˋticular? – ˈThat's ˋCup Final ˳day.]

We ˎ̀can't miss the ˇCup $_{o}$Final.
ThPr ˎ̀ + ;NegFocAnt RhPr > Tr DTh > ˇ$_{o}$RhPr.
(AT 19.26)

The IC on the second *Cup Final* represents a special type of deshading that is associated with emotive repetition, an interesting case of re-evaluating intensification. Further examples follow.

[ˇSorry, Mr $_{o}$Smith. We must ˋgo ˏnow. Or ˇMum'll be$_{o}$gin to $_{o}$think / ˈAndrew's °blown us ˃up / in the ^potting-$_{o}$shed!] – ˏPotting-°shed?! ˏPotting-°shed?! [LaˇBoratory, ^please!] (AT 83.26)

Potting-shed has its genuine predecessor in the immediately relevant preceding context, and is in this sense context-dependent; but it becomes context-independent on account of the disagreement and irritation it is made to convey by re-evaluating prosodic intensification. Note the use of punctuation in the written language and also the soothing effect of the immediately following reaction of another participant in the conversation.

Oh, ˌtake no $_{o}$notice of ˏhim, °Andrew. He's ˋalways $_{o}$putting his $_{o}$foot in it. (AT 83.31)

The emotive character of the soothing words is signalled by the re-evaluating devices (cf. the shifting of the ICs onto *him* and the shading of *putting his foot*).

Perhaps no special comment is needed on the repetition of *Manchester* occurring in the following excerpt.

[He ˌrang up from ˋManchester!] – ^Manchester! [He'd ˎ̀have to be ˇquick / to ˎ̀get to St °Albans in °half an ˇhour. ˉIt's a ˏhundred and °fifty ˋmiles or $_{o}$more.] (AT 93.30)

The occurrence of the rise–fall on *Manchester* is quite in keeping with O'Connor and Arnold's observation that the rise–fall 'is very often used in echoing an immediately prior remark, in order to show how impressed the speaker is, whether favourably or not' (1973: 78). Once again, it is the conveyance of the speaker's attitude that renders *Manchester* context-independent. Another case of emotive repetition is represented by the following example.

[And we ˈdid some ˋriding. – What, ˏall of you? ˈJoan asˏwell? She's ˈnever been ˋon a $_{o}$horse / in her ˋlife!] –

'Even ^Joan. [And ˇwhat's ˇmore, / I 'didn't fall ^off.]

(AT 57.18)

It is Joan herself who repeats her own name in confirmation of what has been said about her!

[We ˏran out of ˋpetrol.] 'Ran out of ˏpetrol? – [ˋYes. Riˋdiculous, / ˋisn't it?]   (AT 53.11)

Each element of the sentence under examination has its genuine predecessor. Nevertheless, the sentence comes to serve as a vehicle of new information. It conveys the speaker's incredulity, his surprise at the absurdity of the event, or perhaps even his low estimation of the other person's efficiency as a driver. The speaker's attitude is not precisely specified, but unmistabably suggested by the intonation; this is borne out by the other person's reaction. Let me add that all the above one-word sentences implement only RhPr and TrPr (see p. 93).

As a re-evaluating procedure, deshading raises the degrees of CD of the elements affected. It operates against the background of perfect correspondence between the non-prosodic CD distribution and the PP distribution. It is particularly sensitive to context dependence, against the background of which it can successfully assert itself.

It must be added, however, that the systemic relations described by the preceding discussions can be somewhat blurred by what may be described as the automatic placement of the IC. Such a placement does not respect the outcome of the interplay of the non-prosodic FSP factors: irrespective of it the IC is placed on the last stressed communicative unit within the field. In this way it can happen that, for instance, the structure *A boy came into the room* can have the IC on *into the room* even if this element has been rendered context-dependent. Under the circumstances, however, automaticity is not strong enough to prove truly functional. The deshading caused by it can only somewhat blur the outcome of the interplay of the non-prosodic factors, but not render it entirely inoperative.

Further notes on shading and the to-be-in-the-know effect

It follows from the foregoing that the post-IC prosodic shade is constituted by the following:

1   elements that are context-dependent and hence carry low degrees of CD; and/or

2   elements that, though context-independent, carry low degrees of CD on account of their semantic character and the character of their semantic relations; and/or

3   context-independent elements that on account of their semantic character and the character of their semantic relations qualify for carriers of the highest degrees of CD and whose presence in the post-IC prosodic shade is therefore highly marked and brings about a re-evaluation of the perspective of the distributional field.

The fact that, like elements of type 1, even elements of type 3 can appear in the post-IC shade creates the impression that the latter present context-dependent information. The wording 'creates the impression' is important, for objectively speaking the type 3 elements are context-independent. It is with this connotation that the verb 'present' is to be understood here.

Let me remind the reader that context dependence and context independence are determined by the immediately relevant verbal and situational context (see pp. 23ff.). Assessing context dependence or independence, the language user goes by the clues found in this contextual sphere. Against the background of phenomena objectively existing in this sphere, the speaker can 'present' context-independent notions as context-dependent and the attentive listener will duly respond, recognizing the true character of such notions. In this way the speaker can employ intonation in successfully manipulating context dependence/independence for his communicative purposes. He may, of course, fail in achieving his aim if the clues used are ambiguous or indistinct, or if the listener is not sufficiently responsive.

The relationship between shading and context dependence/independence is also reflected by the phenomenon that can be referred to as the 'to-be-in-the-know effect'. The following example will illustrate.

> [It's ˋOK for our °holiday in ˇSkye, ₒMarjorie. Mum
> ˇheard from ₒCousin ₒJeannie / this ˋmorning.] But
>   TrPro
> ˈshe' d pre°fer the ˋlast two ₒweeks in ₒAugust /
> ˈThPr +   °Tr   /
> ˌrather than the ˌmiddle °two.   (AT 43.01)
>   ˋₒₒˌ°RhPr.

The three sentences form an opening of a conversation. The times expressed by the expanded and compound object of *prefer* have no predecessors. This renders the information entirely context-independent, and its bearer, the object, can therefore be expected to assert itself as a successful competitor of the verb and to bear the IC. The object does indeed serve as RhPr and does bear the IC, but the IC occurs on the first element of the object (*last*) and puts all the others in the post-IC shade. (The shading takes place within the subfield provided by the object.) The information conveyed by the shaded elements is presented as context-dependent.

It is important to note that the shading is not accompanied by emotive signals. How is the 'presentation' to be accounted for? Let us take three viewpoints into consideration: that of the speaker; that of the initiated listener, who belongs to the same family as the speaker; and that of a stranger, who is a totally uninitiated observer and does not participate in the conversation.

Irrespective of any of the three viewpoints, it is an objective fact that the shaded information is irretrievable from the immediately relevant context. This induces the initiated listener to recall notions to his mind that have not been explicitly mentioned in the conversation but are familiar to him. Being in the know, he accepts the way these context-independent notions are presented to him by the speaker and puts them on a par with genuinely context-dependent information. Assuming that the listener is in the know, the speaker can strike the intimate note. For the uninitiated observer, on the other hand, the shaded information is entirely new. Its shading indicates to him a high degree of intimacy between the two interlocutors. He is well aware of the to-be-in-the-know effect produced by the shading of context-independent information. The absence of the information from the immediately relevant context is appreciated by all three – the speaker, the initiated listener and the unitiated listener–observer – and is an objective basis on which the to-be-in-the-know phenomenon can be established. The speaker decides where the IC falls (see, e.g., Halliday 1967a; Lipka 1977), but in order to achieve his communicative purpose he must observe the laws of the interplay of FSP factors. The final effect depends on the way this interplay has been employed.

Let me add that *Cousin Jeannie* in the second sentence participates in the production of the to-be-in-the-know effect. It has no predecessor and yet occurs in a post-nuclear prosodic shade. (The shade produces the 'presentation' effect, but does not occur after an IC.)

If the to-be-in-the-know effect had not been applied, *Cousin Jeannie* would serve as RhPr and bear the IC. The element *this morning* would duly appear in the shade as a setting. But in the version examined, it serves as a specification. The following fragment of conversation is worth comparing with the one just under discussion.

> [Our ˋholiday in ˇFrance / is ˋoff. – ˎHow's ˋthat?]
>   – I   had a ˈletter from ˋDominique / ˎyesterday.
> ThPr + ;Tr   ˋˋRhPr /   ˎDTh.
> [She says her ˈmother had an ˋaccident.]   (AT 39.22)

No to-be-in-the-know effect is produced here. *Yesterday* is duly shaded as a temporal setting. Let me briefly discuss two more examples.

> [They're ˈgoing over˃seas / ˈearlier than exˋpected. The ˈday after toˋmorrow, in ₒfact. Apparently,
> ˋWilliam had heard a ˇrumour about ₒthat /] beˈfore
>   ˈTrPro
> he beˋgan hisₒleave.   (AT 53.35)
> ThPr ˋRhPr   ₒDTh.
> [It was ˋhandy / ˎhaving the ˎcar.] Like ˇthat,
>   /we
>   ˇDTho/ThPr
> were ˈable to get °quite far aˋfield / from Porˎtree.
>   +   ˈTr   °ˋRhPr /   ˎDTh.
>   (AT 57.12)

The shaded elements *his leave* and *from Portree* have no predecessors. Only the initiated know that William was about to begin his leave and that the holiday-makers were staying at Portree. The to-be-in-the-know effect enables the speakers to throw extra stress on the unexpectedness of William's departure and on the large extent of the area they could visit.

In closing the present section let me recall the discussion of the structure *President Kennedy has been assassinated*. If my interpretation on page 64 is correct, then under the contextual conditions stipulated there (providing for entire context independence of the structure) the unexpected placement of the IC on *assassinated* and the resultant deshading of this element would evoke the to-be-in-the-know effect in the uninitiated listener. He cannot but assume that for one reason or another President Kennedy has been the object of the interlocutors' or at least the speaker's special concern.

The contextual application of the structure with the IC on *assassinated* would be different if not the immediately relevant situational context, but the general objectively existing situation could be characterized by the feeling that some adverse event affecting President Kennedy was imminent. Under these circumstances all the perceivers of the structure including the uninitiated listener would interpret the IC as perspectiving the message not towards the president, but towards what has happened to him. Strictly speaking, the notion of 'President Kennedy' remains irretrievable from the immediately relevant situational context as delimited in this study. Under these contextual conditions the application of the structure under examination points to the borderline sphere (see p. 23) adjacent to that of the immediately relevant context.

Settings and specifications

The enquiry into the relation between the non-prosodic CD distribution and the PP distribution bears out the distinction between the Set-function and the Sp-function. In the spoken language, intonation not only reflects these functions as they have been assigned by the interplay of the non-prosodic FSP factors, but proves capable of consummating this interplay by eliminating potentiality shown in the written language by cases permitting an interpretation of the elements concerned either as specifications or as settings.

No matter whether potentiality is present or not at the non-prosodic level, the following sentences exemplify adverbials that have been put in the post-IC prosodic shade and in this way are unequivocally signalled as settings. They serve as DThs.

'That's how he °talks to `Joan ₒwhen she's at ₒhome.

(AT 85.11)

And 'Jamie's quite a `friendly ₒchap, / ‚once you ₒget to ‚know him. (AT 59.09)

[`Anyway, / you'll ex`cuse me / ‚now, `won't you?] I've got some `cakes in the ₒoven. (AT 87.16)

‚Why did you `come here, / if you ‚feel like ‚that?

(AT 71.27)

The following sentences, on the other hand, contain adverbials whose

representative prosodic feature is a nucleus serving as IC. No matter
whether potentiality is present or not at the non-prosodic level, the
adverbials are unequivocally signalled as specifications by the IC and act
as rhemes proper.

> We'll 'get $^>$off / as 'soon as you $^°$let us come `by.
> (AT 69.20)
> [Will 'you pay the ˌbill, $^°$Dave?] And we'll 'sort it out `later.
> (AT 73.15)
> [It's the `tax-payer's $_°$money.] And some of $^\lor$that / comes
> from `me. (AT 69.08)
> 'Dad's `promised me $_°$one, / be'cause I $^°$won that `prize.
> (AT 97.17)
> No, but it'll `be all $^\lor$right / so $_°$long as I `don't $^°$take it on
> the $^\lor$roads. (AT 97.24)

Each of the following sentences ends in an adverbial put in the post-
IC shade and acting as a setting and a DTh. This adverbial occurs after
another adverbial whose representative prosodic feature is a nucleus
serving as IC. The IC signals the latter as a specification and RhPr. Once
again, the prosodic signalling is unequivocal.

> I was 'talking to Mrs `Jones / at the `paper $_°$shop / the
> ˌother ˌday. (AT 19.14)
> `Dad's taking $^°$Simon and $^\lor$me / to the `speedway / ˌnext
> $_°$Friday ˌevening. (AT 83.18)
> Well, Dad 'used to go $^°$every `week / beˌfore the ˌwar.
> (AT 89.08)

By eliminating potentiality, intonation disambiguates the FSP
function of an element and frequently also the perspective of the entire
distributional field. As it does not create a 'discrepancy' between the two
distributions, elimination of potentiality contributes towards the
establishment of perfect correspondence between them. Seen from this
angle, elimination of potentiality is not an intensification phenomenon.

However, intonation can affect the Set-elements and the Sp-elements
through prosodic intensification, in particular through deshading and
shading. It does not confine itself to reflecting the Set- and Sp-functions
or to disambiguating them. This is illustrated, for instance, by the way
the final adverbials are treated in the following two groups of sentences.

As for the first group, it can be assumed that, in the types of co-text in which they occur below, the final adverbials (*at breakfast, now, in this restaurant, to some extent, somehow*) would normally be treated as settings and accordingly shaded. Their bearing the IC (their deshading) makes them additionally carry various nuances of attitudinal and emphatic meaning. The commas throwing extra emphasis on *in this restaurant* (which, non-prosodically speaking, is context-dependent) and *somehow* are in harmony with the interpretation just offered. The ICs have re-evaluated the settings into specifications.

> [That's the ˇfirst ˇI've ₒheard of a ₒdinner. ˏNobody °ever tells me ˋanything. ˏReally, ₒSimon!] ˋDad was ˇtalking about it / at ˋbreakfast / this ˋmorning. [You ˏjust weren't ˋlistening.] (AT 3.08)
>
> Well, as a ˋmatter of ˇfact, / 'that's why I've °come round ˋnow. (AT 41.09)
>
> 'Now we want to °get a ˋmeal, / in this ˋrestaurant. (AT 67.31)
>
> Still, 'I'm with ˋAndrew / to ˇsome exₒtent. (AT 89.33)
>
> [But ˇdon't ask how the °four of us got ˇin it.] We ˇdid, / ˇsomehow. (AT 57.15)

As for the second group, it can be assumed that, in the types of co-text in which they occur below, the adverbials *to number one, so early* and *to the nearest filling station* would normally be treated as specifications and carriers of the highest degree of CD and bear the IC. They would serve as rhemes proper. But they have been affected by re-evaluating intensification, the IC having been shifted onto *soon, you* and *miles*. They have been moderated to DThs serving as settings.

> [Yes, that ˇnew ˇSquallies ₒnumber / sounded ˋvery ₒgood. ˇI ₒreckon / it's their 'best ˇyet.] It'll ˋsoon get to ₒnumber ₒone in the ˏcharts. [I bet.] (AT 9.08)
>
> [ˋHullo, / ˏJoan.] ˏWhat's brought ˋyou round ₒhere so ₒearly? (AT 39.20)
>
> [Near the 'northern °end of Loch ˋLomond we ₒwere. –] And of ˋcourse, / it was ˋmiles / to the ˏnearest ˏfilling °station. (AT 53.18)

It follows that intonation efficiently signals settings and specifications.

But intonation is also a powerful instrument of emotive intensification and moderation. In this capacity, it can emotively intensify a setting into a specification and, vice versa, emotively moderate a specification into a setting. Deshading and shading are the main devices used in such intensification and moderation, respectively. I trust that the present discussion has sufficiently illustrated these operations of intonation within the interplay of FSP factors. It may be asked whether it is always possible to draw an exact dividing line between unintensified non-reevaluated (unintensified) settings and non-reevaluated (unmoderated) specifications on the one hand, and re-evaluated (intensified) settings and re-evaluated (moderated) specifications on the other. Knowing that language is not a rigid system, but a system with a centre and a periphery, we can assume that it is not always possible to draw such a line. In any case, a more exact description of the types of cases involved in the processes of shading and deshading remains pending.

More thoughts on the prosodic implementation of the subject and on potentiality

The preceding section has demonstrated how intonation removes potentiality by unequivocally deciding whether an adverbial is to perform the Set-function or the Sp-function. This section offers some comments on intonation removing potentiality by unequivocally deciding whether a subject is to perform the Ph-function or the B-function. I have chosen for discussion three types of examples. All three represent borderline cases.

I	The tide was in.	(MacCarthy 1956: 60)
	The teams are coming out.	(AT 1971: 08)
	The inevitable thing happened.	(Lewis 1977: 54)

If the subjects of the three sentences were context-dependent and the verbs context-independent, the sentences would be unequivocally perspectived towards the verbs, which would perform the Q-function and the subjects the B-function. On the other hand, the sentences would be unequivocally perspectived towards the subjects if the latter were context-independent; the verbs, expressing existence or appearance, would then perform the Pr-function, and the subjects the Ph-function.

But in the contexts in which the sentences appear, uncertainty arises as to the contextual status of the subjects. True enough, the information conveyed by them does not occur in the immediately relevant preceding verbal context, nor is it suggested by the immediately relevant situational context so forcibly as to become a matter of the interlocutors' common immediate concern (see p. 25), nor does it refer to items that though inconspicuous are considered to be always part of the immediately relevant context (see p. 24). This assessment permits to regard the subjects as context-independent.

But at the moments concerned, the referents of the subjects can be understood as the only ones suggested by the situation and/or inevitably emerging on the scene. Only they are not suggested by the immediately relevant situational contexts so forcibly as to become objects of the interlocutors' common immediate concern (see p. 25). This assessment permits to regard the subjects as context-dependent.

If these observations are correct, the uncertainty as to the adequate assessment is due to the referents occurring in the borderline area between the immediately relevant portion and the rest of the situational context (see p. 23). This leads to potentiality, which in the spoken language is removed by the placement of the IC either on the subject or on the verb. In the tonetically transcribed texts from where the examples are quoted, the case is decided by placing the IC on the verb, inducing it to perform the Q-function and the subject the B-function.

2   Another borderline type is illustrated by the following sentences. They are all entirely context-independent.

> In every country, dogs bite.
> When the cow flies, her tail follows.
> Extremes meet.
> Old vessels must leak.

In contrast with the type discussed above, there is no need for intonation to disambiguate; without its aid, the perspective of the structures adduced is unequivocal. This is due to the proverbial character of the information conveyed. In a generalizing manner, a characteristic (quality) is ascribed to a phenomenon. The interpretative arrangement naturally places the context-independent characterization after the phenomenon to be characterized. The communication is perspectived towards the characterization. The subject performs the B-function and the notional component of the verb the Q-function.

This perspective is in keeping with the communicative role of the proverb consisting in recalling an experience well known and generally accepted as valid. The perspective has, in fact, been determined and petrified outside the immediately relevant context, and is ready to be introduced at any time into the immediately relevant context. This places the information in the borderline area between the immediately relevant context and the wider context of situation and experience.

3   The following note has been suggested by a group of sentences in Bolinger (1987: 132–3):

> My mother was ill.
> My mother was in pain.
> My mother made it necessary.

Each sentence is entirely context-independent and a possible reply to a question asking a man to account for his being late. By placing the IC on *My mother*, Bolinger indicates the way the reply is perspectived. It is the man's mother who is presented as the cause of the late arrival. This means that *My mother* performs the Ph-function, which prevents the verb (*was*, *made*) from being interpreted as performing the AofQ- or Q-function and entails its interpretation as a Pr-element. In consequence, the elements *ill*, *in pain* and *necessary* are considered to express background information and to perform the Set-function.

Whereas the placement of the intonation centre on *My mother* unequivocally implements a Ph-perspective, the perspective of the written sentence is not so unequivocal under the contextual conditions stipulated. An interpretation preferring the Q-perspective cannot be ruled out: cf. *My mother* (B) *was* (AofQ) *ill* (Q); *My mother* (B) *was* (AofQ) *in pain* (Q); *My mother* (B) *made* (Q) *it* (context-dependent element, Set) *necessary* (Sp). Under the circumstances, the written sentence becomes a case of potentiality in contrast with the spoken sentence.

A context-dependent subject rules out the Ph-perspective; a context-independent subject, on the other hand, may be affected by the tendency to present a context-independent phenomenon first within a separate field before another field is perspectived to a quality or qualities ascribable to this phenomenon (see p. 68). This tendency is not restricted to a context-independent subject linked with a verb of appearance/existence and (possibly) an adverbial expressing the spatial background and/or an adverbial expressing the temporal background.

An exact assessment of the force of this tendency must be left to further research. It is in operation not only in European languages: in his *Beknopte javaansche Grammatica* (1941: 93), Uhlenbeck makes the following highly relevant observation: 'It is an important principle in Javanese that nothing can be communicated about a person or thing if the existence of this person or thing is unknown to the listener' (my translation).

By removing potentiality, intonation can indeed 'sway the choice' or 'tip the balance', to use Bolinger's apt wording, but it does not operate independently of the non-prosodic FSP factors. Further research into these factors may reveal that what has so far been considered a case of potentiality may be accounted for by their unequivocal interplay.

The particular problems discussed here have in fact also been taken up, for instance, by Allerton (1978), Gussenhoven (1983, 1984) and Faber (1987). An analysis that would evaluate their interpretations from the point of view of the theory of FSP has to remain pending.

Functional sentence perspective, intonation and emotiveness

Dealing with re-evaluating prosodic intensification, I have devoted a good deal of attention to emotiveness in FSP. An important question can be raised in this connection. In what way exactly does FSP participate in rendering a sentence emotive? This question is quite legitimate, because emotiveness is frequently co-signalled on more than one linguistic plane (see Schubiger 1935: 45; Grepl 1967: 126). An example will help to clarify the matter.

> [And the ˇhospital ˳thinks / I 'need to catch °up on my
> ˋsleep. ˇSleep?! It's 'really dis˷gusting, Mrs ˳Brown.]
> ˋLunchtime   it ˳was/when she ˏfinally ˳came
>   ˋRhPr ThPR ˳+ ;Tr /
> ˳down˷stairs to°day.   (AT 85.04)
>   '˳∕°DTh.

The sentence under examination is clearly emotive; so is the immediately relevant preceding context. Note the emotive repetition of *sleep*, the fall–rise conveying resentful dissent (see O'Connor and Arnold 1973: 66–71), the highly marked simultaneous use of the question and exclamation marks at the level of written language, the choice of words at the lexical plane (the assertive *really* and the disapproving *disgusting*), and even the use of the vocative *Mrs Brown*, which is meant to lend additional emphasis to the preceding disparaging words. The adverb *finally* has an opprobrious connotation of 'at long last' and, above all, the order of words markedly deviates from the normal arrangement, producing an unmistakably emotive effect. What about the non-prosodic CD distribution and the PP distribution? (In the analysis below, the degrees of CD are presented as determined by the interplay of non-prosodic FSP factors.)

The ThPr, *it*, carries the lowest degree of CD and is unstressed. The RhPr, *Lunchtime*, carries the highest degree of CD and bears the IC. The DTh, *when she finally came downstairs today*, the representative prosodic feature of which is a non-IC nucleus, exceeds in CD and in PP the ThPr, on the one hand, and is exceeded in CD and in PP by the RhPr, on the other. The fact that it does not exceed in CD the transitional *was*, which bears unaccented stress, but exceeds it in PP, causes prosodic intensification of the Th and prosodic weakening of the Tr. In consequence, the sentence shows non-reevaluating prosodic intensification.

As for the subfield provided by the diathematic *when*-clause, the correspondence between the non-prosodic CD distribution and the PP distribution is perfect but for the relation of *when* and *she*.

> when   she ,finally $_o$came   down,stairs to °day.
> TrPro ThPr ,TrPro $_o$+ ;Tr   ,RhPr °DTh.

If the observation regarding the operation of linear modification in a spoken sentence (see p. 144) is strictly applied, then, though both *when* and *she* are unstressed, the latter bears a higher degree of PP. Seen in this light, even the subfield shows a degree of non-reevaluating prosodic intensification due to slight prosodic intensification of ThPr.

It is important to note that the correspondence between the non-prosodic CD distribution and the PP distribution would remain the same if the order of words were changed back to normal.

> It   was `lunchtime when she ,finally $_o$came
> ThPr + ;Tr   `RhPr
> down,stairs to°day.
>   ' $_o$, °DTh.

The same applies to the following sentence.

> [But there 'must have been °something `wrong / with the
> `petrol ₒgauge, / because the ⱽnext we ₒknew / the `engine
> had ₒstopped.] Near the 'northern °end of Loch
> `Lomond we ₒwere. (AT 53.15)
> 'ᵒ`DTh ThPr ₒ+ ;Tr.

The correspondence between the two distributions is perfect. It remains
the same even if the order of words, which deviates from the ordinary,
is changed back to normal.

> We were near the 'northern °end of Loch `Lomond.
> ThPr + ;Tr 'ᵒ`RhPr.

This shows that the primary cause of the emotive character of the
sentences under examination is the order of words. FSP follows suit by
proportionately raising the degrees of CD in the emotive versions, but,
strictly speaking, remains a secondary force in signalling emotiveness.
One last example must suffice.

> [It was 'quite an ex´perience, / ₐgoing to the ₐspeedway. –
> Yes, it `was exₒciting, / `wasn't it?]
> ⁻Such tre ₓmendous `speeds they ₒgo at on their
> `RhPr ThPr ₒ+ ;Tr
> ₒmotorbikes. (AT 87.31)
> ₒDTh.

The correspondence between the two distributions, which but for the
non-reevaluating prosodic intensification of the DTh is well-nigh
perfect, remains the same even if the order of the words is changed back
to normal. Note the conspicuous prosodic intensification of RhPr
imposed upon the well-nigh perfect correspondence. This intensification
raises the degrees of CD, but does not change the mutual relations of the
elements in regard to the distribution of CD. It is the marked order of
words that plays the leading role in rendering the sentence emotive.

It is evident that intonation becomes a vehicle of emotiveness through
what has been termed here prosodic intensification. It is especially the
re-evaluating prosodic intensification that proves to be a powerful means
of emotiveness in the spoken language.

Intonation of questions

In English questions the relationship between the non-prosodic CD distribution and the PP distribution is the same as in English declarative sentences. It follows that, for instance, the bearers of the foci of the written questions that were discussed on page 98 and are re-adduced below will correspond to the IC bearers of the spoken counterparts.

When will Father go with Peter *to London*?
When will Father go *with Peter* to London?
When will Father *go* with Peter to London?
When will *Father* go with Peter to London?
When *will* Father go with Peter to London?
When will Father go with Peter to London?
Will Father go with Peter *to London*?
Will Father go *with Peter* to London?
Will Father *go* with Peter to London?
Will *Father* go with Peter to London?
Will Father go with Peter to London?

Intonation reflects the interplay of the non-prosodic FSP factors by placing the IC on the element assigned by them the highest degree of CD.

German and Czech interrogative sentences behave in the same way (Firbas 1976); but an interesting problem is posed by the intonation of the interrogative sentences in Slavonic languages. The Czech way of intoning the interrogative sentence cannot be regarded as typically Slavonic. I have discussed the problem of the Slavonic question in an extensive paper (Firbas 1976), which was prompted by a thought-provoking enquiry into the FSP of the Slavonic question by Helena Křížková (1972).

Following Mathesius, Křížková regards the *wh*-word and the finite verb form as conveyers of RhPr (see this volume, p. 98). They perform this function no matter where they occur in the question or whether they bear the IC. Like Mathesius, Křížková applies the questioner's criterion of known and unknown information and regards the *wh*-word and the finite verb as the only bearers of unknown information in the sentence (see this volume, p. 98). (For convenience I use the term '*wh*-word' also in reference to Slavonic languages, although it does not reflect the actual phonic implementation of the Slavonic words; cf. Slovak *kto* for 'who' and Slovak *co* for 'what'.)

According to Křížková, the typical Slavonic *wh*-question opens with the *wh*-word, which bears the IC. In the typical *yes–no*-question the IC is borne by the finite verb, which does not necessarily occur in front position. Deviations from these basic types are due either to the need specially to emphasize a particular element or to a tendency to place the IC automatically on the last element. Křížková finds that this tendency blurs the difference between questions that select, and those that do not select, one particular element for special emphasis.

But an analysis of the copious material collected by Křížková in her study bears out the interpretation that regards the *wh*-word or the ME as RhPr (the focus of the question) only in the absence of successful competitors. It is significant that the IC occurring on another element than the *Wh*-word or the finite verb unequivocally signals the RhPr (focus of the question). For instance, in the Russian questions

Kuda ty   sobirajeshsya *vecherom?*
Where you go-you   in-the-evening
A   *ty*   kuda   sobirajeshsya vecherom.
And you   where go-you   in-the-evening

the ICs unequivocally signal *vecherom* and *ty* as rhemes proper. (*Vecherom* is unequivocally signalled as a specification and *ty* as a conveyer of the context-independent semantic feature of selection.) On the other hand, it is equally significant that the IC occurs on the *wh*-word or on the finite verb (i) if they convey the focus, or (ii) if the focus is conveyed by another element but signalled with sufficient adequacy (unequivocally) by the interplay of non-prosodic means so that there is no need for the disambiguating aid of the IC. For instance, in the Slovak question structure

Kedy si   bol   naposledy v   kine?
When you   were   last-time in   cinema?

v kine is RhPr (focus of the question) if it is context-independent. It functions as a specification and carries the highest degree of CD; but it does not bear the IC. (*Naposledy* serves as a setting.)

It follows that in Slavonic languages the congruence between the question focus and the IC remains vital if the unequivocal signalling of the question focus is jeopardized. Viewed in this light, what has been regarded as a blurring tendency is in fact a clarifying tendency aiming at providing an unequivocal signal of the question focus.

But how are we to account for the IC in Slavonic questions that occurs on a *wh*-word or a finite verb not acting as question focus, this role being performed by another element and signalled with sufficient adequacy by non-prosodic means? Recalling that from the questioner's point of view the *wh*-word or the finite verb because of its ME is the only element that conveys unknown information, we can regard them as conveying the speaker's rheme. We can then speak of a prosodic intensification of the speaker's rheme. What is intensified is the speaker's appeal to the interlocutor for providing the missing information. In regard to the FSP of the question, however, this intensification remains non-reevaluating. This is due to its stereotyped character in the Slavonic languages inolved. It is a constant feature of the question or at least always present when the question focus is signalled with sufficient adequacy by non-prosodic means.

10 Analyses of two spoken texts

In this chapter I will analyse two spoken texts extracted from longer conversations. The first is taken from Arnold and Tooley (1972) and the second from the *Corpus*. The analyses will also include some statistics. Special attention will be paid to the frequencies of the types of relationship between the non-prosodic CD distribution and the PP distribution.

In the diagnoses concerning the relation between the two distributions, the following new abbreviations are introduced: PERF (perfect) CORR (correspondence), N-R (non-reevaluating) INT (intensification), R (re-evaluating) INT (intensification), and DESH (deshading). The abbreviation N-R INT always denotes the selective type of non-reevaluating prosodic intensification (see p. 159).

In each case the abbreviation is followed by one of the following symbols: o (indicating absence of post-IC prosodic shade); 1 (indicating the presence of a post-IC prosodic shade made up of one or more context-dependent communicative units); 2 (indicating the presence of a post-IC prosodic shade made up of one or more context-independent communicative units occurring in the shade on account of their semantic character); 3 (indicating the presence of a post-IC prosodic shade produced by re-evaluating prosodic intensification); 1 + 2 (indicating the presence of a post-IC prosodic shade made up of one or more communicative units of type 1 and one or more communicative units of type 2); 0.2 (indicating the presence of a post-IC prosodic shade that arises within a communicative unit that provides a distributional subfield and stands last within the basic distributional field; the shaded units are of type 2).

The symbol 0.2 – and likewise, for instance, the symbols 0.1 and 0.3 – indicates that the IC shades only part of the final communicative unit in which it occurs. The two texts analysed here contain only 0.2 cases.

For 0.1 and 0.2 cases, see Firbas 1987c, which examines a larger portion of the conversation of which the first text analysed here forms a part.

Analysis of the first text

The first text is taken from Arnold and Tooley (1972: 34–7). It is adduced below in the normal spelling, with Arnold and Tooley's tonetic marks and my FSP analysis. The basic distributional fields are numbered. An asterisk added to the number indicates that the field is specially commented upon. The comments immediately follow the text.

Mrs BROWN
    But `Joan, /          `how did you $_o$lose
TrPro `ThPro / `TrPro ;RhPr + ThPr $_o$DTho
$_o$the $_o$money?
    $_o$DTh.   (1)*   N-R INT, 1 + 2
                What `happened?
DTh ;TrPro ;QFocA   ` + ;RhPr.
                                (2)   PERF CORR, 0

JOAN
    `Well,                  you $_o$see, /    I  `sneezed.
`TrPro  (ThPr  $_o$ + ;RhPr)  $_o$TrPro / ThPr ` + ;RhPr.
                                (3)   PERF CORR, 0

Mrs BROWN
    Joan,   `do   have
ThPr ThPr ; + ;CFocA > `ThPr ; + ;RhPr + ;Tr > DTho
a $_o$bit of $_{o'}$sense.
RhPr >   ,DTh.
                                (4)   R INT, 3
    You   `can't   lose $_o$money / by ,sneezing.
ThPr ` + ;RhPr DTho $_o$DTho /   ,DTh.
                                (5)*   PERF CORR, 1

SIMON
            ‿Joan $_o$can.
ThPr > ‿RhPr + ;RhPr > $_o$ + ;DTh.
                                (6)*   R INT, 3
        'Clever `girl, / my ,sister.
        [+]   '`RhPr /   ,ThPr.
                                (7)*   PERF CORR, 1

JOAN

Well,   we   were in `Oxford $_o$Street, / near `Selfridges.
TrPro ThPr + ;Tr   `$_o$Rh /              `RhPr.

(8)   PERF CORR, O

I   'felt   a `sneeze coming $_o$on.
ThPr ' + ;Tr (`RhPr $_o$ + ;Tr) `$_o$RhPr.

(9)*   PERF CORR, 0.2
(PERF CORR, 2)

So   I 'opened my °bag >quickly, /
TrPro ThPr ' + ;Tr   °Rh   >RhPr /

(10)   PERF CORR, O

and 'pulled out a `hanky.
' + ;Tr   `RhPr.

(11)   PERF CORR, O

I   `must have   °pulled out   my ˇnotecase /
ThPr   ˋ +   ° + ;Tr   ˇRh /
`with it.
DTh > `RhPr.

(12)*   R INT, DESH, O

(1)* The loss of money is a context-dependent notion. The field shows non-reevaluating prosodic intensification, because the transitional *did* is prosodically less prominent than ThPr, *you*, and the diathematic *lose* and *money*.

(5)* The sentence shows perfect correspondence between the two distributions. The notions of 'loss', 'money' and 'sneezing' occur in the post IC-shade on account of their context dependence. Nevertheless, the intonation pattern proportionately raises the degrees of CD by adducing the sentence to carry the additional meaning of incredulity and surprise. The pause also plays its part in throwing emphasis on *by sneezing*.

(6)* Both the notion of 'Joan' and that of 'ability' are retrievable. Owing to the interplay of the non-prosodic FSP factors, the only rhematic piece of information is therefore the counterassertion, conveyed by *can*. The re-evaluating prosodic intensification of *Joan* is in keeping with the speaker's taunting his sister; see his remark conveyed by the preceding sentence.

(7)* The verbless sentence contains no TMEs. The function of TrPr is vicariously signalled by intonation (see p. 93).

(9)* The notion of 'sneezing' occurs in the immediately preceding

Table 10.1. *Non-prosodic CD distribution and PP distribution in 82 distributional fields*

		%		%		%
PERF CORR	30	36·3 ⎫		59·6 ⎫		
PERF CORR*	16	19·7 ⎪	49		71	86·4
PERF CORR, REC DESH	2	2·4 ⎬				
PERF CORR, REC DESH*	1	1·2 ⎭				
N-R INT	22	26·8	22	26·8 ⎭		
R INT	7	8·6 ⎫				
R INT, DESH	2	2·5 ⎬	9	11·1	9	11·1
Truncated sentences	2	2·5	2	2·5	2	2·5
	82	100·0	82	100·0	82	100·0

context. It is, however, regarded as context-independent here. This is because Joan retells her story, 'beginning at the beginning'. In this way 'a sneeze' is introduced into the narration as a new piece of information.

(12)* The elements *I, pulled out* and *it* (pronominalizing *hanky*) convey retrievable, *must* and *notecase* irretrievable information. Such information, however, is also conveyed by the preposition *with*: the possibility of Joan's having unwillingly pulled out her handkerchief and her notecase at the same time. On account of their relational character, prepositions normally recede into the background and show little prosodic prominence. But if the degree of their prosodic prominence is intensified, the meaning conveyed by them becomes effectively foregrounded. This accounts for the IC on *with* – in other words, for the deshading of *with*, which emphasizes the notion of simultaneity.

As has been pointed out, the analysis of the twelve basic distributional fields of the conversation here examined has been taken over from Firbas 1987c, where an analysis of a further seventy basic distributional fields of the same conversation can be found. As for the relations between the non-prosodic CD distribution and the PP distribution as shown by all the eighty-two distributional fields of the conversation examined, they are reflected by the statistical table, 10.1. With the exception of two truncated sentences and seventeen verbless sentences (indicated by the asterisk in table 10.1), all the remaining sentences are verbal. One case requires special comment: it contains a clause subordinated to a verbless structure; on account of the missing superordinate verb, it has been classed with verbless fields. It should be borne in mind that the statistics are based on the data offered by the representative features of the communicative units within the basic distributional fields.

Table 10.1 reflects two significant facts: the predominating frequency of basic distributional fields displaying perfect correspondence between the non-prosodic CD distribution and the PP distribution (59.6 per cent), and the predominating frequency of basic distributional fields unaffected by re-evaluating prosodic intensification (86.4 per cent). The comparatively low frequency of basic distributional fields showing such re-evaluation (11.1 per cent) is in harmony with the marked character of re-evaluation. Its marked effect is underlined by the variety of types of its implementation.

Analysis of the second text

General analysis

Let me now turn to a portion of a dialogue recorded in the *Corpus* 116 (text S.1.4: tone units 614–52). The two interlocutors are denoted by A and B.

B: I   ‖don't know 'Leslie's △ ˅VIEWS /
          ThPr ‖ + ;NegFocA + ;Tr   '△ ˅RhPr /

                                        (1)   N–R INT, 0

          and   I   ‖sǎID TO ▷him   you ▷know /
          TrPro ThPr ‖ ˅ + ;Tr   ▷DTh (ThPr ▷ + ;RhPr) /

          ‖one of the THǏNGS that'd / ... as to ‖when we 'stop

          LĚCTURING this 'term /
          ... ‖ '˄'RhPr /

                                        (2)   N–R INT, 0.2
                                        (PERF CORR, NO NUCLEUS)

The opening sentence provides a short distributional field. On the other hand, the conjunction *and* introduces a very extensive field including a complex subfield (with further subfields). In relation to the transitional *SAID*, this complex subfield acts as an extensive RhPr. The words *you know* are regarded as an insertion and provide a distributional field of their own. The same applies to *you know* occurring further below in the dialogue.

The complex subfield lacks perfect syntactic organization. It contains two false starts (*one of the* THINGS *that'd*, *if we call all*). They loosen the structure, but do not efface the character of the relations within the complex, which is organized as follows:

‖one of the THÍNGS   that'd /   ·it ‖seems to 'me
           ‖´DTh /   ThPr‖ + ;Tr 'ThPro

it would… LÊCTURING this 'term /
           …⌃'RhPr /
                        (3)   N-R INT, 0.2

Moving one rank further down, we find the following subfield:

it would   'be CON△VĚNIENT / if …LÊCTURING
ThPr   + '+ ;Tr   △ˇRh/
this 'term /
… ⌃'RhPr/
                        (4)   N-R INT, 0.2

which in its turn contains the subfields:

if   we could ‖all ·   if   we ‖could   you
TrPro ThPr   + ‖DTh · TrPro ThPr   ‖+ (ThPr

KNOÝ / ‖[set]
´RhPr) / ‖[set]

"‖MÒRE or ▷less /   a‖gree TOGÉTHER / as to
"‖ˋ ▷Rh /   ‖+ ;Tr   ´Rh /

‖when   we 'stop LÊCTURING THIS 'term   /
(‖TrPro ThPr '+ ;Tr   ⌃RhPr   'RhPr)   RhPr /
                        (5)   N-R INT, 0.2
                    (PERF CORR, 0), (PERF CORR, 2)

(The interpretations of *MORE or less* and *TOGETHER* are tentative.) But the dialogue continues.

A: ‖if   we   could   ▷all what ·
       ‖TrPro ThPr   + ▷DTh   ·

B: A‖GRĖE / as to ‖when   we   △stop· △L̀ECTURING   /
         ‖ˇ + ;Tr /   (‖TrPro ThPr·△+ ;Tr· △ˇRhPr)   RhPr /

                                                        (6)   PERF CORR, o
                                                        (PERF CORR, o)

                    ‖Ì   SÁID /
         ThPr > ‖ˇRh   + ;Tr > ʼ + ;DTh /

                                                        (7)   R INT, 3

A does not properly catch the end of the extensive field as is indicated
by the dummy *what* of his unfinished sentence continued by B. The
continuation assumes the character of recapitulatory repetition.

I said shows re-evaluating intensification, an indication of B's serious
concern with the matter. This is in harmony with the falls on the
intensive *VERY* and *EMBARRASSED* in the following context. The syntactic
rank of the complex field opened by the *because*-clause (see below)
cannot be unequivocally determined. Does the clause belong to the
complex subfield re-opened by the recapitulatory clause, or is it
subordinated to *I said*, or does it open a new complex field in its own
right? In any case, it does open another complex field, the beginning of
which is quite efficiently indicated by *I said*. The structure of this
complex is as follows.

         be‖cause in △PRĖVIOUS YEÁRS / · [əm] you ‖KNÓW   /
         ‖TrPro   △ˇʼDTh / · (ThPr ‖ʼ + ;RhPr) /

         ‖I've been   ˇ"△VERY EMBÀRRASSED   by the FÁCT /
         ‖ThPr+   +   "△ˇTr   /

         that ... "△WELL /
         ʼ ... "△ˇRhPr/

                                                        (8)   N-R INT, o

Let us note that RhPr is constituted by a subfield in which *the FACT* acts
as Th (DTh) and the expanded *that*-clause as Rh (rheme proper). In
terms of their representative features, these two communicative units
display PERF CORR. The subfield provided by the *that*-clause shows
the following structure. (The interpretations of its subfields are adduced
in parentheses.)

‖though   I' m   'not ·   EX△ĂMINING /
(TrPro ThPr +'NegFocA · + ;ᵛRhPr)   DTh /
‖none the LE̅S̅S̅ / · ‖teaching 'seems to △come to an EN̂D /
    ⁻ᵀTrPro / ·   ‖ThPr   '+   △ + ;Tr   ´Rh /

    you ‖KNOŴ   / after a▷bout △six △WE̅EKS /
(ThPr ‖´RhPr) /   ▷△△ᵛRh /

which ‖suits me very " △WE̅LL/
(DTh ‖ + ;Tr ThPr   " △ᵛRhPr) RhPr /

                        (9)   N-R INT, o
            (PERF CORR, o) (PERF CORR, o), (PERF CORR, o)

B concludes with a distributional field provided by a *but*-clause.

    but ·   " I   haven't   'had the △same "GROUNDS
TrPro · "ThPr + ;NegFocA ' + ;Tr   △"ᵛRh

ACTUALLY / for ‖NOT 'going ON̂ /
    ´TrPro /   ‖ᵛ'´RhPr /

                        (10)   N-R INT, o

The noun phrase *for NOT going ON* shows PERF CORR. In the absence
of successful competitors (*going ON* is context-dependent), *NOT* ceases to
act as focus anticipator and expresses itself the negation focus.
    The dialogue continues.

A: but   you ‖   will   have △THIS year /
        TrPro ThPr‖ TrPro + ;Tr   △ᵛRhPr /

                        (11)   N-R INT, o

B: [ə]   I   ‖WI̅LL   have / " ‖TH̅IS 'year /
        ThPr   ‖ᵛTrPro + ;Tr /   " ‖ᵛ'Rh /

        cos   I' m EX‖ĂMINING
        (TrPro ThPr +   ‖ᵛRhPr) RhPr

                        (12)   N-R INT, o
                        (N-R INT, o)

The first part of B's sentence is a recapitulatory repetition (see p. 73). The CD relations as determined by the non-prosodic FSP factors remain the same. So do the PP relations between the communicative units. The prosodic intensification, however, has been further reinforced. Note the intensifications of *will* and *this year*.

B continues:

<pre>
    and   he [?] came   [ləu] ‖he'   s 'very STRONGLY
    TrPro DTh   + ;Tr   ‖DTh + ;Tr   '˅Rh
of the

OPINION /   that   we ‖ALL 'ought to go on TEACHING /
     / (TrPro ThPr ‖ ˅Rh   '+   ⁺ + ;DTh /

to the ‖end of △TERM   /
        ‖△ ˅RhPr) RhPr /
</pre>

$$(13) \quad \text{N–R INT, o}$$
$$(\text{N–R INT, o})$$

Together with the attributive *that*-clause, the noun OPINION constitutes one communicative unit, which serves as RhPr. The noun OPINION itself, however, is prosodically backgrounded, bearing a lower degree of PP than STRONGLY, which together with *very* serves as an intensive. The prosodic backgrounding of *go on TEACHING* is primarily due to context dependence. It contributes towards greater PP of ALL.

<pre>
A: REALLY /
       ⌃RhPr /
B: and   he ‖thinks   it'   s 'rather 'scandalous
       TrPro TrPr ‖ + ;Tr (ThPr + ;Tr   "Rh

       that   we   △DON'T   /.
       [TrPro ThPr △ ˅ + ;NegFocA ;RhPr] RhPr) RhPr /.
</pre>

$$(14) \quad \text{PERF CORR, o}$$
$$(\text{PERF CORR, o}), [\text{N–R INT, o}]$$

<pre>
       [ɑ:] ‖HE [sə]   ‖HE   'said /
       ‖ ˅ThPr   ‖ ˅ThPr '+ ;Tr /
</pre>

The verb *said* introduces a quotation of Leslie's words vehemently criticizing the dons. The vehemence has already been underlined by the prosodic intensification of *very STRONGLY* and by the adjective *scandalous*. In the quotation, which follows, it is underlined by the prosodic intensification of *AMAZED* and *STILL*. The rise in PP shown by *HE* fits in with all these prosodic intensifications. The verb *said* serves as a transitional element in relation to the field provided by the quotation.

‖I' m A△MÁZED /   that ‖dons   should △STÌLL BE /
‖ThPr+ △ˇ + ;Tr / (TrPro ‖DTh   + △ˇTrPro + /
− [əm]− pre‖paring their 'lectures at the 'end of the
            + ;Tr   'Rh
'summer   Tᴇᴿᴹ   /
        "ˇRhPr)   RhPr /
                    (15)   N-R INT, o
                           (N-R INT, o)
   and   I ‖   said   well   I   don't 'really
TrPro ThPr ‖ + ;Tr (TrPro ThPr + ;NegFocA 'TrPro
   think   this 'makes any △DIFFERENCE   /
   + ;Tr [DTh ' + ;Tr   △ˇRhPr]   RhPr) RhPr /
                    (16)   PERF CORR, o
                           (N-R INT, o), [PERF CORR, o]

Prosodic features of the finite verb

Concentrating on the finite verbs in the short section taken from the *Corpus*, we find that their total number is thirty-three. Only eight are competitorless and become rhemes proper. It is worth noticing that five of them (in fields 2, 5, 7, 8, 9) occur in short sentence structures (distributional fields) interrupting the flow of communication as insertions; cf. *You know, I said.* (To be distinguished from the same combination of words well integrated in the flow of communication; cf. *I am sure you know what I mean.*) Under these circumstances, only three competitorless verbs (9, 12, 14) serve as rhemes proper in 'ordinary' distributional fields. The rest of the thirty-three verbs, twenty-five in all, concur with successful competitors and are transitional. Through their TMEs, all the thirty-three verbs perform the function of TrPr.

Table 10.2 *Prosodic-level FSP functions of the finite verbs examined* (*1*)

	DTh	Tr	RhPr
Non-nuclear	–	27	1
Non-IC nucleus	1	4	–
IC nucleus	–	–	6

As for the prosodic implementation, one of the eight rhemes proper (7) is re-evaluated to DTh and bears a non-IC nucleus. With one exception (2), the remaining seven rhemes proper are all IC bearers. (The exception is due to one occurrence of the *You know* structure in the post-IC prosodic shade.)

Out of the twenty-five transitional verbs, twenty-one bear a non-nuclear prosodic feature and four a non-IC nucleus. The non-IC nuclei (2, 6, 12, 15) are cases of non-reevaluating prosodic intensification.

As for the verbal auxiliary, let me just add that in one case (14) it conveys RhPr; it does so in the absence of the verbal notional component and any other competitors, and bears the IC. Otherwise the auxiliary remains within the transitional sphere, showing non-reevaluating prosodic intensification in three cases (bearing a non-IC nucleus in field 12 and a more prominent non-nuclear feature than the verbal notional component in fields 1 and 11).

The results of this analysis of the FSP functions of the thirty-three finite verbs at the prosodic level can be tabulated as in table 10.2

The analysis just offered testifies to the tendency of the verb to perform a non-rhematic (in an overwhelming majority of cases, transitional) function.

The objection could be raised that the thirty-three finite verbs represent a very small group not permitting reliable generalization. But the tendency of the verb towards non-rhematicity is also borne out by the statistics covering the entire dialogue S.1.4 in the *Corpus*. The number of finite verbs occurring in this dialogue amounts to 809.

For the purpose in hand these statistics have been simplified in the following way. They are concerned with (i) whether the finite verbs are rhematic or non-rhematic, special note being taken of such as owe their status to re-evaluating prosodic intensification; and (ii) whether they bear the IC nucleus or a non-IC nucleus or a non-nuclear prosodic feature.

Table 10.3 *Prosodic-level FSP functions of the finite verbs examined* (2)

	Non-Rh	RhPr	
Non-nuclear	513	8	
Non-IC nucleus	61	–	
IC nucleus	–	227	
	574 (70.95%)	235 (29·04%)	809 (100%)

The simplifications adopted mean the following. 1 As rhematicity is opposed to non-rhematicity, no distinction is made between thematicity and transitionalness, let alone between various degrees of thematicity or transitionalness. But let me recall that the role of the verb in the thematic section is very much restricted, and that categorial exponents (through the TMEs) invariably perform the function of TrPr. What is relevant to the present statistics is whether within its distributional field the verb expresses or does not express the piece of information towards which the field is perspectived.

Let me recapitulate that such information is expressed by the verb (i) through its notional component if no successful competitor is present, or (ii) through its categorial exponent(s) if in the absence of successful competitors even its notional component has ceased to act as one, or (iii) in the presence of competitors, through its notional component or its categorial exponent(s) re-evaluated to RhPr by prosodic intensification.

2 When the finite verb form bears more than one prosodic feature (which happens when it consists of more than one word), only the most prominent of them has been recorded. This is as rule borne by the notional component. The comments, however, will state the number of cases in which the most prominent feature has appeared on an auxiliary.

As the presence of re-evaluating prosodic intensification is opposed to its absence, no distinction is made between prefect correspondence, and non-selective or selective non-reevaluating prosodic intensification. Only the Non-Rh > RhPr and the RhPr > Non-Rh re-evaluations are taken into account.

Carried out on the lines indicated, the statistics yield the results shown in table 10.3 concerning the prosodic features of the finite verb form and its FSP status in the spoken distributional field. Out of the 227 rhemes proper (the IC nucleus group), 188 are conveyed by verbal notional components and 39 by auxiliaries. Out of these 227 rhemes proper, fourteen (notional components and four auxiliaries) owe their status to re-evaluating prosodic intensification. With one exception, all the 61 non-IC nucleus bearers are notional components.

It is significant that the Non-Rhs do not bear IC nuclei. Their prosodic feature is either non-nuclear or a non-IC nucleus. With the exception of eight cases, the rhemes proper are all IC nucleus bearers. The eight non-nuclear rhemes proper, however, are not difficult to account for. Each of them occurs within a distributional field provided by a *You know* structure that is syntactically unrelated to what precedes and to what follows, and acts as an insertion (see p. 201). Within its field, each RhPr is prosodically more prominent than the Non-Rh, but the field itself is prosodically backgrounded. This accounts for the absence of an IC-nucleus within it (ibid.).

Let me add some more comment on the verb in the *You know* type of insertion. (In the dialogue, two other word pairs, *I see* and *I say*, act in the same way as *I know* if serving as insertions.) In all (forty-one) cases the verb is context-independent, competitorless and therefore conveying RhPr. If not shaded (in thirty-three cases), the insertion has an IC nucleus, which in a majority of cases (twenty-seven) actually occurs on the verb; see items 5, 8 and 9 of the dialogue section. The occurrence of the IC on the subject (in six cases) is due to re-evaluating prosodic intensification; cf.

‖which was ex'tremely △NÌCE of him / − ‖but [ə:] – he △DÒESN'T 'want to 'do [ð] / ‖YǑU 'know /
(*Corpus* S.1.4: 1010–11)

The re-evaluation intensifies the speaker's appeal to the listener to draw the conclusion hinted at himself.

As with tags and unfinished sentences, the type just discussed forms a peripheral group within the corpus offered by the dialogue. If these three groups are excluded from the statistics, the tendency of the verb to perform a non-Rh function becomes even more prominent. Before giving the statistics so altered, let me briefly comment on the tag questions and the unfinished sentences.

In all the tag questions (seventeen in all), the verbal element expresses RhPr and bears the IC (cf. *CGEL* 810). But in two of what the *CGEL* would regard as another type of reduced question (*CGEL* 133), the IC occurs on the pronominal subject. Let us note that in contrast with the

Table 10.4 *Prosodic-level FSP functions of the finite verbs examined (3)*

	Non-Rh	RhPr	
Non-nuclear	477	–	
Non-IC nucleus	54	–	
IC nucleus	–	180	
	531 (74·68%)	180 (25·32%)	711 (100%)

subjects of the tag questions, the subjects of the two reduced questions are context-independent on account of the contrast they convey. They act as successful competitors of the verbal element; cf.

$$\|\text{I} \quad \triangle\text{think} \quad {}'\text{we} \quad \overset{\backprime}{\text{COULD}} \quad /$$
$$\|\text{ThPr} \triangle + ;\text{Tr ('ThPr} \overset{\backprime}{\,} + ;\text{RhPr) RhPr} /$$
$$\|\text{don't} \quad \text{YO}\acute{\text{U}}$$
$$\| + ;\text{Tr};\text{NegFocA} \, {}^{\nearrow}\text{RhPr}$$

(*Corpus* S.1.4: 225–6)

PERF CORR

A natural spontaneous dialogue does not consist exclusively of perfectly organized structures. In the dialogue under examination, forty finite verbs – fully or only partly implemented – occur in structures that are to be regarded as fragmentary. In none of them does the verb serve as RhPr, but performs a non-rhematic (as a rule, transitional) function in an unfinished distributional field. In a majority of cases (thirty-three) it bears a non-nuclear prosodic feature. In six cases it bears a non-IC nucleus showing non-reevaluating prosodic intensification. For examples, see the false starts in items 3 and 13 in the dialogue section analysed.

Let us now look at the statistics covering all the finite verbs of the dialogue examined to the exclusion of the verbs of the three groups discussed above (see table 10.4).

It is certainly significant that the FSP functions performed by the verb in the spoken sentence tallies with the degrees of PP it carries. This observation, however, applies also to all the cases covered by table 10.3 above. It applies also to the eight rhemes proper that are recorded by table 10.3 as not bearing an IC nucleus, for, though not bearing a nucleus, they do bear the most prominent prosodic feature within their fields. In this way the FSP function they perform tallies with the degree of PP.

Frequencies of the types of correspondence between the non-prosodic distribution of communicative dynamism and that of prosodic prominence

It may be asked how frequent the cases of perfect correspondence, those of selective non-reevaluating prosodic intensification and those of re-evaluating prosodic intensification are in the dialogue under examination. In order to answer this question, I have subjected to statistical analysis the section of the dialogue extending from tone unit 684 to the end, i.e. tone unit 1227. Excluding incomplete fields, the statistics cover (i) basic distributional fields and (ii) subfields of all ranks as provided by subordinated clauses. The prosodic features taken into account are those representing the communicative units within their fields.

The section contains 387 basic distributional fields. In terms of representative features, 251 (64·86 per cent) of them show perfect correspondence, 118 (30.49 per cent) selective non-reevaluating prosodic intensification and 18 (4.65 per cent) re-evaluating prosodic intensification. The frequency of perfect correspondence would be lower if one-word sentences (108 in all) were not counted. Then 166 (54.97 per cent) of the basic distributional fields would show perfect corre-spondence, 118 (39.07 per cent) selective non-reevaluating prosodic intensification and 18 (5.96 per cent) re-evaluating prosodic intensifi-cation. The frequency of perfect correspondence would be still lower if tags and insertions of the *You know* type were not counted. The respective frequencies and percentages would then be: 143 (51.25 per cent), 118 (42.30 per cent) and 18 (6.45 per cent). The subfields, ninety in all, yield the following frequencies and percentages: 35 (38.89 per cent), 49 (54.45 per cent) and 6 (6.66 per cent).

Of particular interest are the results yielded by the analysis of the fields showing selective non-reevaluating prosodic intensification. In this connection let me concentrate on the 118 basic fields showing such intensification and add a summarizing statement concerning the forty-nine subfields coming under the same heading.

Dealing with selective non-reevaluating prosodic intensification, we have to bear in mind that prosodic intensification is linked with prosodic weakening. Elements prosodically weakened permit other elements to be selected for prosodic intensification. Out of the 118 basic fields, 105 show

Table 10.5 *Selective non-reevaluating prosodic intensification of 105 distributional fields*

	Intensified Th-elements	Weakened Tr-elements	Number of fields		
(i)	1p	1	21	21	
(ii)	2	1	49 ⎫ 57		
(iii)	2p	2	8 ⎭		105
(iv)	3	1	18 ⎫		
(v)	3	2	8 ⎬ 27		
(vi)	3p	3	1 ⎭		

prosodic weakening of the Tr permitting the prosodic intensification of the Th and twelve show prosodic intensification and prosodic weakening taking place within the Tr. It is only in one basic field that the selective non-reevaluating prosodic intensification operates exclusively within the Th. It is worth noticing that the section most frequently affected by weakening is the Tr. The elements not involved in the intensification and weakening process show perfect correspondence between the non-prosodic CD distribution and the PP distribution. It is significant that among such elements are those that constitute the Rh.

The weakened transitional elements are represented by a verbal auxiliary and/or a notional component of the finite verb and/or a conjunction and/or a sentence adverb, the last two being TrPro.

Features causing prosodic intensification

Let me now take a closer look at the prosodic features that within the 105 basic distributional fields under examination cause the prosodic intensification of the thematic elements, on the one hand, and those causing the prosodic weakening of the transitional elements, on the other. They are shown in table 10.5. The degrees of PP are indicated as follows: 1, 2 and 3 stand for absence of stress, non-nuclear stress and non-IC nuclear stress, respectively; an added 'p' (1p, 2p, 3p) indicates intensification through position. (Of two prosodic features of the same rank, the one occurring later displays a rise in PP; see p. 144). In table 10.5 each numeral indicator stands for the highest degree present within the intensified or the weakened section of the field.

The 105 basic distributional fields showing selective non-reevaluating prosodic intensification fall into six groups, which can be reduced to three. The following six sentences illustrate the six groups. In all of them Th is affected by prosodic intensification through the prosodic weakening of Tr. The Th–Rh relationship as signalled by the non-prosodic distribution is perfectly reflected by the PP distribution.

Since I am dealing with basic distributional fields, I shall discuss the examples in terms of the representative features of the communicative units of these fields. The subfields will be at least touched upon below (p. 201). Each example is introduced by the number of its group and the abbreviations of the element(s) intensified and the element(s) weakened. The numbers following the abbreviations stand for the degrees of PP. The numbers following the tone units examined are those assigned by the *Corpus* (S.1.4).

(i)   *ThPr – 1p, TrPro – 1*

       but   it   ‖does in F̀ACT /   (832)
       TrPro ThPr ‖ + ;Tr ˋRhPr /

(ii) *ThPr – 2, TrPr (+) – 1*

    ‖he' s SUR△PRI   SED/ that ‖we're PRE△PARING 'them /
                                        (660–1)

    ‖ThPr +   △ˋ + ;Tr/   ‖△ˇ'RhPr /

(iii) *ThPr – 2p, TrPro – 2 (and TrPr (+) – 1)*

     so ‖probably   [j] △you   will 'have "△more
       ‖TrPro   △ThPr   + '+ ;Tr
     SCRÍPTS / than ‖I shall 'have in △two △special
     "△ˊRh /

            ‖SÙBJECTS /   (865–6)
     ‖'△△△ˋRhPr /

(iv) *DTh – 3, TrPr (+) – 1 and TrPro – 1*

       but   ‖she' s △been 'rather [ə] – E△LÙSIVE /
       TrPro ‖ThPr +   △ +   '△ˋRhPr /

     as 'far as 'I'm CONCÉRNED /   (909)
              "ˊDTh /

(v)   *ThPr – 3, Tr – 2*

        ‖HÈ [Sə] ‖HÈ   'said / ‖I'm A△MÀZED , that ‖dons
        ‖ˋThPr ‖ˋTrPr   '+ ;Tr /   /

    should △STÌLL be / – [əm] – pre‖paring their
              /

'lectures at the 'end of the 'summer TĔRM /   (648–51)
　　　　　　‖△`‖△`‖'''ᵛRhPr /

(vi)　*DTh – 3p, TrPro – 3*

in "‖FȦCT 'Joseph / with"‖out being "△ȦSKED /　‖did
"‖`TrPro 'ThPro /　　　　　"‖"△ᵛDTh / ‖ + ;Tr

　　　it HIM"△SĔLF /   (1004–6)
　ThPr　"△`RhPr /

Table 10.6 *Frequencies of prosodic features on intensified thematic and weakened transitional elements*

		1	1p	2	2p	3	3p
(i)	Th	–	60	–	–	–	–
	Tr	40	–	–	–	–	–
(ii–iii)	Th	–	6	50	10	–	–
	Tr	67	2	12	–	–	–
(iv–v–vi)	Th	–	–	19	–	28	1
	Tr	25	–	10	–	1	–

The list of possible combinations of features would be longer if all the concurring features of lower prominence were enumerated. Table 10.6 gives at least the total frequencies of all the prosodic features as they occur on the intensified thematic and on the weakened transitional elements. The distinctiveness of the effect produced by the intensification and the weakening depends on the degrees of PP involved. A low degree of obviousness as displayed by group (i) brings the PP distribution close to perfect correspondence with the non-prosodic CD distribution. On the other hand, an obvious intensification of the Th and an obvious weakening of one or more transitional elements effectively indicate non-reevaluating prosodic intensification.

Table 10.7 shows which elements are affected by the prosodic weakening in the group of fields under discussion. Let me add that the fifty-five TrPr bearers are twenty-six auxiliary and twenty-nine non-auxiliary verb forms (the latter being represented by the verb *to be* in twenty-three, and by other verbs in six cases). The twenty-six cases TrPr bearers are sixteen auxiliary and ten non-auxiliary verb forms (the latter being represented by the verb *to be* in seven and by other verbs in

Table 10.7 *Elements affected by prosodic weakening in the 105 basic fields under discussion*

			%
Bearer of TrPr (+)	55 ⎫		
Bearer of TrPr (+), together with another transitional element	26 ⎬	81	77·14
TrPro element	24 ⎭	24	22·86
Total	105	105	100·00

three cases). The TrPro within the group of twenty-four cases is implemented in twenty-two cases by a conjunction and in two cases by a sentence adverb.

It is worth noticing that in an overwhelming majority (77.14 per cent) of the 105 fields under examination it is the bearer of TrPr that, either on its own or together with another transitional element, constitutes a point of prosodic weakness within the field. In the remaining cases (22.86 per cent), which come close to perfect correspondence between the non-prosodic CD distribution and the PP distribution, it is a TrPro element that shows prosodic weakening.

It can hardly be due to chance that selective non-reevaluating prosodic intensification predominantly involves the weakening of transitional elements (see p. 206), in particular the bearer of TrPr. The prosodic weakening of TrPr is not at variance with its serving as a link and simultaneously as a boundary between the Th and the Non-Th. Through selective non-reevaluating prosodic intensification, the elements to be linked can receive greater prosodic prominence than the element(s) establishing the link. The function of TrPr is in fact only promoted thereby.

Taking into account that, if present in the field, the DTh is always the most prosodically prominent element in the Th and the RhPr always the most prosodically prominent element in the Non-Th, we find that the prosodic weakening of TrPr or of even a wider Tr lends greater PP to the DTh (or in its absence to another thematic element), on the one hand, and to the RhPr, on the other. A distinct prosodic intensification of the DTh (or in its absence another thematic element) linked with a distinct prosodic weakening of TrPr or even a wider Tr effectively balances the Th against the Rh with the RhPr as its most prominent element and IC bearer.

The above conclusions are based on an investigation of basic distributional fields. Considerations of space prevent me from offering an equally detailed analysis of distributional subfields. It would yield a similar picture.

It is not without interest to note that all the subfields in the above examples show selective non-reevaluating prosodic intensification and that in each case Th is intensified through the weakening of TrPr and, if present, a TrPro-element. All these subfields come under the heading of type (ii).

(ii) *ThPr – 2, ThPro – 2p, TrPr (+) – 1p, TrPro – 1*

that ‖we' re PREPˇARING 'them /
TrPro ‖ThPr + △ˇ + ;RhPr 'ThPro /

(ii) *ThPr – 2, TrPr (+) – 1p, TrPro – 1*

than ‖I shall 'have in two △special △SUˊBJECTS /
TrPro ‖ThPr + ' + ;Tr △△ˊRhPr /

(ii) *ThPr – 2p, TrPr (+) – 1, TrPro – 2*

as 'far as 'I' m CONCEˊRNED /
'TrPro 'ThPr + ˊRhPr /

(ii) *ThPr – 2, TrPr (+) – 1*

‖I' m A△MAˋZED / that ‖dons
‖ThPr + △ˋ + ;Tr /

should △STˋILL be / – [əm] – pre‖paring their
/

'lectures at the 'end of the 'summer TEˇRM /
‖△ˋ‖''ˇRhPr /

(ii) *DTh – 2, TrPr (+) – 1p, TrPro – 1*

that ‖dons should △STˋILL be / – [əm] –
TrPro ‖DTh + △ˋTrPro + /
pre‖paring their
‖ + ;Tr
'lectures at the 'end of the 'summer TEˇRM /
'Rh ''ˇRhPr /

It has been shown that the TMEs serve as a simple FSP signal. Let me repeat that the way this signal is treated by non-selective prosodic intensification is not at variance with its function of acting as a link/boundary between the Th and the Non-Th.

The relevance of degrees of prosodic prominence to functional sentence perspective

Have the foregoing analyses of single sentences and stretches of text disproved or corroborated the assumption that the degrees of PP have relevance to FSP? At this point it is important to note that though not doubting the phonetic reality of the degrees of stress, Szwedek maintains that 'only nuclear stress has a function and in this it is opposed not only to the lack of stress but also to the lower degrees of stress' (1986: 34; and see *passim*). In his view, it has not yet been proved that communicative functions can be ascribed to the degrees of stress beyond this dichotomy (1986: 34).

As for the correlation between the gamut of CD and the gamut of PP, it must be remembered that the numbers of degrees of CD and PP depend on the given distributional field. Both gamuts are expandable. In terms of interpretative arrangement, the degrees of CD keep on rising as long as the development of the communication within the distributional field has not been completed. As for the gamut of degrees of PP, let me recall that it can be expanded owing to the operation of linear modification which lends different prominence to prosodic features of the same phonic status. The gamut of degrees of PP is further expandable through the modifications caused by special configurations of prosodic features. If in the interpretative arrangement a constant gradual rise in CD as determined by the non-prosodic FSP factors corresponds to a constant gradual rise in PP, the distributional field shows perfect correspondence between the non-prosodic CD distribution and the PP distribution. Types of non-reevaluating intensification and re-evaluating intensification are assessed against the background of this perfect correspondence. As for the number of the thematic and the non-thematic functions, it depends on the structure of the distributional field. Strictly speaking, none of these functions is invariably linked with one particular prosodic feature, although it may show a more or less distinct tendency to associate with such a feature (e.g., a RhPr with nuclear stress). This is due to the fact that both the concept of CD and that of PP are relational concepts. It is the gradient relation between the degrees that matters.

Against the outlined network of relations between the non-prosodic CD distribution and the PP distribution, the investigator can decide on the degree of delicacy with which to approach this network in accordance with the aim of the investigation. The investigator can, for instance, choose to study the relation between the bearer of the most prominent prosodic feature and all the bearers of the less prominent features (see Szwedek's approach mentioned above), or limit the investigation in another way (see tables 10.5, 10.6 and 10.7). In my approach I would, however, always do so against the background of the entire network of relations.

An enquiry into the relationship between the non-prosodic CD distribution and the PP distribution shows that the degrees of PP perform a significant role in FSP as implemented in the spoken language; in other words, they perform important communicative functions. This is the conclusion that can be drawn from the preceding chapters. It does not substantiate Szwedek's pessimistic view that 'although it is possible to distinguish four degrees of stress (as has been done by phoneticians), no communicative functions have been found to reflect this differentiation' (1986: 64).

11 Some special issues concerning functional sentence perspective in the spoken language

The foregoing discussions enable me to formulate my view of the contextual applicability of the spoken sentence structure, answer the question whether CD can be equated with PP, summarize the role of intonation in FSP, subscribe to Vachek's assessment of the relationship between the written language and the spoken language, account for the concept of potentiality and assess the role of the contextual factor in FSP.

Functional sentence perspective and the contextual applicability of the spoken sentence structure

Discussing FSP in written communication, I posed the question of the contextual applicability in FSP of the written semantic and grammatical sentence structure. Let me now add a note on FSP contextual applicability in the spoken language. An enquirer into contextual applicability is free to choose the structure, the applicability of which he wishes to assess; but in doing so, he has to determine which features are to be regarded as constitutive, i.e. as identifying the structure.

Examining the contextual applicability in FSP of a written sentence structure on pages 110–14, I regarded the words used, their syntactic implementation, their linear arrangement and – if employed – their typographical intensification (its italicization, for instance) as such constitutive features. A different word and/or another syntactic implementation and/or a change in word order and/or a difference in typographical intensification would have created a different sentence structure.

Examining the contextual applicability in FSP of a spoken sentence structure, I exclude from the features just enumerated the signals of typographical intensifications, but add the PP distribution. The presence of the PP distribution narrows the contextual applicability of the structure. Not invariably, but frequently, it restricts the operation of the structure to one instance level:

> ˋAll this ˇtravelling / makes me   ˋravenous.
> ˋˇDTh   / + ;Tr ThPr ˋRhPr.

For instance, the structure *We ˋcan't miss the ˇCup ₒFinal* can operate either on an ordinary first-instance level where *the Cup Final* is context-independent (a), or on a re-evaluating first-instance level, where *the Cup Final* is a carrier of context-dependent information and simultaneously also of recapitulation, a piece of context-independent information (b). Re-evaluating instance levels are additionally created within the first-instance sphere by the spoken language.

> We   ˋcan't   miss the   ˇCup   ₒFinal.
> ThPr ˋ+ ;NegFocAnt Tr   ˇₒRhPr. (a)
> ThPr ˋ+ ;NegFocAnt RhPr > Tr DTh > ˇₒRhPr. (b).

Similarly, the structure *ˇHe's looking ₒpleased with himself* operates either on an ordinary first-instance level when the shaded elements convey context-dependent information, or on a re-evaluating first-instance level when *looking* and *pleased* convey context-independent information.

> ˇHe'   s   looking
> ˇRhPr   +   + ;DTho
> ThPr > ˇRhPr+   + ;Tr > + ;DTho
>   ₒpleased with himself.
>   ₒDTh   DTho. (a)
> RhPr > ₒDTh   ThPro.(b)

The PP distribution is a powerful signal of FSP. Nevertheless, as has been shown, it does not operate independently of the non-prosodic signals.

By normally restricting the applicability of a structure to one instance level, intonation reduces the frequency of potentiality almost to a minimum. That it does not do so invariably (p. 183) is not surprising. Not even the spoken language is a rigidly closed system.

Let me add just one more note on FSP contextual applicability in the spoken language. It concerns sentences operating on the basic instance level. Szwedek criticizes Bílý, who in principle advocates an FSP approach as presented in this study and my previous writings, for wanting 'to reconstruct the intonation of an isolated (context-free) sentence' (1986: 36; cf. Bílý 1981: 43). He finds that such an attempt reflects 'the fundamental contradiction between the basic assumption of FSP, which is context dependency, and the concept of context-free (isolated) sentences' (Szwedek 1986: 36). This critique is based on a misunderstanding. What is meant by an 'isolated' or 'context-free' written sentence in Bílý's argument is a sentence neither preceded nor followed by verbal context, nor taking over any information from the immediately relevant situational context. In an act of communication such a sentence simultaneously represents an opening and a closing sentence of a text. In the approach advocated by Bílý and myself, such a sentence is context-independent and operates on the basic instance level.

Now it must be remembered that the basic instance level is not determined without regard to context (see p. 112). It must also be remembered that if not further qualified 'context independence' means zero dependence on (independence from) the immediately relevant context (see p. 31). Zero dependence on (independence from) the immediately relevant context does not exclude dependence on the part of context extending beyond the immediately relevant sphere; see p. 112). Let me recall that it is the elements independent of the immediately relevant context that actually develop the communication.

When reading out (intoning) a sentence operating on the basic instance level, we must naturally take into consideration the non-prosodic CD distribution as determined by the interplay of linear modification and the semantic factor. No elements that are dependent on the immediately relevant context as delimited in my writings and through which the contextual factor operates are present on the basic instance level.

Can communication dynamism be equated with prosodic prominence?

Commenting on my formulation 'the distribution of degrees of CD over the sentence elements (the signalling of degrees) is an outcome of an interplay of three factors: context, semantic structure, linear arrangement' (Firbas 1971: 138), Lötscher thinks that the statement on the interplay of the three factors makes sense only when CD is equated with PP ('Akzentuierungsstärke', accentual intensity, in Lötscher's terms); only then can it be interpreted to say that sentence stress is determined by context, semantic structure and word order. He quotes my interpretations (in Firbas 1974: 21) as evidence for my frequently deducing the distribution of CD directly from the stress (intonation) pattern of the sentence. He concludes that such short-circuiting deduction of the degree of CD from the degree of PP can only mean an equation of CD with PP, and that the degree of CD is a redundant concept (Lötscher 1983: 72–3).

This is the passage from Firbas (1974: 21) quoted by Lötscher:

Not all types of semantic content, however, are capable of signalling degrees of CD in the way indicated above. This is borne out by the following examples, each of which contains a contextually independent indirect and a contextually independent direct object: *He gave a boy an apple, He gave an apple to a boy*. Of the two objects, the one occurring later evidently carries a higher degree of CD. Similarly, a contextually independent infinitive of purpose will carry a lower degree of CD when occurring initially than when occurring finally: *In order to meet his friend, he went to Prague, He went to Prague in order to meet his friend*.

It is important to note that the syntactic elements involved are not regarded as severed from, but linked with, certain types of semantic content. The purpose of the passage is to demonstrate that, in contrast with types of semantic content whose CD is in principle unaffected by sentence position (linear modification) and which are illustrated in the paragraphs preceding the passage, there are types of semantic content which are affected by sentence position and whose different positions perspective the sentence in different ways. This is exemplified by the members of the pairs adduced in the passage.

Concentrating on the effect produced by linear modification, the passage does not discuss the degree of CD of each element. It assumes the knowledge of the arguments offered in the discussion immediately preceding, which recalls the roles played in FSP by the semantic character of the personal pronoun and that of the verb–direct object combination. The context dependence/independence of the elements concerned is also duly considered. All the three non-prosodic FSP factors are taken into account and it is demonstrated how their interplay operates in determining the distribution of degrees of CD. This is the setting in which the passage in question appears. It is unjustified to claim that the distribution of CD has been directly deduced from the accentual structure, in other words the distribution of PP. The distribution of PP is not mentioned in the passage at all.

The accentual structure (PP) ascribed by the critic to the sentences under examination corroborates the interpretation offered at the level of the written language. Intonation, which is absent from the inventory of the means of the written language, indeed reflects the CD distribution as determined by the interplay of the non-prosodic FSP factors. But although it does not operate independently of these factors, it is not a mere reflecter of the degrees of CD as they are determined by them. It also acts as a non-reevaluating or a re-evaluating intensifier of the degrees of CD.

The concept of CD cannot therefore be equated with the concept of PP. Doing so denies the written language the capability of signalling degrees of CD, and prevents the spoken language from being viewed as capable of intensifying them in various ways. The equation of the concept of CD with that of PP does not do justice to the role played by PP in FSP.

Summarizing the role of intonation in functional sentence perspective

Another observation concerning the role of intonation in FSP comes, for instance, from Keijsper, who maintains: 'The basic misunderstanding in many publications on FSP is that they attempt to show that the accentuation and/or word order of a sentence is the *consequence* of the fact that some elements are the theme and others the rheme' (1985: 71; italicized by Keijsper).

What is a consequence of what in my approach? I will first concentrate on the written language and introduce my reply with another three questions. Is linear modification the consequence of degrees of CD? Are the semantic characters of an element (its semantic character and the character of the semantic relations into which it enters) the consequence of a degree of CD? Is the operation of the immediately relevant context the consequence of a degree of CD? The answers are in the negative. It is the outcome of the interplay of the three factors mentioned that determines the degrees of CD and their distribution over the written sentence, i.e. its FSP. The degrees of CD and ultimately FSP (the theme and the non-theme in general, and all the thematic and all the non-thematic functions in particular) are the consequence of the interplay. It is not the other way round.

However, language is not only produced; it is also received and perceived. The language user therefore keeps on changing roles, alternately acting as encoder and decoder. A correct encoding and decoding of FSP presupposes the knowledge of the code, consisting in the laws of the interplay of factors, which leads to the production of simple or complex signals of CD. No matter in which direction the language user proceeds – no matter whether he acts as encoder or decoder – he (as a rule subconsciously) appreciates that a degree of CD is the outcome (consequence) of the interplay of the FSP factors. The cause–consequence direction does not change with the change of the language user's roles. There is no circularity involved.

Acting as decoder of FSP, the recipient naturally goes by the signals offered by the sentence. For the sake of the clarity of the argument let me recall that in regard to a written sentence element, the signalling role is performed by the following (i) the formal (syntactic) implementation of the element and the formal (syntactic) implementation of its relation to other elements, these implementations serving as vehicles of the semantic content of the element and of its semantic character; and/or (ii) the position of the element in the linear arrangement; and/or (iii) its relation to the immediately relevant context depending on the presence or absence of a predecessor in or from this section of context. From the viewpoint of the decoder of a written sentence, the phenomena (i), (ii) and (iii) represent the means (devices) of FSP whose interaction signals the degree of CD carried by a written sentence element.

I have so far not mentioned accentuation, or intonation for that matter, because it is not present in the written form of language. Turning to intonation, I must repeat here the gist of the argument presented in the preceding section. As a participant in the interplay of FSP factors, intonation cannot operate independently of the other FSP factors. It asserts itself in its specific contributory way if it effects prosodic intensification, non-reevaluating or re-evaluating, and thereby raises the degree of CD already assigned to the element by the non-prosodic factors.

The decoder of the spoken sentence naturally goes by the prosodic features which serve as means and signals of FSP in the spoken language. But evaluating them he does so in relation to the non-prosodic means of FSP. Even in the spoken language, the cause–consequence direction in regard to degrees of CD remains the same both for the encoder and the decoder.

Let me add that Keijsper's interpretation of the theme and the rheme results from the interaction of three factors: accentuation, word order and the phenomenon ensuring that accents have a certain scope (Keijsper 1985: 145). Let me also add that Keijsper argues that 'the theory of Functional Sentence Perspective as it was devised by Mathesius and developed by his followers fails to account for the phenomena it studies' (ibid.: 143). As the present study does not offer a survey of the state of the art (see p. xi), I cannot discuss Keijsper's approach as much as it would deserve, but at least some of her objections are further dealt with in the two following sections. They concern a very important problem: that of the relationship between the written and the spoken language. Keijsper does not view this problem in the same way as I do.

Written language and spoken language

Keijsper correctly states that in dealing with written texts I do not deal with accentuation, but regards this as a drawback which testifies to the inadequacy of my approach. She insists that in describing the FSP of a sentence the investigator should proceed from accentuation. But accentuation is not a means of the written language. Keijsper is aware of this, but is consistent in adding accentuation to written sentences when interpreting them. In doing so, she does not regard the written language as a form of language in its own right. In her view, an analysis of FSP in a text that is available only in written form 'must be preceded by a reconstruction of the accentuation' (1985: 83). Such a reconstruction, however, can never be fully reliable (ibid.). Keijsper appreciates the existence of means employed by the written language to signal FSP, but regards them as mere cues for the missing accentuation. In a description of FSP, they should be subordinated to accentuation (1985: 84).

Keijsper's attitude to the written language is reminiscent of that of de Saussure, who regarded writing as a mere registration of spoken utterances, depreciating the specific functions served by the written language (see Vachek 1989: 103; Luelsdorff 1989: xii). I subscribe to the results of Vachek's extensive enquiries into the written language (e.g., 1989). They have established the spoken language and the written language as two language norms which 'differ not only materially (phonic vs. graphic substance) but...also functionally' (ibid.). Whereas Keijsper denies the written language the capability of direct correlation with content, i.e. without the mental or actual addition of accent (Keijsper 1985: 84), Vachek demonstrates that the written text can convey its meaning directly (1989: 100). 'No *détour* via the spoken utterances is absolutely necessary in deciphering' a written text (1989: 22; italicized by Vachek).

Not regarding the written language as a system in its own right, Keijsper does not regard the non-prosodic means of FSP as constituting a system either. But as I have attempted to show, these means participate in an interplay forming a system. Accentuation – or PP, in my terms – is absent from the written text and joins the systemic interplay of FSP means only in the spoken language, i.e. also in the process of transposing written utterances into spoken utterances. This process (and, vice versa, naturally also that of transposing spoken utterances into written utterances) is a linguistic fact established by Haas (see Haas 1970 and Vachek 1989: 206). Haas aptly speaks of 'phono-graphic translation'.

In transposing written utterances into spoken utterances, one can hardly subordinate the non-prosodic means of FSP to accentuation (PP). In adding accentuation to the written utterance, the transposer must let himself be guided by the outcome of the interplay of the non-prosodic means. Accentuation (the PP distribution) can reflect it or intensify it in a non-reevaluating or re-evaluating way, but can do so only against the background of perfect correspondence between the non-prosodic CD distribution and the PP distribution. I do not think that an approach can be regarded as inadequate if it accounts for the operation of FSP means within the written language without having recourse to accentuation (PP distribution), which operates outside it.

All this is relevant to the discussion of potentiality as sometimes displayed by a written sentence and removable through accentuation (PP distribution) at the level of the spoken language.

Potentiality revisited

Keijsper reacts to my concept of potentiality by quoting an example (from Firbas 1978: 43; requoted here on p. 109 and below) and by drawing the conclusion that the concept 'proves that a theory of FSP which treats a given accentuation as a consequence of placing an unaccented unit in a given context, is inadequate' (1985: 64).

> ... but those who seized Jesus took him away to the house of Caiaphas, where the scribes and elders had gathered (Moffatt: Matt. 26.57)

The gist of my argument in Firbas 1978 is that the contextual status of *the scribes and elders* is not unequivocal (see this volume, p. 109). Hence the possibility of perspectiving the *where*-clause either to the subject or to the verb.

As I see it, no accentuation (PP distribution) accompanies the written sentence. Under these circumstances, accentuation (PP distribution) comes into existence only in the course of 'grapho-phonic translation'. The two possible 'translations', each offering another perspective, only bear out the existence of the phenomenon of potentiality in the written language. But Keijsper's formulation is based on the assumption of the non-existence of the written language as a language system in its own right.

Potentiality in FSP is a linguistic fact. Language is not a rigidly closed system. It is a system that has its centre and its periphery (Daneš 1966; Vachek 1966). Potentiality occurs on its periphery. An approach can hardly be declared to be inadequate when it takes this phenomenon into account and is capable of demonstrating its existence.

The contextual factor revisited

Let me concentrate on at least one more problem raised by Keijsper. I have attempted to demonstrate the importance of context dependence/independence (retrievability/irretrievability from the immediately relevant context) for FSP. It is not without interest that Keijsper comes to the conclusion that the differentiation between given and new serves no useful purpose and can therefore be abolished (1985: 73). She bases her argument on the fact that not only new, but also given, information can be singled out for special attention by accentuation (ibid.: 72). In support of her argument she adduces two passages. One runs as follows (ibid. 64).

> We were waiting for the train, but it was late that day. John became nervous and went away to buy some cigarettes. Just as he left the station, the train arrived.

Keijsper points out that in *the train arrived* either *train* or *arrived* could be singled out by accentuation for special attention; 'train' can receive special attention in spite of its having been mentioned; the different accentuations convey different meanings.

The other passage (1985: 66) is taken from a Russian story by Suskin. The story is about a Jakovlev, an unruly person, who comes to his village after a time of absence. He gets irritated by the cool reception he receives from his former mates. He tries to re-establish contact, but does so in an outrageous way, insulting people and provoking a fight. He is ignored. The story ends with the following words (I am quoting Keijsper's English translation):

> Just at that moment the theatre group arrived. And everybody went to watch the theatre group.

Keijsper finds it probable that in reading the closing sentence aloud the reader is expected by the author to accentuate *the theatre group*. She emphasizes that *watch* could be accentuated instead, but it is the first accentuation that makes the most perfect story (ibid.). It is important to note that *the theatre group* conveys information retrievable from the immediately preceding sentence.

I agree that, like *the train, the theatre group* can be devoid of accentuation (the IC, in my terms) or bear it. But this does not prove the irrelevancy of the fact that the two are carriers of retrievable information. It is against the background of their retrievability that special effects are achieved by intonation. The IC on *the theatre group* is an instance of deshading producing the recapitulatory or summarizing effect (discussed here on pages 173–4, and also, e.g., in Firbas 1980: 131; 1985: 36–8). It is not irrelevant that the sentence closes the narration. The deshading offers a summarizing appraisal of the situation. The IC on *the train* shades *arrived*, which the non-prosodic CD distribution unequivocally determines as RhPr. A shift of the IC onto *the train* is due to re-evaluating prosodic intensification, which produces a special communicative effect. In the passage examined, the IC on the second occurrence of *the train* underlines the perhaps disastrous, or in any case disagreeable, consequence of John's nervous behaviour: the arrival of the train while he was absent from the station.

While I find that the PP distribution is highly sensitive to context, Keijsper refuses to take context into consideration. She holds that as accentuation can be studied directly in speech and as it is the formal correlate of an aspect of content (1985: 84), it is not necessary to have recourse to context: 'In speech we do not need the context to enable us to hear the accents' (1985: 83).

In the present study, I have attempted to demonstrate that it is through participation in the development of the communication that a semantic content becomes informational. Through occupying a place in this development it acquires a particular informational aspect or informational value, in other words a degree of CD. Assessing the informational aspects carried by the elements of a spoken sentence, i.e. their degrees of CD, the decoder cannot go by the accents (features of PP, in my terms) alone, for they do not operate independently of other signals, including those offered by the immediately relevant context. The deshading and shading effects produced in the two sentences discussed above depend on such contextual signals.

As for the silent reader, it must be borne in mind that, not having recourse to intonation, but merely guided by the interplay of non-prosodic FSP factors, he may of course give the first and the second sentence under discussion the summarizing and the emotive inter-pretation, respectively. But in the absence of intonation from the interplay of FSP factors, the clues suggestive of these interpretations are only potentially present in the written text.

The contextual factor is hierarchically superior both to linear modification and to the semantic factor. Intonation does not operate independently of the interplay of the non-prosodic FSP factors in which the contextual factor plays the dominant role. As has been shown intonation is highly sensitive to the immediately relevant context. Seen in this light, it is understandable why the phenomenon of FSP is sometimes referred to as the contextual organization of the sentence.

Epilogue

The present study has attempted to demonstrate that any linguistic element – as long as it conveys some meaning – participates in the development of the communication. The extent to which it contributes to this development determines its degree of communicative dynamism. Elements conveying some meaning serve as carriers of CD and are hierarchically organized in the structure of language. The distribution of degrees of CD over the elements serving as sentence constituents induces the sentence to function in a definite perspective. The sentence constituent carrying the highest degree of CD is the one towards which the sentence is perspectived. With due alterations, the same applies to structures of lower ranks: subordinate clauses, semiclauses and noun phrases. In each case, the structure is induced to function in a definite perspective owing to the distribution of degrees of CD over its constituents.

In examining the function of a linguistic element in the act of communication, the present study approaches the element from the semantic, syntactic and FSP points of view (cf. Daneš' three-level approach to syntax; Daneš 1964). The degree of CD carried by an element determines the place of the element in the development of the communication, the development being reflected in a gradual rise in CD, which need not necessarily coincide with the actual linear arrangement.

The degree of CD is a communicative value acquired by the element in the act of communication. The study establishes the factors – the formative forces – whose interplay determines the degrees of CD carried by the elements. It also establishes the signals yielded by this interplay. The interplay performs a crucial role in the establishment of the theme and the non-theme and of the parts constituting these two sections of the sentence.

Further enquiry into the interplay of FSP factors will extend our knowledge of FSP, which proves to constitute a system. It may also contribute to a better understanding of potentiality, which operates on the periphery of the FSP system, and perhaps even find that what has so far been regarded as a type of potentiality is in fact the outcome of an unequivocal interplay of FSP factors. As for intonation, it joins the interplay of FSP factors at the level of the spoken language. Through prosodic intensification, it raises the degrees of CD as they are determined by the interplay of non-prosodic factors.

An examination of elements from the three viewpoints mentioned above (semantic, syntactic and FSP) enables us to contribute towards a better understanding of the relation of semantics and syntax on the one hand and FSP on the other.

References

Abbreviations

BSE   *Brno Studies in English* (Brno: Masaryk University)
JL   *Journal of Linguistics* (Cambridge: Cambridge University Press)
SMFPUB   *Studia Minora Facultatis Philosophicae Universitatis Brunensis* (Brno: Masaryk University)
TLP   *Travaux Linguistiques de Prague* (Prague: Academia)

Adamec, P. 1966. *Porjadok slov v sovremennom russkom yazyke* (Word order in present-day Russian), Prague: Academia.
Allerton, D. J. 1978. 'The notion of "givenness" and its relations to presupposition and theme', *Lingua* 44: 133–68.
Arnold, G. F. and O. M. Tooley (1971). *Say it with rhythm 2*, London: Longman.
   (1972). *Say it with rhythm 3*, London: Longman.
Bauer, J. and M. Grepl 1980. *Skladba spisovné češtiny* (*Syntax of standard Czech*), *3rd edn, Prague*: SPN.
Bílý, M. 1981. *Intrasentential pronominalization and functional sentence perspective* (Lund Slavonic Monographs 1), Lund: Lund University.
Bogusławski, A. 1977. *Problems of the thematic–rhematic structure of sentences*, Warsaw: Państwowe Wydavnictwo Naukowe.
Bolinger, D. L. 1952. 'Linear modification', *Publications of the Modern Language Association of America* 67: 1117–44.
   1965. *Forms of English*, Cambridge, Mass.: Harvard University Press.
   1987. 'More views on "Two views of accent"', in Gussenhoven, Bolinger and Keijsper, 124–46.
Boost, K. 1955. *Neue Untersuchungen zum Wesen und zur Struktur des deutschen Satzes*, Berlin: Akademie.
Breivik, L. E. 1983. *Existential THERE*, Bergen: University of Bergen.
Chafe, W. L. 1974. 'Language and consciousness', *Language* 50: 111–33.
   1976. 'Givenness, contrastiveness, definiteness, subjects, topics and points of view', in Li (ed.), 26–56.

Chamonikolasová, J. 1985. 'The internal structure, communicative value and prosodic weight of the English object', *BSE* 16: 49–61.

Chládková, H. 1979. 'English and German equivalents of the Czech adverb of manner examined from the point of view of functional sentence perspective', *BSE* 13: 61–104.

Collins Cobuild English language dictionary 1985. London: Collins.

Cooper, Ch. R. and S. Greenbaum (eds.), 1986. *Studying writing: linguistic approaches* (Written Communication Annual, 1), Beverly Hills: Sage.

Contreras, H. 1976. *A theory of word order with special reference to Spanish* Amsterdam: North Holland.

Crystal, D. 1969. *Prosodic systems and intonation in English*, Cambridge: Cambridge University Press.

  1985. *A dictionary of linguistics and phonetics*, 2nd edn., Oxford: Blackwell.

Crystal, D. and D. Davy 1975. *Advanced conversational English*, London: Longman.

Crystal, D. and R. Quirk 1964. *Systems of prosodic and paralinguistic features in English*, The Hague: Mouton.

Daneš, F. 1957. *Intonance a věta ve spisovné češtině* (Intonation and sentence in present-day standard Czech), Prague: Academia.

  1960. 'Sentence intonation from a functional point of view', *Word* 16: 34–54.

  1964. 'A three-level approach to syntax', *TLP* 1: 225–40.

  1966. 'The relation of centre and periphery as a language universal', *TLP* 2: 9–21.

  1968. 'Some thoughts on the semantic structure of the sentence', *Lingua* 21: 55–69.

  (ed.) 1974a. *Papers on functional sentence perspective*, Prague: Academia.

  1974b. 'Functional sentence perspective and the organization of the text', in Daneš (ed.), 106–28.

  1985. *Věta a text* (Sentence and text), Prague: Academia.

  1987. 'On Prague School functionalism in linguistics', in Dirven and Fried (eds.), 3–38.

Daneš, F., M. Grepl, Z. Hlavsa, *et al.* 1987. *Mluvnice češtiny 3 (Skladba)* (A grammar of Czech 3 (Syntax)), Prague: Academia.

Dirven, R. and V. Fried (eds.), 1987. *Functionalism in linguistics*, Amsterdam: Benjamins.

Dobrzyńska, T. and J. Janus (eds.), 1983. *Tekst i zdanie* (Text and sentence), Wrocław: Ossolineum.

Dvořáková, E. (= Golková, E.) 1964. 'On the English and Czech situational adverbs in functional sentence perspective', *BSE* 4: 129–42.

van Ek, J. A. and N. J. Robat 1984. *The student's grammar of English*, Oxford: Blackwell.

Enkvist, N. E. 1981. 'Experiential iconicism in text strategy', *Text* 1: 97–111.

Ertl, V. 1926. *Gebaurova Mluvnice česká pro školy střední a ústavy učitelské*

(Gebaur's Czech grammar for secondary schools and teachers' training colleges), 9th edn, newly adapted by Václav Ertl, Prague: Unie.

Faber, D. 1987. 'The accentuation of intransitive sentences in English', *JL* 23: 341–58.

Firbas, J. 1956. 'Poznámky k problematice anglického slovního pořádku z hlediska aktuálního členění větného' (Notes on the problems of English word order from the point of view of functional sentence perspective), *SMFPUB* A4: 93–107.

1957. 'Some thoughts on the function of word order in old English and modern English', *SMFPUB* A5: 72–100.

1961. 'On the communicative value of the modern English finite verb', *BSE* 3: 79–104.

1965. 'A note on transition proper in functional sentence analysis', *Philologica Pragensia* 8: 170–6.

1966. 'Non-thematic subjects in contemporary English', *TLP* 2: 239–56.

1968. 'On the prosodic features of the modern English verb as means of functional sentence perspective', *BSE* 7: 11–48.

1971. 'On the concept of communicative dynamism in the theory of functional sentence perspective', *SMFPUB* A19: 135–44.

1974. 'Some aspects of the Czechoslovak approach to problems of functional sentence perspective', in Daneš (ed.), 11–37.

1975. 'On the thematic and the non-thematic section of the sentence', in Ringbom (ed.), 317–34.

1976. 'A study on the functional perspective of the English and Slavonic interrogative sentences', *BSE* 12: 9–56.

1978. 'K problematice tématu výpovědi' (On problems concerning the theme of the utterance), in Mayenowa (ed.), 29–46.

1979. 'A functional view of "ordo naturalis"', *BSE* 13: 29–59.

1980. 'Post-intonation-centre prosodic shade in the modern English clause', in Greenbaum, Leech and Svartvik (eds.), 125–33.

1981. 'Scene and perspective', *BSE* 14: 37–91.

1983a. 'On bipartition, tripartition and pluripartition' in the theory of functional sentence perspective', in Dobrzyńska and Janus (eds.), 67–79.

1983b. 'On some basic issues of the theory of functional sentence perspective (comments on Alexander Szwedek's critique)', *BSE* 15: 9–36.

1984. 'Carriers of communicative dynamism', *Prague Studies in English* 18: 63–73.

1985. 'Thoughts on functional sentence perspective, intonation and emotiveness', *BSE* 16: 11–48.

1986a. 'On the dynamics of written communication in the light of the theory of functional sentence perspective', in Cooper and Greenbaum (eds.), 40–71.

1986b. 'A case-study in the dynamics of written communication' in Kastovsky and Szwedek (eds.), 859–76.

1987a. 'On the delimitation of the theme in functional sentence perspective,' in Dirven and Fried (eds.), 137–56.

1987b. 'On two starting points of communication', in Steele and Threadgold (eds.), vol. 1, 23–46.

1987c. 'Thoughts on functional sentence perspective, intonation and emotiveness', part 2, *BSE* 17: 9–49.

1987d. 'On some basic issues of the theory of functional sentence perspective (on Wallace L. Chafe's view on new and old information and communicative dynamism)', *BSE* 17: 51–9.

1988. 'On the role of the parts of speech in functional sentence perspective', in Klegraf and Nehls (eds.), 96–109.

1989. 'Degrees of communicative dynamism and degrees of prosodic prominence', *BSE* 18: 21–66 and appendix.

Firbas, J. and E. Golková, 1975. *An analytical bibliography of Czechoslovak studies in functional sentence perspective*, Brno: Masaryk University.

Gimson, A. C. 1970. *An introduction to the pronunciation of English*, 2nd edn, London: Arnold.

Golková, E. 1983. 'On adverbials of agency in English and Czech', *BSE* 15: 37–48.

1985. 'On English adverbials of agency in the penultimate sentence position', *BSE* 16: 63–71.

Greenbaum, S. and J. Whitcut 1988. *Guide to English usage*, London: Longman.

Greenbaum, S., G. Leech and J. Svartvik, (eds.), 1980. *Studies in English linguistics for Randolph Quirk*, London: Longman.

Grepl, M. 1967. *Emocionálně motivované aktualizace v syntaktické struktuře výpovědi* (Emotively motivated cases of foregrounding in the syntactic structure of the utterance), Brno: Masaryk University.

Grünberg, M. 1967. *The West-Saxon gospels*, Amsterdam: Scheltema and Holkema.

Grzegorek, M. 1984. *Thematization in English and Polish*, Poznań: Mickiewicz University.

Gussenhoven, C. 1983. 'Focus, mode and the nucleus', *JL* 19: 377–417.

1984. *On the grammar and semantics of sentence-accents*, Dordrecht: Foris.

Gussenhoven, C., D. Bolinger and C. Keijsper 1987. *On accent*, Bloomington: Indiana University Linguistics Club.

Gutknecht, Ch. (ed.), 1977. *Grundbegriffe und Hauptströmungen der Linguistik*, Hamburg:

Haas, W. 1970. *Phono-graphic translation*, Manchester: Manchester University Press.

Hajičová, E. 1975. *Negace a presupozice ve významové stavbě věty* (Negation and presupposition in the semantic structure of the sentence; English summary), pp. 124–47, Prague: Academia.

Hajičová, E. and P. Sgall 1982. 'Functional sentence perspective in the Slavonic languages and in English', *Juzhnoslovenski filolog* 38: 19–79.

Hajičová, E. and J. Vrbová 1981. 'On the salience of the elements of the stock of shared knowledge', *Folia Linguistica* 15: 291–303.

1982. 'On the role of the hierarchy of activation in the process of natural language understanding', in Horecký (ed.), 107–13.

Halliday, M. A. K. 1967a. *Intonation and grammar in British English*, The Hague: Mouton.

1967b. 'Notes on transitivity and theme in English II', *JL* 3: 199–244.

1970. *A course in spoken English: intonation*, London: Oxford University Press.

1985. *An introduction to functional grammar*, London: Arnold.

Hatcher, A. G. 1956. *Theme and underlying question, two studies in Spanish word order*, Supplement to *Word* 12.

Hladký, J. 1969. 'A note on the quantitative evaluation of the verb in English', *BSE* 8: 95–8.

Horecký, J. (ed.), 1982. *Coling 82. Proceedings of the ninth international conference on computational linguistics*, Prague: Academia.

Horová, E. 1976. 'On position and function of English local and temporal adverbials', *BSE* 12: 93–123.

Hruška, J. 1981. 'Translation and the problems of functional sentence perspective', *Philologica Pragensia* 24: 122–39.

Jellinek, H. M. 1913–14. *Geschichte der neuhochdeutschen Grammatik von den Anfängen bis auf Adelung*, Heidelberg: Winter.

Kastovsky, D. and A. Szwedek (eds.), 1986. *Linguistics across historical and geographical boundaries*, vol. 1, Berlin: Mouton de Gruyter.

Keijsper, C. E. 1985. *Information structure*, Amsterdam: Rodopi.

Kingdon, R. 1958a. *The groundwork of English intonation*, London: Longmans, Green.

1958b. *English intonation practice*, London: Longmans, Green.

Klegraf, J. and D. Nehls (eds.), 1988. *Essays on the English language and applied linguistics on the occasion of Gerhard Nickel's 60th birthday*, Heidelberg: Groos.

Křížková, H. 1972. 'Kontextové členění a typy tázacích vět v současných slovanských jazycích' (Contextual organization (functional sentence perspective) and types of interrogative sentence in contemporary Slavonic languages), *Slavia* 41: 241–62 (Prague).

Krushel'nitskaya, K. G. 1961. *Ocherki po sopostavitel'noĭ grammatike nemeckogo i russkogo yazykov* (Contrastive grammatical studies in German and Russian), Moscow: Izdatel'stvo literatury na inostrannych yazykach.

Kuchařová-Blažková, E. 1980. 'Emotivní slovosled ve staré angličtině' (Emotive word order in old English), unpublished dissertation, Brno: Masaryk University.

Kuno, S. 1972. 'Functional sentence perspective: a case study from Japanese and English', *Linguistic Inquiry* 3: 269–320.

Lewis, J. W. 1977. *People speaking*, London: Oxford University Press.

Li, Ch. N. (ed.), 1976. *Subject and topic*, New York: Academic Press.

Lipka, L. 1977. 'Functional sentence perspective, intonation and the speaker', in Gutknecht (ed.), 133–41.

Longman dictionary of contemporary English, 2nd edn, 1987. Harlow: Longman.

Lötscher, A. 1983. *Satzakzent und funktionale Satzperspektive im Deutschen*, Tubingen: Niemeyer.

Luelsdorff, Ph. A. 1989. 'Introduction', in Vachek 1989, ix–xix.

Lutz, L. 1981. *Zum Thema 'Thema'*, Hamburg: Hamburger Buchagentur.

Lyons, J. 1968. *Introduction to theoretical linguistics*, Cambridge: Cambridge University Press.

MacCarthy, P. A. D. 1956. *English conversation reader*, London: Longmans, Green.

Mathesius, V. 1911. 'O potencionálnosti jevů jazykových', *Věstník Královské české společnosti nauk 1911–12, třída filozoficko-historicko-jazykozpytná*, no. 2 (February), 1–14 (Prague). See Mathesius 1964.

1928. 'On linguistic characterology with illustrations from modern English', *Actes du Premier Congrès International de Linguistes à la Haye*, 56–63 (Leiden: Sijthoff). Reprinted in Vachek (ed.), 1964, 59–67.

1936. 'On some problems of the systematic analysis of grammar', *Travaux du Circle Linguistique de Prague* 6: 95–107.

1941. 'Základní funkce pořádku slov v češtině' (The basic function of word order in Czech), *Slovo a slovesnost* 7: 169–80.

1942. 'Ze srovnávacích studií slovosledných' (From comparative word-order studies), *Časopis pro moderní filologii* 28: 181–90, 302–7 (Prague).

1947. *Čeština a obecný jazykozpyt* (Czech language and general linguistics), Prague: Melantrich.

1964. 'On the potentiality of the phenomena of language', translation of Mathesius 1911 by Vachek, in Vachek (ed.), 1–32.

1975. *A functional analysis of present-day English on a general linguistic basis*, transl. L. Dušková, ed. J. Vachek, Prague: Academia.

Mayenowa, M. R. (ed.), 1978. *Tekst, język, poetika* (Text, language, poetics), Wrocław: Ossolineum.

Mukařovský, J. 1941. *Kapitoly z české poetiky* (Chapters from Czech poetics) vol. I, Prague: Melantrich.

Newmark, P. 1988. *A textbook of translation*, New York: Prentice Hall.

Nosek, J. 1985a. 'The parts of speech in functional sentence perspective', *Kommunikativ-funktionale Sprachbetrachtung, Wissenschaftliche Beiträge* F 59: 117–8 (Halle an der Saale: Martin-Luther-Universität Halle-Wittenberg).

1985b. 'The parts of speech in the functional sentence perspective', *Kommunikativ-funktionale Sprachbetrachtung, Teil III, Arbeitsberichte und wissenschaftliche Studien*, no. 109: 25–32 (Halle an der Saale: Martin-Luther-Universität Halle-Wittenberg).

O'Connor, J. D. O. and G. F. Arnold (1973). *Intonation of colloquial English*. 2nd edn, London: Longman.

Palmer, H. E. 1924. *English intonation with systematic exercises*, Cambridge: Heffer.

Paul, H. 1920. *Prinzipien der Sprachgeschichte*, 5th edn, Halle an der Saale: Niemeyer.

Poldauf, I. 1954. 'Podíl mluvnice a nauky o slovníku na problematice slovesného vidu' (Grammar and lexicology in the discussion of verbal aspect), *Studie a práce lingvistické* 1: 200–23 (Prague: Academia).

Quirk, R., S. Greenbaum, G. Leech and J. Svartvik 1972. *A grammar of contemporary English*, London: Longman.

1985. *A comprehensive grammar of the English language*, Harlow: Longman.

Quirk, R. and C. L. Wrenn, 1955. *Old English grammar*, London: Methuen.

Reichling, A. 1961. 'Principles and methods of syntax: cryptoanalytical formalism', *Lingua* 10: 1–17.

Ringbom, H. (ed.), 1975. *Style and text: studies presented to Nils Erik Enkvist*, Stockholm: Skriptor AB.

Schubiger, M. 1935. *The role of intonation in spoken English*, Cambridge: Heffer.

1958. *English intonation, its form and function*, Tübingen: Niemeyer.

Sgall, P., E. Hajičová and E. Buráňová, 1980. *Aktuální členění věty v češtině* (Topic/focus articulation of the Czech sentence), Prague: Academia.

Sgall, P., E. Hajičová and J. Panevová, 1986. *The meaning of the sentence and its semantic and pragmatic aspects*, Prague: Academia.

Šmilauer, Vl. 1966. *Novočeská skladba* (Modern Czech syntax), Prague: Statní pedagogické nakladatelství.

Steele, R. and T. Threadgold (eds.), 1987. *Language topics*, Amsterdam: Benjamins.

Svartvik, J. and R. Quirk (eds.), 1980. *A corpus of English conversation*, Lund: Gleerup.

Svoboda, A. 1968. 'The hierarchy of communicative units and fields as illustrated by English attributive constructions', *BSE* 7: 49–85.

1981. *Diatheme*, Brno: Masaryk University.

1983. 'Thematic elements', *BSE* 15: 49–85.

1987. 'Functional perspective of the noun phrase', *BSE* 17: 61–86.

1989. *Kapitoly z funkční syntaxe* (Chapters from functional syntax), Prague: Statní pedagogické nakladatelství.

Szwedek, A. 1986. *A linguistic analysis of sentence stress*, Tübingen: Gunter Narr.

Trávníček, F. 1937. 'Základy českého slovosledu' (Fundamentals of Czech word order), *Slovo a slovesnost* 3: 78–86 (Prague).

Trost, P. 1962. 'Subjekt a predikát' (Subject and predicate) (Acta Universitatis Carolinae, Philologica 3), *Slavica Pragensia* 4: 267–9 (Prague: Charles University). See Trost 1987.

1987. 'Subject and predicate', *Explizite Beschreibung der Sprache und*

234   References

automatische Textbearbeitung 14: 145–9 (Prague: Charles University). A translation by P. Sgall of Trost 1962.

Uhlenbeck, E. M. 1941. *Beknopte Javaansche grammatica*, Batavia: Volkslektuur.

1983. 'Linguistics: neither psychology nor sociology', *1983 NIAS lecture*, Wassenaar: NIAS.

Uhlířová, L. 1974. 'O vztahu sémantiky příslovečného určení k aktuálnímu členění' (The relationship between the semantics of adverbials and functional sentence perspective), *Slovo a slovesnost* 35: 99–106.

Urbanová, L. 1984. 'Prozodická realizace anglického určitého slovesa ve spojení s adverbiálním určením z hlediska aktuálního členění' (Prosodic realization of the English finite verb in relation to the adverbial modifiers with regard to FSP), C.Sc. dissertation, Brno: Masaryk University.

Vachek, J. 1958. 'Some notes on the development of language seen as a system of systems', *Proceedings of the eighth international congress of linguistics*, 418–19, Oslo: Oslo University Press.

1966. 'On the integration of the peripheral elements into the system of language', *TLP* 2: 23–37.

1975. *Linguistic characterology of modern English*, Bratislava: Comenius University.

1976. *Selected writings in English and general linguistics*, Prague: Academia.

1989. *Written language revisited*, Amsterdam: Benjamins.

(ed.), 1964. *A Prague School reader in linguistics*, Bloomington: Indiana University Press.

Weil, H. 1844. *De l'ordre des mots dans les langues anciennes comparées aux langues modernes*, Paris: Joubert.

Index

The index is selective in the sense that it does not exhaustively cover all the mentions in the text of the basic concepts of the theory of functional sentence perspective (FSP).